Social Capital and Economic Development

To Tracy, Faith, Kate and our families.
J.I.

To Annemarie, and Joseph and Noreen Kelly.
T.K.

To Varna, my mother, and to the memory of my father.
S.R.

Social Capital and Economic Development

Well-being in Developing Countries

Edited by

Jonathan Isham

Assistant Professor of Economics, Middlebury College, Middlebury, Vermont, USA

Thomas Kelly

Assistant Professor of Economics, Middlebury College, Middlebury, Vermont, USA

Sunder Ramaswamy

Frederick C. Dirks Professor of International Economics, Middlebury College, Middlebury, Vermont, USA

Edward Elgar
Cheltenham, UK • Northampton, MA, USA

Published by
Edward Elgar Publishing Limited
Glensanda House
Montpellier Parade
Cheltenham
Glos GL50 1UA
UK

Edward Elgar Publishing, Inc.
136 West Street
Suite 202
Northampton
Massachusetts 01060
USA

A catalogue record for this book
is available from the British Library

Library of Congress Cataloguing in Publication Data

Social capital and economic development: well-being in
    developing countries/edited by Jonathan Isham, Thomas Kelly
and Sunder Ramaswamy.
        p.   cm.
    Includes index.
    1. Social capital (Sociology)—Developing countries. I. Isham,
Jonathan. II. Kelly, Thomas, 1966– . III. Ramaswamy, Sunder.
HN980.S569   2002
302—dc21

                                                2002017912

ISBN 1 84064 699 3

Typeset by Cambrian Typesetters, Frimley, Surrey

Printed and bound in Great Britain by Biddles Ltd, *www.biddles.co.uk*

Contents

PART III   INVESTING IN SOCIAL CAPITAL IN THE FIELD

Figures

Tables

Preface

Since the mid-1990s, theoretical and empirical research on how social capital affects well-being has blossomed in the fields of economic development, and environmental and natural resource economics. Based on noted theoretical and empirical work in other social sciences, this concept is starting to work its way into the economist's toolkit.

In April 2000, participants in the 21st Annual Conference on Economics Issues at Middlebury College considered the implications of social capital research for the teaching and practice of development economics. Conference participants, drawn from a diverse range of academic and policy viewpoints, shared new research and field experiences as they related to this concept.

The chapters of this volume originated with this conference. Putting a conference together and making it work is no easy task. We would like to acknowledge the wonderful help that we received from Melissa Dalais in taking care of all the details – big and small.

The Christian A. Johnson Endeavor Foundation supported the conference. The Foundation has helped support, not only this annual conference, but also a series of lectures organized by the Department of Economics at Middlebury College: this has helped our economics faculty and students to have much more interaction with colleagues from the wider economic world than is typically possible at most undergraduate institutions. We are extremely grateful to the Foundation for making this possible and would like to thank the president, Julie Kidd, and the holder of the Christian A. Johnson professorship here at Middlebury College, David Colander.

David, with his vast experience in organizing conferences and producing excellent volumes from those proceedings, was also helpful with this volume, with his sage and timely advice. A number of colleagues who took part in the conference helped shape many of the chapters in this volume with their insightful comments. They include Marc Garcelon, Meghan McGuinness, Ellen Oxfeld, Prasanta Pattanaik, Louis Putterman, Umar Serajuddin, Iffath Sharif and Phanindra Wunnava. We would also like to thank Edward Elgar for taking on the project, and, in particular, Francine O'Sullivan, Alexandra Minton, Jennifer Chilton and Caroline Cornish for their wonderful assistance in seeing the project through from start to completion.

We recognized early on that this volume could not simply be a reprinting of the conference presentations, no matter how well the conference went off.

The papers had to fit into a larger theme. This required much rewriting and reworking of the chapters on the part of the authors and the editors. We thank the authors for being prompt in responding to our suggestions. Helen Raiff, with her wonderful eye for detail, served as an excellent editor of all the chapters. Steffy Rompas ably assisted us by cross-checking references and formatting the manuscript.

J.I.

T.K.

S.R.

Contributors

Juan-Camilo Cardenas is an associate professor at the School of Environmental and Rural Studies at *Universidad Javeriana* in Bogota, Colombia. He has conducted field-based research using participatory and experimental methods for the *Instituo de Estudios Ambientales para el Desarrollo, Universidad Javeriana*, the Institute Humboldt for Biodiversity, the *Departamento Nacional de Planeacion* in Colombia and several international agencies. His publications, based on field-based experimental economics and non-market valuation techniques, explore how rural communities cooperate in the local management of natural resources.

Jeffrey P. Carpenter is an assistant professor of economics at Middlebury College. His current research is focused on endogenous social preferences, evolutionary game theory and measuring the effects of social capital on economic outcomes in field settings. This research has been (and is) funded by the National Science, the Russell Sage and the MacArthur foundations. Completed components of this research have been published in the *Journal of Institutional and Theoretical Economics* and are forthcoming in the *Journal of Economic Behavior and Organization, Economic Letters* and *Computational Economics*.

Nat Colletta is currently Director of the Institute for Peacebuilding and Development at George Washington University and teaches at the Centre for Peace and Conflict Resolution, American University and the Georgetown School of Foreign Service. He is a former professor of sociology, anthropology and international education and development at SUNY Buffalo and at the University of Malaysia (as a visiting Fulbright-Hayes lecturer) and was the founding manager of the World Bank Post Conflict Unit and senior spokesperson for the bank on reconstruction and peace building in societies emerging from violent conflict and war.

Michelle Cullen is a consultant at the World Bank, where she specializes in social assessment, study implementation, and project monitoring and evaluation in conflict-affected countries. Michelle has also been commissioned to draft reports for the World Health Organization, the US National Institute for Mental Health and the Commonwealth of Australia. Before joining the bank,

Michelle worked with The Carter Center on its human rights and conflict resolution programmes. She has co-authored a book, several book chapters, and other, smaller publications.

Amrita Daniere is an associate professor of planning and geography at the University of Toronto. Her research interests include urban infrastructure in developing country cities, environmental problems in slum communities, and social capital and community governance issues in urban communities. She is in the midst of conducting a three-year research project based in Bangkok and Ho Chi Minh City on the relationship between social networks, community governance and environmental problems in squatter and slum areas. Her most recent publications can be found in *Economic Development and Cultural Change* and the *Transportation Research Record.*

Christiaan Grootaert is lead economist in the Social Development Department at the World Bank and manager of the Social Capital Initiative, which has undertaken empirical studies on the effects of social capital in 15 countries. He has undertaken research in the areas of measurement and analysis of poverty, risk and vulnerability, education and labour markets, child labour, and the role of institutions and social capital in development. His recent publications include *The Policy Analysis of Child Labor: A Comparative Study* (with H. Patrinos) and *Poverty and Social Assistance in Eastern Europe and the Former Soviet Union* (with J. Braithwaite and B. Milanovic). He is co-author of the recent *World Development Report 2000/2001: Attacking Poverty.*

Kevin Healy is a grant officer for the Inter-American Foundation, a small public-financed foreign aid agency, where he has specialized in the Andean countries of Bolivia, Peru and Ecuador and also funded grassroots development projects in Mexico, Nicaragua, Costa Rica, Honduras and Panama. He is currently an adjunct professor in the Elliott School of International Affairs of George Washington University and has also been an adjunct professor at Georgetown University, American University and the School of Advanced International Studies of Johns Hopkins University (SAIS). He is the author of *Llamas, Weavings and Organic Chocolate, Multicultural Grassroots Development from the Andes and Amazon of Bolivia, Caciques y Patrones, una Experiencia de Desarrollo Rural en el Sud de Bolivia* and 15 chapters in edited volumes.

Jonathan Isham is an assistant professor of economics and an affiliated member of the Environmental Studies Program at Middlebury College. His current research is focused on the institutional determinants of performance of community-based water projects in rural Indonesia; estimating the demand for water among poor households in urban Cambodia; the role of social capital in the diffusion of information among agricultural households in rural Tanzania; the social foundations of poor economic growth in resource-rich countries; and the effect of local social capital on environmental outcomes in Vermont. He has articles published or forthcoming in *Economic Development and Cultural Change*, the *Journal of African Economies*, the *Quarterly Journal of Economics*, the *World Bank Economic Review* and six chapters in edited volumes.

Thomas Kelly is an assistant professor of economics, and a cooperating member of the Latin American Studies Program and the Environmental Studies Program, at Middlebury College in Middlebury, Vermont. His areas of research are economic development, poverty and inequality, environmental problems and food security in developing countries. He is the author of studies examining the relationship between poverty and environmental problems in developing countries, the economic causes of tropical deforestation, and alternative strategies for sustainable agricultural development in Mexico. His most recent research has focused on the effect of structural adjustment on poverty in Mexico, much of which is summarized in his recent book from Ashgate Publishing, *Poverty and Adjustment in Mexico*. He is currently working on an evaluation of poverty alleviation programmes in Mexico and Brazil, and on a study of the economic determinants of farm biodiversity loss in Southeast Mexico. Professor Kelly is on the editorial board of *Revista de Economía*.

José Molinas teaches development economics and macroeconomics at both undergraduate and graduate level at the Catholic University of Asuncion (Paraguay), where he has also been the academic director of the Master Program in Economics. He wrote a dissertation on the developmental role of the collective action sector for achieving economic growth and poverty alleviation, using a combination of formal modelling, econometric methods, and historical and institutional analysis. His research fields include social capital, rural development, political economy of social service delivery, poverty and applied macroeconomics. He has published articles on the determinants of success for peasant cooperatives, rural land markets, internal migration, the macroeconomics of financial crisis and the impact of balance of payment liberalization on growth, income distribution and poverty. His publications have appeared (or will appear) in *World Development, El Trimestre Económico*, the ECLAC *Desarrollo Productivo Series*, as a working paper of the ILO, and as book chapters. His research has been funded by the Inter-American Foundation, the Organization of American States, the Kellogg Institute, the United Nations Development Program, the Interamerican

Development Bank, the World Bank, the Economic Commission for Latin American and the Caribbean (ECLAC), the International Labor Office (ILO) and the Japan International Cooperation Agency, among other agencies.

Anchana NaRanong is teaching at the Graduate School of Public Administration and directing the Master of Public and Private Management Program (Nakornratchasima Campus), National Institute of Development Administration (NIDA), Thailand. She was a research specialist at the Thailand Development and Research Institute (TDRI) and an Honorary Fellow on the Program in Agrarian Studies, Institution for Social and Policy Studies, Yale University. Her research work focuses on poverty, environment and health care for the poor and disadvantaged in Thailand. She was a team leader and project manager for the *Voices of the Poor* Study in Thailand.

Deepa Narayan is senior advisor in the Poverty Reduction and Economic Management Network of the World Bank. She is also the lead author and team leader for *Voices of the Poor*, a multi-country research initiative. She has over 20 years' development experience in Asia and Africa and has worked for NGOs, national governments and the UN system. She has published extensively on community-driven development, participation, social capital and empowerment. Among her recent publications are *Voices of the Poor: Can Anyone Hear Us?*, New York: Oxford University Press, *Voices of the Poor: Poverty and Social Capital in Tanzania*, World Bank, and 'Cents and Sociability: Household Income and Social Capital in Rural Tanzania', in *Economic Development and Cultural Change*.

Gi-Taik Oh is a research consultant at the World Bank. For over a decade, he has undertaken empirical research and data management in the areas of poverty, gender, labour, health, welfare, energy and institution issues, using various survey data from ten countries. He is a co-author on many research working papers at the World Bank. His recent paper, 'Costs of Infrastructure Deficiencies for Manufacturing in Nigerian, Indonesian and Thai Cities' (with K.S. Lee and A. Annas), was published in *Urban Studies*.

Sunder Ramaswamy is the Frederick C. Dirks Professor of International Economics, and Chair of Economics at Middlebury College. His research interests are in the areas of development economics, international trade and applied microeconomics. His books include *The Economics of Agricultural Technology in Semiarid Sub-Saharan Africa*, with John H. Sanders and Barry I. Shapiro (Johns Hopkins University Press, 1996, 1997) and *Economics: An Honors Companion*, with Kailash Khandke, Jenifer Gamber and David Colander (MaxiPress, Richard D. Irwin Publishers, 1995). He is one of the three series editors of the *Middlebury College Bicentennial Series on International Studies*, forthcoming with the University Press of New England. He is also the editor (with Jeffrey Cason) of *Development and Democracy: New Perspectives on an Old Debate*, forthcoming with the University Press of New England, and has contributed numerous chapters in various books as well as articles either published or forthcoming in journals such as *Agricultural Economics, Agricultural Systems, Applied Economics, Comparative Economic Studies, Economic Development and Cultural Change, Economics Letters, Environment* and the *Journal of Development Economics*.

Paul Streeten is Professor Emeritus of Economics of Boston University and founder and chairman of *World Development*. Among his recent books are *Development Perspectives, First Things First, Thinking about Development, The UN and the Bretton Woods Institutions* (co-editor) and *Globalisation: Threat or Opportunity?*

Anand Swamy is an assistant professor in the economics department at Williams College, Middlebury, Vermont. His research focuses on factor markets in the developing world, especially their institutional underpinnings. His publications include a 'A Simple Test of the Nutrition-based Efficiency Wage Model' and 'The Hazards of Piecemeal Reform: British Civil Courts and the Credit Market in Colonial India' (with Rachel Kranton), both published in the *Journal of Development Economics*.

Lois M. Takahashi is the Harvey Perloff Visiting Associate Professor in the Department of Urban Planning at UCLA. Her research spans several areas, including human service delivery for homeless individuals and persons living with HIV/AIDS, the NIMBY (Not In My Back Yard) syndrome, and environmental management in rapidly developing areas (in Southeast Asia, and in rural areas in the western United States). Her book on the NIMBY syndrome was published in 1998 by Oxford University Press.

Michael Woolcock is a social scientist with the Development Research Group at the World Bank, and an adjunct lecturer in Public Policy at Harvard University's Kennedy School of Government. He is the author of several papers on social capital and economic development and the founding moderator of the World Bank's e-mail discussion group on social capital. His forthcoming book, *Using Social Capital: Getting the Social Relations Right in the Theory and Practice of Economic Development*, will be published by Princeton University Press in 2003.

Abbreviations

AT	Adelman–Taft index
BMA	Bangkok Metropolitan Authority
BRAC	Bangladesh Rural Advancement Committee
CDC	Commonwealth Development Corporation
CDE	*Centro de Documentación y Estudios*
CPES	*Centro Paraguayo de Estudios Sociológicos*
CPR	common-pool resource
DGEEC	*Dirección General de Estadísticas, Encuestas y Censos*
H	High pay-off tables
HL	Asymmetric groups
HLO	higher-level organization
IFAD	International Fund for Agricultural Development
IMF	International Monetary Fund
INAH	Institute of Anthropology and History
L	Low pay-off tables
LLI	Local Level Institutions
LSMS	Living Standards Measurement Survey
MWA	Metropolitan Waterworks Authority
NGO	Non-governmental organization
O & M	Operations and maintenance
OECD	Organization for Economic Cooperation and Development
PRI	*Partido Revolucionario Institucional*
PTA	Parent Teacher Association
PWA	Provincial Waterworks Authority
PWD	Public Works Department
RTLMC	*Radio et Télévision Libre des Mille Collines*
S	Symmetric baseline groups
VCM	voluntary contribution mechanism

PART I

The History and Scope of the Concept of
Social Capital in Development Economics

1. Social capital and well-being in developing countries: an introduction

Jonathan Isham, Thomas Kelly and Sunder Ramaswamy

> What are human investments? Can they be distinguished from consumption? Is it at all feasible to identify and measure them? What do they contribute to income? Granted that they seem amorphous compared to brick and mortar, and hard to get at compared to the investment accounts of corporations, they assuredly are not a fragment; they are rather like the contents of Pandora's box, full of difficulties and hope. (Theodore Schultz, 1961, in his address to the American Economic Association on human capital)

Forty years after the introduction of the concept of human capital in the corpus of economics, the related concept of social capital has taken hold. From an economist's perspective, social capital – like human capital before it – is a concept with much appeal and promise, but full of definitional and operational ambiguities. The concept creates challenges and opportunities for researchers, practitioners and teachers. The chapters in this volume explore these challenges and opportunities.

In assembling this volume, we asked contributors from a diverse range of academic and policy viewpoints to share new research and field experiences. Although these chapters are informed by excellent research on social capital in the developed world (for example, Putnam, 1993, 2000), the volume itself focuses on the developing world. As development and environmental economists, we feel that a volume dedicated to social capital and well-being in developing countries meets an urgent need in academic and policy quarters. The economics discipline, both scholarly and popular, continues to focus mostly on problems and challenges faced by the industrialized world (Basu, 1997). Both conceptually and operationally, we feel that economists have an obligation to draw our discipline's collective attention to 'what needs to be done' to improve the lives of the poor.

In this introductory chapter, we highlight the thematic connections among the chapters that comprise the rest of the volume. The first section of the chapter discusses the rise of the concept of social capital within the discipline of economics. The second section uses a household production framework to explore the conceptual relationship between social capital and well-being. The third section discusses the ideal conditions for investing in social capital. The fourth section summarizes each of the subsequent chapters.

THE RISE OF SOCIAL CAPITAL

A new Pandora's box, for better or for worse, has been opened. Despite scepticism among many mainstream economists (highlighted by Streeten in Chapter 3), the concept of social capital – defined by Woolcock in Chapter 2 as 'the networks and norms that facilitate collective action' – has worked its way into the market place of economic ideas.

The recent evidence of this trend is striking. A 'keyword' search of all journals in *EconLit*, the most frequently used database of references in economics, shows that citations for 'social capital' have grown rapidly over the last decade, doubling each year since the late 1990s (Figure 1.1).[1] In 2000, social capital has about a quarter of the absolute number of citations as human capital. (The related concept, 'social networks', had only begun to show any growth.)

In fact, this recent growth of interest in social capital compares favourably with growth of interest in human capital in the years after that concept was introduced. 'Human capital' appeared as a keyword in 12.2 per cent of all 'capital' citations in *EconLit* in 1969, about a decade after being formally introduced by Schultz (1960). 'Social capital' appears as a keyword in 7.4 per cent of all 'capital' citations in *EconLit* in 2000, about a decade after being formally introduced by Coleman (1990). The establishment of a new subcategory in the *Journal of Economic Literature*, 'Social Norms and Social Capital' is further evidence of the discipline's revealed preference for this term.

Many prominent economists are alarmed by this trend (Arrow, 2000; Solow, 2000). While acknowledging the importance of the 'social dimension of development', these and other sceptics question whether the term 'social capital', with inconsistent and ambiguous definitions throughout the social science literature, can adequately capture the complexities of such a dimension.

Some of the loudest criticism concerns the appropriateness of the capital metaphor: are networks and norms really forms of 'capital'? In this regard, too, the concept of social capital compares favourably with the concept of human capital, which faced similar resistance when first introduced by Theodore Schultz. Both human and social capital are composed of durable aspects of human behaviour that accumulate through an identifiable production process: the 'household production' of knowledge and social interactions, respectively (Becker, 1996). Both are acquired through a form of effort that

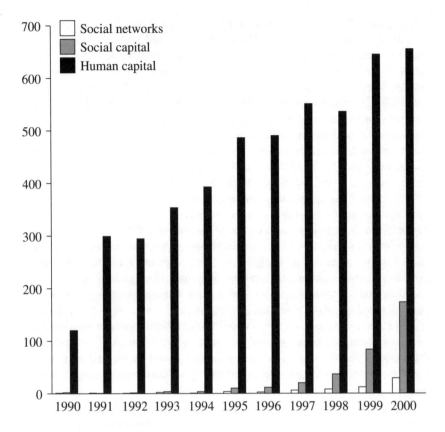

Figure 1.1 Citations with social capital, human capital and social networks in EconLit

puts a limit on their accumulation: knowledge acquisition and social interactions both require time or resources, which are only finitely available. Both exist in a variety of forms: human capital comprises different forms of formal education and on-the-job experience; social capital comprises different forms of social networks and social norms. Both can generate large positive or negative externalities: the accumulation of levels of knowledge and the social networks of one's neighbours can have positive or negative effects on one's own economic decisions. Finally, an economic value can be placed on both: the net present value of the incremental income stream associated with access to knowledge and to recurrent and patterned social interactions, respectively (Collier, 2002).

On the other hand, certain aspects of networks and norms do not capture the strict sense of the term 'capital' as applied to physical goods that are factors of production; this is also true for formal education and on-the-job experience. There is certainly no standard way to account for depreciation – how do social networks and stocks of knowledge depreciate without use? (Ostrom, 2000) – nor for whether they can be used at different rates. More critically, without a set of market prices to determine their relative value, it is not possible to aggregate social interactions determined by networks and norms into a meaningful measure of a stock of capital (Dasgupta, 2000).[2]

There is related criticism concerning measurement: how can one measure the quantity and quality of social networks and norms, as researchers measure formal education and on-the-job experience? Putnam's pioneering approach (1993) focused on the quantity and quality of associational membership and activity. In the development context, Narayan and Pritchett (1999) and Grootaert *et al.* (Chapter 5, present volume) exemplify this approach, where the quantity and quality of associational activities are used to test empirically the effect of social capital on different economic outcomes. Indeed, household-level survey instruments are now regularly incorporating measures of social capital: for example, most World Bank household survey instruments have included questions about social networks and norms since the successful 'Local Level Institutions Project' (World Bank, 1998). However, measurement of networks and norms can be troublesome. Glaeser *et al.* (2000) and Carpenter (Chapter 7, present volume) show how hypothetical and 'warm glow' biases, among others, can cast doubt on self-reported measures of trust and reciprocity.

Of course, the growing acceptance of social capital in the market place of ideas does not imply that critics' questions about conceptual and measurement issues have been completely answered. We are convinced, however, that the concept enhances the analysis of the determinants of well-being in developing countries. Indeed, the growing theoretical and empirical literature on social capital has helped to fuel a resurgence of interest in the social dimensions of development (Woolcock, present volume, Chapter 2). A range of new research shows that communities endowed with a rich capacity to form social networks and adhere to social norms are in a stronger position to resolve disputes (Schafft and Brown, 2000), share useful information (Isham, forthcoming), implement successful development projects (Galasso and Ravallion, 2001) and alleviate poverty (Moser, 1996; Kozel and Parker, 2000).

We believe that Dasgupta (2000) puts it well: 'The concept of social capital is useful insofar as it draws our attention to those particular institutions serving economic life that might otherwise go unnoted. Once attention is drawn to them, we need to try to understand them and find ways of improving them or building around them.'

SOCIAL CAPITAL AND WELL-BEING

Development is a process of expanding the real freedoms that people enjoy (Sen, 1999).[3] In particular, it requires the removal of major sources of 'unfreedom': poverty as well as tyranny; poor economic opportunities as well as social deprivation; neglect of public facilities as well as the intolerance or overactivity of repressive states.

Development enables greater well-being: an expanded set of economic opportunities, better health, more education and greater political and civil liberties. Well-being, as conceived of by Amartya Sen and Partha Dasgupta, is a measure of actual and potential quality of existence: it encompasses both the attainments of an individual and the choices that she enjoys.[4]

Sen (1985) introduced the term in the development context by noting that the quality of a person's existence encompasses 'being' and 'doing' (what Sen calls 'functionings') from an available set of choices (what Sen calls 'capabilities'). For example (as in Grootaert *et al.* in Chapter 5 of the present volume), the standard of living of members of a family in Burkina Faso can be partially assessed by observing whether the entire family is healthy and the school-age children are literate. The entire family is able to stay healthy because the head of the household has the choice of borrowing from a community lending institution, and school-age children are literate because they have the choice of attending a community-supported school.

Muellbauer (1987) illustrated how Sen's notion of well-being is conceptually related to the household production model. In the household production framework, commodities – the 'primary objects of consumer choice . . . that directly contribute to utility' (Michael and Becker, 1973) – are produced by market goods and time. Broadly interpreted, these commodities are similar to the 'functionings' that increase an individual's well-being: they are 'beings' and 'doings' that are chosen from a constrained set of capabilities to function, which are in turn derived from a set of available market goods and services and a set of environmental, physical and social inputs. Again, using the example of a family in Burkina Faso, good health and literacy are 'produced' in part by purchases of household goods and the allocation of family time for health care and school attendance.

We can illustrate the connections among household production, well-being and social capital with one equation that represents the utility of a household that is optimizing over a range of commodities. Let the utility of household i at time t be $U_{it} = U(Z_i(X_i, T_i, W_i))$, where household allocations of vectors of market goods (X_i) and time (T_i) produce a vector of commodities (Z_i) that yields utility. Deaton and Muellbauer (1980) and Betancourt (1996) detail how the environmental, physical and social inputs can be seen as fixed inputs into the household production decision. Accordingly, let W_i be a vector of fixed inputs that affects this production of commodities: these fixed inputs include forms of physical capital, environmental conditions and forms of social capital. For example, a rural household in Indonesia will need to use fewer market goods and less time to obtain clean water when it can depend on productive forms of physical capital (a system of working standposts), good environmental conditions (a reliable water source) and productive forms of social capital (social norms that facilitate collective maintenance) (Isham and Kähkönen, 2002).

In Chapter 3 of the present volume, Paul Streeten distinguishes among different aspects of social capital: consumption goods (non-durable and durable), non-durable production goods, and durable capital goods (for marketed and non-marketed activities). Following the household production framework, these aspects of social capital include commodities that directly yield utility (making a new friend or enjoying activities of a soccer club); productive inputs into commodity production (joining a peasant organization, as discussed by Molinas in Chapter 6 of the present volume); and fixed inputs into commodity production (community lending institutions and effective parent-teacher associations, as discussed by Grootaert *et al.* in Chapter 5).

Streeten notes that one of the distinguishing aspects of social capital is that these aspects are interdependent: 'we may enter a club for pleasure, companionship, or self-interest but in the process we acquire the trust and the skills that bring substantial economic benefits'. In other words, household production of social investments by an individual in one period – as both consumption and production goods – will accumulate into forms of social capital that are available in future periods, as fixed inputs into future household production by this individual and by others.

Specifically, many forms of privately generated social investments are likely to yield productive spillovers as forms of bonding, bridging and linking social capital. In Chapter 2, Woolcock illustrates how 'bonding' social capital refers to relations among family members, close friends and neighbours; 'bridging' social capital refers to relations among more distant associates and colleagues who have somewhat different demographic characteristics irrespective of how well they know one another; and 'linking' social capital refers to alliances with sympathetic individuals in positions of power. In Chapter 4, Narayan focuses on two comparable aspects of social capital: cross-cutting ties that characterize social relations in informal or formal voluntary groups and networks characterized by heterogeneity of membership that distinguish social groups; and the interaction between formal and informal institutions.

The household production-based view of social capital and well-being is also consistent with the reality that selected elements of the social structure can have negative spillovers (discussed by Streeten in Chapter 3), as in the case of norm reinforcement by the Mafia in southern Italy (Gambetta, 1988).[5]

In addition, it is also consistent with the reality that selected elements of the social structure can have positive effects on some economic outcomes and negative effects on other economic outcomes. In some settings village-level ethnic homogeneity may increase intra-village information flows about improved technologies. In the same setting, it may also decrease the resolution of inter-village collective action dilemmas. For example, Grootaert (1999) illustrates how village homogeneity can have both positive and negative effects on economic outcomes in rural Indonesia.

In a manner that is consistent with this conceptual approach, the chapters in this volume explore how social capital – as a fixed input into household production – affects well-being. Many of the chapters focus on one of the four aspects of well-being emphasized by Sen (UNDP, 1990 and subsequent years) and Dasgupta (Dasgupta and Weale, 1992; Dasgupta, 1993): real purchasing power, education, health and freedom to choose.

- *Real purchasing power*: in Chapter 5, Grootaert *et al.* present evidence that the incidence of consumption crises in Burkina Faso is substantially lower in villages in which community lending institutions are active. In Chapter 11, Healy demonstrates how social capital in Bolivia, in the forms of democratic assemblies, rule by consensus, rotating leadership and egalitarian ethos, has been mobilized to support the growth of the cacao market.
- *Education*: in Chapter 5, Grootaert *et al.* present evidence that community participation in parent–teacher associations in Burkina Faso is associated with substantially higher rates of school attendance.
- *Health*: in Chapter 10, Daniere *et al.* discuss how access to sanitation services in five Bangkok slums critically depends on social integration and linkages with external authorities.
- *Freedom to choose*: in Chapter 8, Cardenas presents empirical evidence from field experiments in Colombia, which shows that voice and loyalty among members within a group improve outcomes through communication and self-government. In Chapter 12, Colletta and Cullen show that conflict in war-torn Cambodia, Guatemala, Rwanda and Somalia has often been caused by social exclusion, inequality and indignity.

INVESTING IN SOCIAL CAPITAL TO IMPROVE WELL-BEING

Designers and supervisors of development projects and policy can no longer ignore forms of social capital that are likely to affect economic outcomes (Dasgupta, 2000). For example, in villages with high levels of inequality, norms that discourage social contacts between the rich and the poor would hinder the flow of public information about agricultural practices from the rich to the poor; in countries with few cross-cutting ties among ethnic groups, public health programmes may be coopted by the controlling elite.

Taking social capital into account, however, poses an immediate challenge to policy makers: how can one assess the composition of social capital in a target area? In Chapter 9, Isham promotes 'social assessments', field-based investigations of the social processes that affect local development outcomes (World Bank, 1996), as a cost-effective means of analysing characteristics of local social structures. In Chapters 7 and 8, Carpenter and Cardenas make the case that experiments among potential recipients of development assistance are a promising method for assessing various forms of social capital. Overall, the information provided by social assessments or experiments can help to provide information on which villages will, *ceteris paribus*, have higher expected returns to public investments. This is also true at the state level. In Chapter 12, Colletta and Cullen illustrate, with case studies of the four war-torn countries of Cambodia, Guatemala, Rwanda and Somalia, how disastrous conflicts can result from social exclusion, inequality and indignity. The implementation of a country-level development strategy is likely to be more effective when such country-level social conditions are documented and subsequently frame the strategy formation.

Under what guidelines should policy makers act on knowledge gained from assessments of local social structures and of country-level social conditions? First, we underline that one must follow the principle of 'first, doing no harm' (Ostrom, 1990; Narayan and Pritchett, 1999). As noted by Daniere *et al.* in Chapter 10 of the present volume, complex social relations that exist in even the least socially integrated groups can be detrimentally affected by poorly designed (if well intentioned) planning initiatives. This may be particularly true in very poor communities: households that are struggling to meet basic needs are less likely to respond to incentives designed to create social capital (for example, to gather regularly to initiate and support a local primary school).

In Chapter 4, Narayan stresses that development assistance dedicated to increasing well-being should support existing social organizations and promote cross-cutting relationships among exclusionary groups: this includes investments for building the strength of organizations of the poor and for directly facilitating cross-cutting ties. However, if investments in social capital are to be undertaken – for example, by training a local women's self-help group or by cofinancing a national-level NGO – the expected net benefits of such investments, like all potential development investments, should be compared to the expected net benefits of alternative investments. In Chapter 9, Isham explores this point by focusing on potential investments in the delivery of local services, like clean water and sanitation.

In Chapter 12, Colletta and Cullen illustrate how to follow these investment principles in the case of humanitarian relief. They argue that, when local abilities to utilize social capital are identified, humanitarian assistance should strengthen both primary (bonding) social capital and bridging networks. However, international agents should not overload local capacity by giving too much work or money to such efforts: in other words, when the marginal returns to investments in social capital have substantially diminished.

CHAPTER SUMMARIES

The chapters after this introduction are arranged in the thematic fashion: the history and scope of the concept of social capital in development economics; empirical and experimental evidence on social capital and well-being; and policy implications for investing in social capital in the field. We hope that the contributions in each of these chapters will help scholars, practitioners and teachers to sharpen their analysis of the ways social capital can affect the pursuit of improved well-being in the developing world.

The rest of the chapters in Part I frame the history, scope and the complexities surrounding the use of 'social capital' as it pertains to economic development. In Chapter 2 ('Social capital in theory and practice: where do we stand?'), Michael Woolcock synthesizes the recent theoretical and empirical literature on social capital and economic development. He reviews the challenges of defining and measuring social capital, and discusses the strengths and weaknesses of different disciplinary approaches to the term. Woolcock suggests that proven research strategies – qualitative and quantitative – should inform the design of new instruments to measure social capital, thereby improving our understanding of the way social capital affects well-being. He argues that social capital should provide a framework and a discourse that permits a common conversation among representations from different disciplines, methodologies and sectoral backgrounds. Moreover, he encourages policy makers to support interdisciplinary educational programmes that incorporate 'clean models' and 'dirty hands' and nurture rigorous depth and sympathetic breadth of knowledge about the role of social capital in improving well-being.

In Chapter 3 ('Reflections on social and antisocial capital'), Paul Streeten acknowledges the difficulty of defining, measuring and implementing the concept of social capital, yet exhorts sceptical development economists to take a second look at the concept. To clarify the concept, Streeten argues that social capital comprises consumption goods (non-durable and durable), non-durable production goods, and durable capital goods (for marketed and non-marketed activities). He emphasizes the potential negative effects of what he calls 'antisocial capital' on development outcomes, and then proposes that productive social capital should be nurtured and promoted at a global level. Streeten concludes with a list of novel suggestions for future research in this area.

In Chapter 4 ('Bonds and bridges: social capital and poverty'), Deepa Narayan summarizes theoretical and empirical evidence that shows how the concept of social capital improves the analysis of the social dimension of development. Narayan then focuses on two aspects of social capital: cross-cutting ties that characterize social relations in informal or formal voluntary groups and networks; and the interaction between formal and informal institutions. She presents case studies to demonstrate four possible combinations (comprising high and low cross-cutting ties, and well and poorly functioning states) and illustrates how high levels of cross-cutting ties and a well-functioning state best facilitate economic growth and well-being. She argues that outside interventions intended to increase well-being must account for existing social organizations and promote cross-cutting relationships among exclusionary groups.

The chapters in Part II provide empirical and experimental evidence, with different measures of social capital, on critical linkages between social capital and well-being. In Chapter 5 ('Social capital, education and credit markets: empirical evidence from Burkina Faso'), Christiaan Grootaert, Gi-Taik Oh and Anand Swamy empirically examine the effects of different forms of social capital on the performance of educational institutions and the functioning of credit markets in Burkina Faso. Using household survey data, the authors find that community participation in parent–teacher associations is associated with substantially higher rates of school attendance, and the incidence of consumption crises – as indicated by distress sales – is substantially lower in villages in which community lending institutions are active. The authors conclude by suggesting ways to increase active involvement in parent–teacher associations and establishment of stronger active community lending institutions.

In Chapter 6 ('The interactions of bonding, bridging and linking dimensions of social capital: evidence from rural Paraguay'), José Molinas empirically investigates forms of bonding, bridging and linking social capital in rural communities in Paraguay. With survey data from households and peasant committees, he explores the determinants of successful committee performance and attendance as well as peasants' decisions to join a local committee. He shows that informal interactions among households and strong linking strategies of peasant committees can strengthen bridging and bonding social capital, as measured by committee performance and membership attendance. He concludes by arguing that policy makers can catalyse virtuous circles of poverty alleviation by understanding the nature of bonding, bridging and linking relationships in local communities.

In Chapter 7 ('Measuring social capital: adding field experimental methods to the analytical toolbox'), Jeffrey Carpenter makes the case that laboratory experiments should complement the use of policy-oriented surveys in economics (and other social sciences). Carpenter shows that, while surveys can effectively frame policy-related issues and capture demographic data, economic experiments can validate survey results by providing incentive compatibility to elicit truthful responses. He then details four experiments: the 'trust' game, which measures trust and reciprocity; the 'ultimatum' game, which measures norms of fairness and reciprocity; the 'dictator' game, which measures generosity; and the 'voluntary contribution' game, which measures individuals' propensity to cooperate. While they are designed to test the predictive power of game-theoretic models, Carpenter illustrates how these games can be used to measure forms of social capital.

In Chapter 8 ('Rethinking local commons dilemmas: lessons from experimental economics in the field'), Juan-Camilo Cardenas argues that pessimism about commons dilemmas should be reconsidered in light of recent theoretical models, fieldwork and experimental work on common-pool resources (CPR). With data from field experiments conducted in rural CPR settings in Colombia, Cardenas demonstrates that many institutional factors determine whether groups can approach the socially optimal management of a CPR. In particular, an institutional setting that permits communication among homogeneous agents, without the intervention of a regulator, can promote relatively effective 'governing of the commons'. He concludes by suggesting that policy-oriented researchers should design field experiments that encourage active contributions of actual CPR users and that educators should involve students in classroom experiments to create a deeper understanding of sustainable management of a CPR.

The chapters in Part III explore the conditions under which investments in social capital can significantly improve well-being. In Chapter 9 ('Can investments in social capital improve local development and environmental outcomes? A cost–benefit framework to assess the policy options'), Jonathan Isham considers potential investments in development projects whose principal objective is the improved delivery of local services, such as the provision of clean water to a village. In this context, Isham cautions against blindly investing in social capital as a panacea for all development ills. He calls for a cost–benefit-oriented approach to potential investments in social capital that follows three guidelines. First, potential investments in social capital should be considered alongside potential investments in physical and human capital during the planning phase of most development projects. Second, since social capital can be a substitute or a complement to other potentially productive inputs, assessments of prevailing forms of social capital in a target area are likely to be valuable, even when direct investments in social capital are not anticipated or called for. Finally, guided by social assessments and the likely benefits and costs of potential investments in social capital, designers of development projects should recommend that investments not be undertaken in certain regions with very low levels of social capital – unless guided by equity considerations.

In Chapter 10 ('Social capital and environmental management: culture, perceptions and action among slum dwellers in Bangkok'), Amrita Daniere, Lois Takahashi and Anchana NaRanong explore the connection between social capital and environmental management in five of Bangkok's urban slums. The authors analyse how the capacity of low-income groups for collective environmental action is affected by geographic locale, income, security of tenure, relationship with other low-income settlements, and forms of social capital. Differences in environmental management among these slums critically depend on differences in social integration and linkages with external authorities. According to the authors, it is critical that the prevailing forms of community-level social capital be assessed prior to project implementation.

In Chapter 11 ('Building networks of social capital for grassroots development among indigenous communities in Bolivia and Mexico'), Kevin Healy presents two case studies of indigenous organizations that utilize social capital to promote grassroots development. The case of *El Ceibo*, a Bolivian peasant federation of 37 community-based service cooperatives, demonstrates how democratic assemblies, rule by consensus, rotating leadership and egalitarian ethos have been mobilized to support the growth of the cacao market in Bolivia. The case of *museos communitarios*, a community-based museum movement in Oaxaca, Mexico, illustrates how external agents have assisted the linking process that supplies the necessary financial capital for the growth of local museums. Healy argues that policy makers must acknowledge the importance of cultural change and thereby consider investments in social capital (such as the training of local personnel) to support this social process.

In Chapter 12 ('Resilient communities: building the social foundations of human security'), Nat Colletta and Michelle Cullen use case studies from four war-torn countries – Cambodia, Guatemala, Rwanda and Somalia – in order to identify conditions that reinforce exclusionary 'bonding' social capital, as opposed to nurturing exclusionary 'bridging' social capital. Colletta and Cullen show how conflict often results from exclusion, inequality and indignity, and then analyse the post-conflict recovery and growth of the four countries. They argue that peace-building efforts, in addition to economic reconstruction and the rebuilding of physical infrastructure, should try to foster social cohesion; and that the development process in these regions must revitalize productive social capital in order to lay the foundations for future sustained improvements of well-being.

We conclude by stressing the need for humility in attempting to define and measure forms of social capital and in attempting to assess and invest in social capital. The social dimensions of development are indeed extraordinarily complex. However, in order to improve well-being in developing countries, we think that such attempts are well worth the effort. We believe that the chapters in this volume provide guidance in this difficult but hopeful direction.

NOTES

1. This search of *EconLit* was conducted on 20 May 2002.
2. Aggregating all private and public investments is, in theory, a way to measure the increase of an economy's capital stock in a given period. In practice, this too is very challenging, particularly in the context of the developing world. For a discussion, see Pritchett (2000).
3. While Sen's ideas are widely accepted, there are a number of scholars who would argue that 'freedom' is a cultural construct, and the way in which 'freedom of choice' is typically expressed in development economics, and adopted by economists in general, is highly restrictive. Marglin and Marglin (1990) best capture these alternative critiques.
4. Dasgupta (1993) defines well-being as a function of 'utility (because it is the most reliable approximation of her rational desires), and an index of the worth to her of the freedom she enjoys'.
5. In a recent letter to *The Economist* on multilateral interventions to support civil society, Robert Wade dryly observes: 'Unkind people might observe that al-Qeda is an NGO, and one with extraordinary levels of social capital' (*The Economist*, 13 October 2001).

REFERENCES

Arrow, Kenneth J. (2000), 'Observations on social capital', in Partha Dasgupta and Ismail Serageldin (eds), *Social Capital – A Multifaceted Perspective*, Washington, DC: World Bank.

Basu, Kaushik (1997), *Analytical Development Economics*, Cambridge, MA: MIT Press.

Becker, Gary (1996), *Accounting for Tastes*, Cambridge, MA: Harvard University Press.

Betancourt, Roger R. (1996), 'Growth capabilities and development: implications for transition processes in Cuba', *Economic Development and Cultural Change*, **44** (2), 315–31.

Coleman, James S. (1990), *Foundations of Social Theory*, Cambridge, MA: The Belknap Press of Harvard University Press.

Collier, Paul (2002), 'Social capital and poverty', in Christiaan Grootaert and Thierry van Bastelaer (eds), *The Role of Social Capital in Development*, Cambridge: Cambridge University Press.

Dasgupta, Partha (1993), *An Inquiry into Well-Being and Destitution*, Oxford, UK: Clarendon Press.

—— (2000), 'Economic progress and the idea of social capital', in Partha Dasgupta and Ismail Serageldin (eds), *Social Capital – A Multifaceted Perspective*, Washington, DC: World Bank.

Dasgupta, Partha and Martin Weale (1992), 'On measuring the quality of life', *World Development*, **20** (1), 119–31.

Deaton, Angus and John Muellbauer (1980), *Economics and Consumer Behaviour*, Cambridge: Cambridge University Press.

Galasso, Emanuela and Martin Ravallion (2001), 'Decentralized targeting of an anti-poverty program', Policy Research Working Paper no. 2316, World Bank, Washington, DC.

Gambetta, Diego (1988), 'Mafia: the Price of Distrust', in Diego Gambetta (ed.), *Trust: Making and Breaking of Cooperative Relationships*, Oxford: Basil Blackwell.

Glaeser, Edward L., David Laibson, José A. Scheinkman and Christine L. Soutter (2000), 'Measuring trust', *Quarterly Journal of Economics*, **65**, 811–46.

Grootaert, Christiaan (1999), 'Social capital, household welfare and poverty in Indonesia', Local Level Institutions Working Paper No. 6, World Bank, Washington, DC.

Isham, Jonathan (forthcoming), 'The effect of social capital on technology adoption: evidence from rural Tanzania', *The Journal of African Economies*.

Isham, Jonathan and Satu Kähkönen (2002), 'How do participation and social capital affect community-based water projects? evidence from central Java, Indonesia', in Christiaan Grootaert and Thierry van Bastelaer (eds), *The Role of Social Capital in Development*, Cambridge: Cambridge University Press.

Kozel, Valerie and Barbara Parker (2000), 'Integrated approaches to poverty assessment in India', in Michael Bamberger (ed.), *Integrating Quantitative and Qualitative Research in Development Projects*, Washington, DC: World Bank, pp. 59–68.

Marglin, Frederique and Stephen Marglin (eds) (1990), *Dominating Knowledge*, Oxford: Clarendon Press.

Michael, Robert T. and Gary S. Becker (1973), 'On the new theory of consumer behavior', *Swedish Journal of Economics*, **75**, 378–96.

Moser, Caroline (1996), *Confronting Crisis: a comparative study of household responses to poverty and vulnerability in four poor urban communities*, Environmentally Sustainable Development Studies and Monograph Series 8, Washington, DC: World Bank.

Muellbauer, John (1987), 'Professor Sen on the standard of living', in Geoffrey Hawthorn (ed.), *The Standard of Living*, Cambridge, UK: Cambridge University Press.

Narayan, Deepa and Lant Pritchett (1999), 'Cents and sociability: household income and social capital in rural Tanzania', *Economic Development and Cultural Change*, **47** (4), 871–97.

Ostrom, Elinor (1990), *Governing the Commons: The Evolution of Institutions for Collective Action*, New York: Cambridge University Press.

—— (2000), 'Social capital: a fad or a fundamental concept?', in Partha Dasgupta and Ismail Serageldin (eds), *Social Capital – A Multifaceted Perspective*, Washington, DC: World Bank.

Pritchett, Lant (2000), 'The tyranny of concepts: CUDIE (cumulated, depreciated, investment effort) is not capital', *Journal of Economic Growth*, **5**, 361–84.

Putnam, Robert (1993), *Making Democracy Work*, Princeton, NJ: Princeton University Press.

Putnam, Robert (2000), *Bowling Alone*, New York: Simon and Schuster.

Ray, Debraj (1998), *Development Economics*, Princeton, NJ: Princeton University Press.

Schafft, Kai and David Brown (2000), 'Social capital and grassroots development: the case of Roma self-governance in Hungary', *Social Problems*, **47** (2), 201–19.

Schultz, Theodore W. (1960), 'Capital formation by education', *The Journal of Political Economy*, **68** (6), 571–83.

Sen, Amartya (1985) 'Well-being. agency and freedom', *The Journal of Philosophy*, **82** (4), 169–221.

—— (1999), *Development as Freedom*, New York: Alfred Knopf.

Solow, Robert (2000), 'Notes on social capital and economic performance', in Partha Dasgupta and Ismail Serageldin (eds), *Social Capital – A Multifaceted Perspective*, Washington, DC: World Bank.

Streeten, Paul (1995), *Thinking about Development*, New York: Cambridge University Press.

UNDP (1990 and subsequent years), *The Human Development Report*, Oxford: Oxford University Press.

Woolcock, Michael (1998), 'Social capital and economic development: toward a theoretical synthesis and policy framework', *Theory and Society*, **27** (2), 151–208.

World Bank (1996), *World Bank Participation Source Book*, Washington, DC: World Bank.

World Bank (1998), 'The local level institutions working study: overview and program description', Washington, DC: World Bank.

2. Social capital in theory and practice: where do we stand?

Michael Woolcock[1]

'It's not what you know, it's *who* you know.' This common aphorism sums up much of the conventional wisdom regarding social capital. It is wisdom supported by empirical evidence, but also borne out in our everyday experience: In good times, we draw on the skills, insights and resources of others to pursue individual and common goals; when we fall upon hard times, our friends and family are often our final 'safety net'. Gaining membership to exclusive clu⌐s requires inside contacts; close competition for jobs and contracts is often won by those with 'friends in high places'. Less instrumentally, some of our happiest and most rewarding hours are spent talking with neighbours, sharing meals with friends, participating in religious gatherings and volunteering on community projects.

The nature and extent of our social relationships have an important impact on our lives but they are especially significant for the poor: with little by way of material assets, modest income or formal education, the poor are left to devise survival and mobility strategies that draw on (or in some cases circumvent) their social capital. This chapter introduces the recent theoretical and empirical literature on social capital as it pertains to economic development, with a particular focus on its significance for teaching and practice. It seeks to address four questions: (1) what is social capital, (2) how do different disciplines conceptualize and measure it, (3) how do any disciplinary similarities and differences influence development theory and research, and (4) how might an awareness of the strengths and weaknesses of these different approaches lead to a more integrated approach to the teaching and practice of economic development?

The chapter begins by examining the remarkable resurgence of interest over the last decade in the social dimensions of development in general and the idea of social capital in particular. It then provides a basic primer on social capital and a brief survey of the empirical evidence. Next it provides a response to several recurring criticisms of the concept of social capital and explores approaches to social capital theory, research and policy taken by the different social science disciplines. It concludes by calling for a renewed commitment to interdisciplinary and multi-method research on development issues among educators and practitioners.

THE DECLINE AND RISE OF THE SOCIAL DIMENSIONS OF DEVELOPMENT

Over the last ten years there has been a resurgence of interest in the social and institutional dimensions of economic development (World Bank, 1997, 2000b). Work in this field was pioneered by Hirschman (1958) and Adelman and Morris (1967), who detailed the critical role of formal and informal institutions in a range of development outcomes. In general, the issues that these authors raised were intellectually 'crowded' out – and neglected in the policy arena – until the late 1980s. During the 1970s and 1980s, Cold War rhetoric and ideological dichotomies (state planning versus free markets) dominated development discourse in First and Second World countries, while elites in the Third World (and many of their western scholarly counterparts) tended to blame forces beyond their borders for poor domestic performance.[2] For more than 30 years, then, the role of national and local institutions – political, legal and social – was largely neglected.

A number of geopolitical factors contributed to an academic and policy turnaround in the 1990s: the fall of communism, the rise of ethnic conflict, the difficulties of creating market institutions in transitional economies, financial crises in Mexico, East Asia, Russia and Brazil, the enduring scourge of poverty in the most prosperous economies and the continued overuse of selected natural resources such as the fisheries in the Northern Atlantic and the forests of South America and sub-Saharan Africa. Meanwhile, policy makers, foreign investors and aid agencies alike finally began to recognize that corruption, far from 'greasing the wheels' in weak institutional environments, was in fact imposing serious and measurable net costs (World Bank, 1998), and that weak local and state institutions could lead to potentially alarming overuse of natural resources (World Bank, 1992). Faced with the glaring evidence that orthodox theories had neither anticipated these difficulties nor offered safe passage through them, attention returned to the social and institutional determinants of development and environmental outcomes.

This was the demand side of the story. On the supply side, a remarkable series of publications gave social scientists greater confidence to address these long-neglected themes. In economics, Nobel laureate Douglass North (1990) argued that formal and informal institutions (the legal structures and normative 'rules of the game') were crucial to understanding economic performance. The pioneering work of Joseph Stiglitz, Amartya Sen and Mancur Olson on (respectively) incomplete information, well-being and institutional rigidities also continued to be influential (Stiglitz, 1998; Sen, 1999; Olson, 2000). In political science, Robert Putnam (1993) showed that the density and scope of local civic associations laid the foundations for the widespread dissemination of information and social trust, thereby creating conditions that underpin effective governance and economic development. Robert Wade (1988) and Elinor Ostrom (1990) delineated the importance of social relations and local institutions in the maintenance of common property resources, including the management of watersheds and fisheries in developing countries.[3] In sociology, Peter Evans (1992, 1995, 1996) demonstrated that whether a state was 'developmental' or 'predatory' was crucially dependent on both the capacity of its public institutions and the nature of state–society relations.[4] By the late 1990s, the development literature on institutional capacity, social networks and community participation inspired by these works began to coalesce around a general framework loosely held together by the idea of 'social capital'.[5] Not everyone in the field of development uses or even likes this term, to be sure, but the language and concepts surrounding social capital can be fruitfully deployed to provide a common reference point for scholars and prac-titioners who otherwise conduct their activities using largely disparate discourses.

DEFINING AND CONCEPTUALIZING SOCIAL CAPITAL

Intuitively, the basic idea of 'social capital' is that one's family, friends and associates constitute an important asset, one that can be called upon in a crisis, enjoyed for its own sake or leveraged for material gain. In the development literature, those communities endowed with a rich stock of social networks and civic associations have been shown to be in a stronger position to confront poverty and vulnerability (Moser, 1996; Narayan, 1997; Kozel and Parker, 2000), resolve disputes (Schafft and Brown, 2000) and share beneficial information (Isham, forthcoming). As several econometric studies have shown, diffuse sets of social ties are crucial to the provision of informal insurance mechanisms (Coate and Ravallion, 1993; Townsend, 1994) and have important impacts on the success of development projects (Isham, Narayan and Pritchett, 1995, Galasso and Ravallion, 2001).

Conversely, the *absence* of social ties can have an equally important impact. A defining feature of being poor is that one is not a member of – or is even actively excluded from – certain social networks and institutions. Narayan's (2000) exhaustive global study of the poor's explanations of their plight strongly implicates (among other things) the absence of organizations enabling those living in poverty to voice their collective interests and aspirations. Varshney (2001) shows that, where cross-cutting associational ties bring Hindus and Muslims together in India, conflict is addressed constructively and rarely descends into violence; where such ties are lacking, there are no established channels for anticipating or dealing with difference. Barr (1998) reports similar findings among firms in Africa: poor entrepreneurs have a limited and circumscribed set of 'protection' networks, while the non-poor have a more diverse set of 'innovation' networks (see also Fafchamps and Minten, 1999). There is also evidence to suggest that, in many poor communities, women primarily possess intensive protection networks, while men have access to more extensive innovation networks (Narayan, 2000).

Our intuition about the concept of social capital also recognizes an additional, less hopeful feature. Social ties have costs as well as benefits; normative expectations regarding the usefulness of education to young girls, for example, can impede their quest to continue schooling.[6] In short, the social ties we have can be both a blessing and a blight, while those we do *not* have can deny us access to key resources. These features of social capital, well documented by empirical evidence, have important implications for economic development.

Social capital has entered debates about economic performance on its ambitious claim to constituting an independent, and hitherto underappreciated, factor of production. The classical economists identified land, labour and *physical* capital (that is, tools and technology) as the three basic factors shaping economic growth, to which in the 1960s neoclassical economists such as Theodore Schultz and Gary Becker introduced the notion of *human* capital, arguing that a society's endowment of educated, trained and healthy workers determines how productively the orthodox factors can be utilized. The latest equipment and most innovative ideas in the hands or mind of the brightest, fittest person, however, will amount to little unless that person also has access to others to inform, correct, assist with and disseminate their work. Life at home, in the boardroom, or on the shop floor is both more rewarding and productive when suppliers, colleagues and clients alike are able to combine their particular skills and resources in a spirit of cooperation and commitment to common objectives. In essence, where human capital resides in individuals, social capital resides in relationships (Lin, 2001).[7] Though beginning from a different theoretical standpoint, many economists have also conceptualized social capital in relational terms, using the language of externalities, public goods and transaction costs.

Much of the broader interest in social capital, however, has been fuelled by a conceptualization that includes not only networks and social relations, but also psychological dispositions (such as social skills, cooperation and honesty) and political measures ('rule of law', 'contract enforceability', 'civil liberties' and so on).[8] This more inclusive approach is appealing to some because of the existence of large, cross-national data sets (for example, the World Values Survey, Freedom House scores), which permit 'social capital' (now measured by country-level 'trust' and 'governance' scores) to be entered into macroeconomic growth regressions.[9] Such studies make for provocative reading, but the collective panoply of micro and macro measures of 'social capital'[10] – and their correspondingly eclectic theoretical moorings – has led many critics to accuse social capital of having become all things to all people, and hence nothing to anyone.

What to do? One approach has been to refer to macroinstitutional issues under a separate banner, calling them instead 'social capabilities' or 'social infrastructure' (for example, Koo and Perkins, 1995; Temple and Johnson, 1998; Hall and Jones, 1999). The virtue of this strategy is that it relieves social capital of its mounting intellectual burden, analytically and empirically disentangling micro-community and macroinstitutional concerns. The vice is that it removes a convenient discursive shorthand for the social dimensions of development vis-à-vis other factors of production (cf. 'human capital', 'financial capital') and treats as separate what is more accurately considered together (see below). A second approach has been to call for a more tightly focused micro definition of social capital (Portes, 1998; Putnam, 2000), to advocate a 'lean and mean' conceptualization focusing on the *sources* of social capital – that is, primarily social networks – rather than its *consequences* (which can be either positive or negative, depending on the circumstances), such as trust, tolerance and cooperation. The upside of this approach is that it is more or less clear about what is, and what is not, social capital, making for cleaner measurement and more parsimonious theory building; the downside is that it tends to overlook the broader institutional environment in which communities are inherently embedded.

So is social capital a micro phenomenon, a macro phenomenon, both or does it not matter?[11] The strategy first outlined in Woolcock (1998) has been to acknowledge the merits of each approach and to attempt a synthesis that builds on the following definition of social capital: social capital refers to the norms and networks that facilitate collective action. This definition of social capital focuses on its sources rather than its consequences, on what it *is* rather than what it *does* (Edwards and Foley, 1997). (Without this distinction, as Portes, 1998, points out, an argument could be put forward that successful groups were distinguished by their dense community ties, failing to consider the possibility that the same ties could be *preventing* success in another otherwise similar group.)

Accordingly, social capital makes most sense when it is understood as a relational (that is, sociological), rather than psychological[12] or political variable.[13] If we are to be true to the dicta of scholarship – namely, that the reliability and validity of data (whether qualitative or quantitative), their analysis and interpretation constitute the central focus of our deliberations – then the broader definition is becoming increasingly untenable, because the best and most coherent empirical research on social capital, *irrespective of discipline*, has operationalized it as a sociological variable (see Foley and Edwards 1999). Furthermore, if 'social capital' is facile or distracting, as some maintain (for example, Fine 1999, 2000), then this, too, should be demonstrated empirically, not refuted polemically. Given the ever-accumulating weight of evidence documenting the significance of social capital, however, the burden of proof is rapidly shifting to the detractors. One virtue of adopting a relatively narrow definition is that it encourages supporters and sceptics alike to play by the same rules. Another virtue is that it allows us to rule *in* several decades' worth of careful research by sociologists and economists on communities, networks and associations that, while not deploying the social capital terminology as such, nonetheless most certainly can and should be read as foundational work in this field.

In order to accommodate the range of positive and negative outcomes associated with our intuitive understanding of the concept of social capital, it is necessary to recognize the multidimensional nature of its sources. The most common and popular distinction – drawing on Cooley's (1909) notion of primary (and Durkheim's writings on secondary) groups, and Granovetter's (1973) work on 'strong' and 'weak' ties – is between 'bonding' and 'bridging' social capital (Gittell and Vidal, 1998). The former refers to relations between family members, close friends and neighbours, the latter to more distant associates and colleagues who have somewhat different demographic characteristics,[14] irrespective of how well they know one another.

Bonding and bridging are horizontal metaphors: they imply tight or loose connections between people. Social capital also has a vertical dimension, which can be called 'linkages'. As Fox (1996), Heller (1996) and Bebbington (1999) have stressed, poverty is largely a function of powerlessness and exclusion, so a key task for development practitioners and policy makers is to ensure that the activities of the poor not only 'reach out' but are also 'scaled up'. An important component of this strategy entails forging alliances with sympathetic individuals in positions of power (Brown and Fox, 1998), an approach Hirschman (1968) wryly calls 'reform by stealth'. This vertical dimension can be called 'linkages' (Woolcock, 1999; World Bank, 2000b). The capacity to leverage resources, ideas and information from formal institutions beyond the community, most notably the state, is a key function of linking social capital.

Building on these concepts of bonding, bridging and linking social capital, the approach adopted in this volume is to argue that different *combinations* of these forms of social capital are responsible for a range of critical development and environmental outcomes. These distinctions have particular significance for understanding the plight of the poor in developing countries, who typically have a close-knit and intensive stock of bonding social capital that they leverage to 'get by' (Briggs, 1998; Holzmann and Jorgensen, 1999), a modest endowment of the more diffuse and extensive bridging social capital typically deployed by the non-poor to 'get ahead' (Barr, 1998; Narayan, 1999) and almost no linking social capital enabling them to gain sustained access to formal institutions such as banks, insurance agencies and the courts (World Bank, 2000b).[15] It is important to stress again that bonding, bridging and linking social capital also have downsides: strong communal ties can justify cruelty to women and minorities; friends in low and high places who fall foul of the law can bring you down, too ('guilt by association'); and oppressive linking ties, such as those between landlords and peasants, can perpetuate servitude and oppression.

This view of social capital, centred on networks within, between and beyond communities, acknowledges the importance of the institutional context within which these networks are embedded, especially the role of the state. Indeed, the vibrancy or paucity of social capital cannot be understood independently of its broader institutional environment: communities can be highly engaged because they are mistreated or ignored by public institutions (for example, providing credit and security because banks and police refuse to do so) or because they enjoy highly complementary relations with the state (Narayan, 1999). The absence or weakness of formal institutions is often compensated for by the creation of informal organizations (Besley and Coate, 1995; Davis, 1999). Weak, hostile or indifferent governments have a profoundly different effect on community life (and development projects), for example, than governments that respect civil liberties, uphold the rule of law and resist corruption (Isham, Kaufmann and Pritchett, 1997; Kaufmann *et al.*, 1999a).

The importance of institutions is particularly instructive for understanding the plight of minorities and marginalized groups in developing countries and the role of social divisions more generally. One of the most popular empirical measures of social divisions is 'ethno-linguistic fractionalization', which some (for example, Easterly and Levine, 1997) have argued is a significant source of economic stagnation in regions such as Africa. The most recent work, by Collier (1999) and Posner (1999), however, argues that high levels of ethnic fractionalization *per se* are in fact not a concern (indeed, diversity can be an asset); rather, it is the presence of two or three large competing ethnic groups *coupled with weak public institutions* that spells danger.[16] This explains in part why ethnically heterogeneous societies like the USA, Canada, the UK and Australia (and OECD countries in general) have been able to enjoy the fruits of their diversity, while many non-democratic developing countries have not.

SOCIAL CAPITAL AND MODELS OF ECONOMIC GROWTH: GETTING THE SOCIAL RELATIONS RIGHT

This conceptualization of the role of different types and combinations of social networks in development represents an important departure from earlier theoretical approaches, and therefore has important implications for current development research and policy. To see why, it is instructive to briefly review those theories.

Until the 1990s, the major theories of development held rather narrow, even contradictory, views of the role of social relationships in economic development and offered little by way of constructive policy recommendations. In the 1950s and 1960s, for example, modernization theory regarded traditional social relationships and ways of life as an impediment to development. When modernization theorists explained 'the absence or failure of capitalism', Moore (1997) correctly notes, 'the focus [was] on social relations as obstacles'. An influential United Nations (1951) document of the time encapsulated this view; for development to proceed, it proclaimed,

> ancient philosophies have to be scrapped; old social institutions have to disintegrate; bonds of caste, creed and race have to burst; and large numbers of persons who cannot keep up with progress have to have their expectations of a comfortable life frustrated. (Cited in Escobar, 1995)

This view gave way in the 1970s to the arguments of dependency and world-systems theorists, who held social relations among corporate and political elites to be a primary mechanism of capitalist exploitation. The social characteristics of poor countries and communities were defined almost exclusively in terms of their relations to the means of production and the inherent antipathy between the interests of capital and labour. Little mention was made of the possibility (or desirability) of mutually beneficial relationships between workers and owners, of the tremendous variation in success enjoyed by developing countries, or of political strategies other than 'revolution' by which the poor could improve their lot. Communitarian perspectives,[17] on the other hand, with their emphasis on the inherent beneficence and self-sufficiency of local communities, underestimated the negative aspects of communal obligations, overestimated the virtues of isolation and neglected the importance of social relations to constructing effective formal institutions. For their part, neoclassical and public choice theories – the most influential in the 1980s and early 1990s – assigned no distinctive properties to social relations *per se*. These perspectives focused on the strategic choices of rational individuals interacting under various time, budgetary and legal constraints, holding that groups (including firms) existed primarily to lower the transactions costs of exchange;

given undistorted market signals, the optimal size and combination of groups would duly emerge. 'Selective incentives' and third-party enforcement were needed where markets failed to ensure that groups acted to serve collective interests. In the theory of environmental policy, the standard view had been solidified by the early 1970s (Baumol and Oates, 1988): that the proper Pigouvian taxes or equivalent permits were the most cost-effective way to find the socially optimal solution in the presence of production or consumption externalities or the overuse of an open access or common-pool resource.

For the major development theories, then, social relations have been construed as singularly burdensome, exploitative, liberating or irrelevant. Reality, unfortunately, does not conform so neatly to these descriptions and their corresponding policy prescriptions. Events in the post-Cold War era – from ethnic violence and civil war to financial crises and the acknowledgment of widespread corruption and continued environmental degradation on an unprecedented scale – have demanded a more sophisticated appraisal of the virtues, vices and vicissitudes of 'the social dimension' as it pertains to the wealth and poverty of nations.

The social capital literature, in its broadest sense, represents a first approximation to the answer to this challenge. It is a literature to which all the social science disciplines have contributed, and it is beginning to generate a remarkable consensus regarding the role and importance of institutions and communities in development. Indeed, one of the primary benefits of the idea of social capital is that it is allowing scholars, policy makers and practitioners from different disciplines to enjoy an unprecedented level of cooperation and dialogue (Brown and Ashman, 1996; Brown, 1998). In reviving and revitalizing mainstream sociological insights, there has been a corresponding appreciation that different disciplines have a vital, distinctive and frequently complementary contribution to offer to inherently complex problems. Another distinctive feature of the social capital approach is its approach to understanding poverty. Living on the margins of existence, the social capital of the poor is the one asset they can potentially draw upon to help negotiate their way through an unpredictable and unforgiving world. As Dordick (1997) astutely notes, the very poor have 'something left to lose', namely each other. While much of the discourse surrounding poor people and poor economies is one of 'deficits', a virtue of the social capital perspective is that it allows theorists, policy makers and practitioners to take an approach based on 'assets'.

If, as argued here, we should adopt a relatively narrow sociological definition of social capital, but understand it as inherently embedded in an institutional context, where does this leave us in terms of applying social capital to questions of economic growth? What relevance does a social theory of norms and networks have for minders of regional and national economic performance?

This question can be answered in a number of ways, but I will identify four. The first is that social capital, so understood, should mind its own business, focus on communities and leave macroeconomic concerns to the experts. A second response is to search for existing proxies for network size and structure, and simply 'add' them to the catalogue of other variables deemed significant for growth and well-being. A third answer is to do the hard work of integrating serious qualitative and quantitative research strategies into the design of comprehensive new instruments to measure social capital more accurately. A fourth strategy is to take the central ideas underlying the social capital perspective (the 'spirit' of social capital, if you will) and apply them in innovative ways to broader issues of policy economy. Of these answers, the first is overly modest, the second overly ambitious. The third is a desirable long-run objective, the fourth an intriguing possibility with more immediate returns. Needless to say, I cast my lot with champions of answers three and four. In the remaining space, let me sketch these positions in further detail.

TOWARDS NEW, BETTER, MORE COMPREHENSIVE MEASURES

For social capital to become a serious indicator of regional and national well-being, measures of it need to be drawn from large representative samples, using indicators that have been pre-tested and refined for their suitability. Building on the success of the World Bank's local-level institutions project (World Bank, 1998b), such efforts are under way in a number of countries, with the distinct possibility that social capital questions may soon be included in the census of several OECD countries. In developing countries such as Guatemala, the highly acclaimed Living Standards Measurement Survey (LSMS), the standard-bearer for high-quality data on income, expenditure, health and education, has incorporated a social capital module, the first of its kind. Just as this survey will enable us to make reliable national-level estimates of the levels of poverty, education and health, so too will it provide more or less comparable data on social capital. The quantitative measures to be gleaned from this survey of more than 9000 representative households will be complemented by a major qualitative analysis at the village level. If social capital is armed with data of the scale and quality of previous LSMS studies, one can argue that it should be 'mainstreamed' into the range of familiar economic measures used to take the pulse of society (unemployment rates, consumer price indexes, inflation levels, and the like).

It is important to stress that, while gathering 'hard data' is indispensable, the qualitative aspects of social capital should not be neglected. In many respects it is something of a contradiction in terms to argue that universal measures can be used. The best survey instruments for measuring social capital are likely to follow intensive periods in the field in order to capture local idiosyncratic realities.

INCORPORATING THE SPIRIT OF SOCIAL CAPITAL INTO POLITICAL ECONOMY AND PUBLIC POLICY

The policy response to reading the social capital literature should not be a call for governments to provide more choirs and soccer clubs, as readers satirizing Putnam (1993) have tended to infer. Social capital is not a panacea, and more of it is not necessarily better. But the broader message rippling through the social capital literature is that how we associate with each other, and on what terms, has enormous implications for our well-being, whether we live in rich or poor countries. Consequently, a number of important findings that have recently emerged independently from the political economy literature are entirely consistent with the emerging social capital perspective.

To see why, recall the three dimensions of social capital outlined above, and my insistence that they be understood in the context of their institutional environment. If it is true that meagre stocks of bridging social capital make it more difficult for ideas, information and resources to circulate between groups, then it follows that broader economic, social and political forces that divide societies will be harmful for growth. Economic inequality and overt discrimination along gender and ethnic lines, for example, should be harmful for growth. Similarly, if leveraging social capital is an important risk management strategy during times of economic distress (for example, losing a job, enduring crop failure or suffering a prolonged illness), it follows that divided societies will experience greater difficulty managing economic shocks. Moreover, my emphasis on understanding the efficacy of social capital in its institutional context implies that the way communities manage both opportunities and risk will be necessarily dependent on the quality of the institutions under which they live. Rampant corruption, frustrating bureaucratic delays, suppressed civil liberties and failure to safeguard property rights and uphold the rule of law can be expected to force communities back on themselves, demanding that they supply privately and informally what should be delivered publicly and formally. Accordingly, in countries where these conditions prevail, there should be little to show for even the most well-intentioned efforts to build schools, hospitals and encourage foreign investment (Easterly, 2001).

Recent work by Dani Rodrik (1999a, 1999b) and William Easterly (2001) provides powerful econometric evidence in support of the idea that economic growth in general, and the ability to manage shocks in particular, are the twin products of coherent public institutions *and* societies able to generate what

Easterly calls a 'middle class consensus'. Countries with divided societies (along ethnic and economic lines) and weak, hostile or corrupt governments are especially prone to a growth collapse. When shocks hit, as they did in the mid-1970s and early 1980s, these countries proved unable and/or unwilling to make the necessary adjustments. Lacking well-established precedents, procedures and institutional resources for managing conflict, these economies experienced a major growth collapse from which some have still not recovered (see below).[18]

For students of economic growth in the 1960s, as Rodrik (1999a) correctly notes, it was hard to adjudicate between the merits of different strategies, as all economies (open/closed, natural resources/manufacturing, landlocked/ coastal, temperate/tropical, large/small) did relatively well. The real test came with the oil crises of the 1970s and the global recession of the early 1980s, which produced a growth collapse in the developing economies of Grand Canyon proportions, one that did not end until 1995. The devastating growth collapse of 1975–95 cost the average person in the typical developing country around $2000,[19] and set back by at least a decade the level of economic development that would have been attained had the 1955–74 growth trajectory been maintained. (By comparison, the recent Asian financial crises will appear as temporary, localized and relatively minor. The OECD nations also suffered a growth collapse in the late 1970s/early 1980s; they recovered relatively quickly, but have returned only to the modest growth rate levels more commensurate with their history.)

So, while social capital scholarship *per se* is surely on the safest ground when it speaks to community development issues, the spirit of social capital is also consistent with findings now emerging in studies of macroeconomic growth. It is in this sense that I think social research on economic issues and economic research on social issues is reaching a remarkable – but largely unacknowledged – consensus. More dialogue and diplomacy among social scientists, rather than perennial civil war, might enable us to harness these collective insights in the joint pursuit of a more productive economy and inclusive society.

IMPLICATIONS FOR THE TEACHING AND PRACTICE OF DEVELOPMENT ECONOMICS

A number of important policy and pedagogical implications follow from the above analysis. First, while it is reasonable to argue that something resembling a coherent theory of development is coalescing around the idea of social capital, it would be contrary to the spirit of this emerging tradition to posture itself as yet another 'grand theory' of development, or as a 'master synthesis' of the otherwise diverse social science perspectives. Rather, a distinctive feature of the social capital approach should be that it provides a framework and a discourse that permits a common conversation among representatives from different disciplines, methodologies and sectoral backgrounds. To draw a parallel with religion, the goal is not to create a new faith or to convert other faiths to your own, but rather to create spaces, opportunities and mutually agreed-upon rules of engagement that enable each to learn from the others. Klitgaard (1998) astutely argues that at the cutting edge of current public policy thinking is a recognition that blueprints are out, frameworks that enable diverse stakeholders to forge common solutions are in. Putnam (2000) is right to stress the importance of not letting social capital's marketing department get ahead of its product development, but the real reason for policy caution is not lack of knowledge about core elements of the social capital framework (as outlined above) but rather that to make definitive *a priori* claims about what should or should not be done can defeat the very purpose of getting communities, firms and governments to take responsibility the process of identifying, implementing, sustaining and evaluating appropriate policy solutions.

In any event, the central goal of a social capital-based policy agenda should be the reduction of social and economic divisions, increasing the responsiveness and accountability of public institutions, and encouraging openness to, and interaction among, people from different walks of life. These principles apply as much to families, communities and firms as they do to nations.

Second, for institutions of higher education, one can argue that this key message – the importance of harnessing the insights of different perspectives – paradoxically means that considerable caution needs to be urged regarding the offering of 'interdisciplinary' *courses* in development studies. Such courses always have noble intentions in terms of freeing students from disciplinary constraints and doubtless they sometimes succeed in this. The harsh reality, however, as Smelser (1997) correctly notes, is that interdisciplinary scholarship is perhaps the most lauded but least rewarded academic activity, and for good sociological reasons: we are not trained this way, interdisciplinary work has no organized constituency to recognize and reward it, and the most influential individuals and paradigms in any policy field are solidly grounded in a single discipline.

Successful challenges to those individuals and paradigms therefore requires a two-part strategy: part one entails engaging in what Hirschman (1968) describes as 'smuggling in change': finding sympathetic allies within the existing power structure who are willing to push the frontiers of acceptability; part two entails forging positive coherent alternatives that nonetheless articulate constructively with that power structure. (Most critics of a prevailing system are far clearer about what they are against than what they are for; similarly, as Machiavelli wisely intoned, defenders of orthodoxy are more vigilant and vociferous than advocates of change.) Effectively carrying out both parts of this strategy requires people who are solidly grounded in a single (depth), but who are simultaneously cognizant of a given discipline's inherent limitations, and who know how and where to find complementary perspectives (breadth). Orthodox undergraduate degree programmes in general, and graduate programmes in particular, do a fabulous job perpetuating the former, but a woeful one incorporating the latter. This implies that there is enormous scope for interdisciplinary *programmes* of study, where both the integrity of disciplines is respected and common ground rules are established to encourage healthy competition and cooperation between them (intellectual monopolies are as inefficient as their economic counterparts). Nowhere are these debates more necessary and important than in questions pertaining to the wealth and poverty of nations.

A third implication pertains to the practice of development and environment research and projects. If better policy emerges from political contexts encouraging the input of different stakeholders, and if better students emerge from educational contexts encouraging both rigorous depth and sympathetic breadth, then we should also expect better development research and better development projects from institutional contexts that encourage the integration of different types and sources of knowledge. This is perhaps a truism at one level, but at another it is actually quite radical, because it implies that (a) there are in fact different forms and ways of 'knowing' (the experience of sleeping in a homeless shelter for two weeks, for example, teaches you something that is qualitatively different from data on the homeless downloaded from the web), and (b) harnessing the comparative advantage of different types of knowledge holds enormous potential for intellectual and practical advancement (Klitgaard, 1994). This means that active support should be given to exercises ranging from 'village immersion' programmes for development executives, mentoring programmes for youth in disadvantaged communities and volunteering, to requiring economists who study poverty to actually talk to the poor, and teaching qualitative social scientists how to interpret a regression table: that is, get all sides to recognize the virtues of both 'clean models' and 'dirty hands' (Hirsch *et al.*, 1990).

CONCLUSION

For both countries and communities, then, rich and poor alike, managing risk, shocks and opportunities is a key ingredient in the quest to achieve sustainable economic development. Whether shocks manifest themselves as terms of trade declines, natural disasters, strikes, disputes over access to water, domestic violence or the death of a spouse, those social entities able to weather the storm will be those that are more likely to prosper. A social capital perspective seeks to go beyond primordial 'cultural explanations' for these different response strategies, to look instead for structural and relational features. Development is more than just a matter of playing good 'defence' (or 'getting by'), however; it also entails knowing how to initiate and maintain strategic 'offence' ('getting ahead'). From large public–private partnerships (Tendler, 1995) to village-level development programmes (Bebbington and Carroll, 1999), success turns on the extent to which ways and means can be found to forge mutually beneficial and accountable ties between different agents and agencies of expertise.

It is in this sense that 'getting the social relations right' (Woolcock, forthcoming) is a crucial component of both the means and ends of development. If the idea and the ideals of social capital help move us in this direction – and do so by encouraging and rewarding greater cross-fertilization between disciplines and methodologies and between scholars, practitioners and policy makers[20] – then it more than justifies its place in the new development lexicon. In matters pertaining to the social dimensions of development, it is easy to be cynical, it is even easier to be a true believer; what we need is more critical innovators, those able to bring valid evidence to bear on empirical questions, on the one hand, and who can find ways and means to do with others what they cannot do alone, on the other.

NOTES

1. This chapter draws on and extends material previously published in Woolcock and Narayan (2000) and Woolcock (2001).
2. To be sure, the power of wealthy nations, corporations and individuals to exert disproportionate influence in developing countries remains an important issue, but in the 1960s, 1970s and 1980s the myopic focus by dependency theorists on these 'external forces' trumped most serious efforts to examine 'internal conditions'. Modernization theorists raised some of these concerns, but largely in unhelpful ways, for example by examining national or ethnic 'cultural traits' or levels of 'achievement motivation', which they believed were reflected in patterns and degrees of development. For a review of the more recent literature on culture and development, see Alkire *et al.* (2000).
3. Norman Uphoff also continued to make influential contributions, building on his earlier work with Milton Esman on local organizations (Esman and Uphoff, 1984).
4. For comparable innovative work in anthropology, see Singerman (1995) and Ensminger (1996).
5. See Woolcock (1998) for an overview of the intellectual history of social capital. Extensive social capital citations in fields other than development are presented in Woolcock (1998) and Foley and Edwards (1999).
6. Indeed, an early criticism of the social capital literature was that it failed to appreciate the forms and consequences of these costs. For members of cults, for example, group loyalties may be so binding that attempts to leave result in death; some successful members of immigrant communities have reportedly Anglicized their names in order to divest themselves of obligations to support subsequent cohorts (Portes and Sensenbrenner, 1993). More onerously, the destructive acts of hate groups, drug cartels and terrorist organizations may impose enormous burdens on society as a whole (Rubio, 1997).

7. Human and social capital are complements, however, in that literate and informed citizens are better able to organize, evaluate conflicting information and express their views in constructive ways; schools that are an integral part of community life, nurture high parental involvement and actively expand the horizons of students report higher test scores (Morgan and Sorensen, 1999; cf. Coleman, 1988; Hanifan, 1916).
8. See Temple (2000) for a review of this literature.
9. See, among others, Knack and Keefer (1997), La Porta *et al.* (1997), Knack (1999a), Collier and Gunning (1999).
10. For a summary of various measures of social capital, see Grootaert (1997, Box 3).
11. A third approach has been to dismiss the definitional debate altogether. For researchers such as Knack (1999b), it is a moot question as to whether social capital is, or should be understood as, a micro or macro phenomenon: 'Social capital *is* what social capital scholars *do*.' Just as social scientists do important and rigorous work on 'power' without a universally agreed-upon definition of it, so, too, these writers maintain, we should care less about debating terms and more about applying consistent scholarly standards to evaluating the merits of research on 'social capital'. If the work satisfies rigorous methodological, empirical and theoretical criteria, then definitional issues will take care of themselves.
12. Cf. Krishna and Uphoff's (1999) distinction between 'cognitive' and 'structural' social capital.
13. A relatively narrow definition of social capital does not preclude cross-country comparisons, but the reality is that at this time we simply do not have the data we need to make meaningful statements. I discuss this aspect in more detail below.
14. The standard distinction between 'bonding' and 'bridging' is between those who are 'like you' and those who are 'not like you'. I find this too crude a division – my family and close friends are valued in qualitatively different ways from those individuals in my Rolodex file, for example – which is why I have sought to introduce the third 'linking' dimension that I discuss in the following paragraph.
15. It is important to note that bonding, bridging, and linking social capital are essentially defined demographically, spatially and relationally, not by what they 'do' (the functionalist approach). As it happens, however, they do tend to be strongly associated with certain outcomes (survival, mobility and so on).
16. The 'timing' of the formation of these institutions, that is, when the country became independent, and the conditions under which the transition from colonialism took place also surely matter, but these aspects await further investigation.
17. This perspective encapsulates the views of the South Commission and Amatai Etzioni, among others. On the doctrine of self-reliance, a key theme of communitarians, see Rist (1997).
18. For recent related work on the importance of governance and bureaucratic structures for development, see Tendler (1997), La Porta *et al.* (1998), Campos and Nugent (1999), Kaufmann *et al.* (1999a, 1999b), Rauch and Evans (1999), Evans and Rauch (1999), and Isham *et al.* (2001). For early work relating social capital to growth, see Helliwell and Putnam (1995).
19. This figure represents the difference between the growth rates that prevailed during the 1975–95 period, and the 2.35 per cent rate of growth sustained over 1955–74. The figure is measured in constant 1995 dollars, based on the median economy in 1974, which had a GNP per capita of $730. The growth collapse therefore cost the average person in this economy roughly three times his/her annual income. See Woolcock (1999).
20. Especially among prominent sociologists, who seem reluctant to enter the policy domain. A notable exception is Massey and Espinosa (1997).

BIBLIOGRAPHY

Adelman, Irma and Cynthia Taft Morris (1967), *Society, Politics and Economic Development: A Quantitative Approach*, Baltimore, MD: Johns Hopkins University Press.

Alkire, Sabina, Vijayendra Rao and Michael Woolcock (2000), 'Culture and development economics: theory, evidence, implications', mimeo, The World Bank, Washington, DC.

Barr, Abigail (1998), 'Enterprise performance and the functional diversity of social capital', Working Paper Series 98-1, Institute of Economics and Statistics, University of Oxford.

Baumol, William J. and Wallace E. Oates (1988), *The Theory of Environmental Policy*, 2nd edn, Cambridge: Cambridge University Press.

Bebbington, Anthony (1999), 'Capitals and capabilities: a framework for analyzing peasant viability, rural livelihoods and poverty', *World Development*, **27** (12), 2021–44.

Bebbington, Anthony and Thomas Carroll (1999), 'Induced social capital formation in the Andes: indigenous federations and development', The World Bank, Social Capital Initiative, Washington, DC.

Besley, Timothy and Stephen Coate (1995), 'Group lending, repayment incentives and social collateral', *Journal of Development Economics*, **46**, 1–18.

Briggs, Xavier de Souza (1998), 'Brown kids in white suburbs: housing mobility and the multiple faces of social capital', *Housing Policy Debate*, **9** (1), 177–221.

Brown, L. David (1998), 'Creating social capital: nongovernmental development organizations and intersectoral problem solving', in Walter W. Powell and Elisabeth Clemens (eds), *Private Action and the Public Good*, New Haven: Yale University Press.

Brown, L. David and Darcy Ashman (1996), 'Participation, social capital and intesectoral problem solving: African and Asian cases', *World Development*, **24** (6), 1467–79.

Brown, L. David and Jonathan Fox (1998), *The Struggle for Accountability: The World Bank, NGOs and Grassroots Movements*, Cambridge, MA: MIT Press.

Burt, Ronald (1992), *Structural Holes*, Cambridge, MA: Harvard University Press.

Burt, Ronald (2000) 'The network structure of social capital', in Robert Sutton and Barry Shaw (eds), *Research in Organizational Behavior*, Greenwich, CT: JAI Press.

Campos, Nauro and Jeffrey Nugent (1999), 'Development performance and the institutions of governance: evidence from East Asia and Latin America', *World Development*, **27** (3), 439–52.

Coate, Stephen and Martin Ravallion (1993), 'Reciprocity without commitment: characterization and performance of informal insurance arrangements', *Journal of Development Economics*, **40**, 1–24.

Coleman, James (1988), 'Social capital in the creation of human capital', *American Journal of Sociology*, **94**, S95–120.

Collier, Paul (1999), 'The political economy of ethnicity', *Annual Bank Conference on Development Economics 1998*, Washington, DC: The World Bank.

Collier, Paul and Jan Willem Gunning (1999), 'Explaining African economic performance', *Journal of Economic Literature*, **37** (March), 64–111.

Cooley, Charles Horton (1909), *Social Organization: A Study of the Larger Mind*, New York: Charles Scribner's Sons.

Davis, Wade (1999), 'Vanishing cultures', *National Geographic*, **196** (2), 62–89.

DiPasquale, Denise and Edward Glaeser (1999), 'Incentives and social capital: are homeowners better citizens?', *Journal of Urban Economics*, **45** (2), 354–84.

Dordick, Gwendolyn (1997), *Something Left to Lose: Personal Relations and Survival among New York's Homeless*, Philadelphia, PA: Temple University Press.

Easterly, William (2001) *The Elusive Quest for Growth: Economists Adventures and Misadventures in the Tropics*, Cambridge, MA: MIT Press.

Easterly, William (2001), 'The middle class consensus and economic development', *Journal of Economic Growth*, **6** (4), 317–35.

Easterly, William and Ross Levine (1997), 'Africa's growth tragedy: policies and ethnic divisions', *Quarterly Journal of Economics*, **62** (November), 1203–50.

Edwards, Bob and Michael Foley (1997), 'Social capital and the political economy of our discontent', *American Behavioral Scientist*, **40** (5), 669–78.

Ensminger, Jean (1996), *Making a Market: The Institutional Transformation of an African Society*, New York: Cambridge University Press.

Escobar, Arturo (1995), *Encountering Development: The Making and Unmaking of the Third World*, Princeton, NJ: Princeton University Press.

Esman, Milton and Norman Uphoff (1984), *Local Organizations: Intermediaries in Rural Development*, Ithaca, NY: Cornell University Press.

Evans, Peter (1992), 'The state as problem and solution: predation, embedded autonomy and structural change', in Stephan Haggard and Robert Kaufman (eds), *The Politics of Economic Adjustment*, Princeton, NJ: Princeton University Press, pp. 139–81.

Evans, Peter (1995), *Embedded Autonomy*, Princeton, NJ: Princeton University Press.

Evans, Peter (1996), 'Government action, social capital and development: reviewing the evidence on synergy', *World Development*, **24** (6), 1119–32.

Evans, Peter and James Rauch (1999), 'Bureaucracy and growth: a cross-national analysis of the effects of "Weberian" state structures on economic growth', *American Sociological Review*, **64** (5), 748–65.

Fafchamps, Marcel and Bart Minten (1999), 'Social capital and the firm: evidence from agricultural trade', Working Paper no. 21, The World Bank, Social Capital Initiative, Washington, DC.

Fernandez, Roberto, Emilio Castilla and Paul Moore (2000), 'Social capital at work: networks and employment at a phone center', *American Journal of Sociology*, **105** (5), 1288–1356.

Fine, Ben (1999), 'The developmental state is dead – long live social capital?', *Development and Change*, **30**, 1–19.

Fine, Ben (2000), *Social Capital Versus Social Theory: Political Economy and Social Science at the Turn of the Millennium*, New York: Routledge.

Foley, Michael and Bob Edwards (1999), 'Is it time to disinvest in social capital?', *Journal of Public Policy*, **19**, 141–73.

Fox, Jonathan (1996), 'How does civil society thicken? The political construction of social capital in rural Mexico', *World Development*, **24** (6), 1089–1103.

Fukuyama, Francis (1995), *Trust: The Social Virtues and the Creation of Prosperity*, New York: Free Press.

Galasso, Emanuela and Martin Ravallion (2001), 'Decentralized targeting of an antipoverty program', Policy Research Working Paper no. 2316, The World Bank, Washington, DC.

Gittell, Ross and Avis Vidal (1998), *Community Organizing: Building Social Capital as a Development Strategy*, Newbury Park, CA: Sage Publications.

Granovetter, Mark (1973), 'The strength of weak ties', *American Journal of Sociology*, **78**, 1360–80.

Grootaert, Christiaan (1997), 'Social capital: the missing link?', reprinted April 1998 as working paper no. 3 of the World Bank's Social Capital Initiative (ESD Studies and Monographs Series no. 17), Washington, DC: The World Bank.

Grootaert, Christiaan and Deepa Narayan (1999), 'Social capital in Burkina Faso', The World Bank (Local Levels Institutions Study), Washington, DC.

Hall, Robert and Charles Jones (1999), 'Why do some countries produce so much more output per worker than others?', *Quarterly Journal of Economics*, **114** (1), 83–116.

Hanifan, Lyda (1916), 'The rural school community center', *Annals of the American Academy of Political and Social Science*, **67**, 130–38.

Heller, Patrick (1996), 'Social capital as a product of class mobilization and state intervention: industrial workers in Kerala, India', *World Development*, **24** (6), 1055–71.

Helliwell, John (1996), 'Economic growth and social capital', in Richard G. Harris (ed.), *Asia Pacific Region in the Global Economy: A Canadian Perspective*, Calgary: University of Calgary Press, pp. 21–42.

Helliwell, John and Robert Putnam (1995), 'Economic growth and social capital in Italy', *Eastern Economic Journal*, **21**, 295–307.

Hirsch, Paul, Stephen Michael and Robert Friedman (1990), 'Clean models vs. dirty hands', in Sharon Zukin and Paul DiMaggio (eds), *Structures of Capital: The Social Organization of the Economy*, New York: Cambridge University Press.

Hirschman, Albert (1958), *The Strategy of Economic Development*, New Haven: Yale University Press.

Hirschman, Albert (1968), *Journeys Toward Progress: Studies of Economic Policy-Making in Latin America*, New York: Greenwood Publishing Group.

Holzmann, R. and S. Jorgensen (1999), 'Social protection as social risk management: conceptual underpinnings for the Social Protection strategy paper', Social Protection discussion paper no. 9904, Washington, DC: World Bank.

Isham, Jonathan (forthcoming), 'The effect of social capital on technology adoption: evidence from rural Tanzania', *The Journal of African Studies*.

Isham, Jonathan, Daniel Kaufmann and Lant Pritchett (1997), 'Civil liberties, democracy and the performance of government projects', *World Bank Economic Review*, **11** (2), 219–42.

Isham, Jonathan, Deepa Narayan and Lant Pritchett (1995), 'Does participation improve performance? Establishing causality with subjective data', *World Bank Economic Review*, **9** (2), 175–200.

Isham, Jonathan, Michael Woolcock, Lant Pritchett and Gwen Busby (2001), 'The varieties of rentier experience: how natural resource endowments and social institutions affect economic growth', mimeo, Middlebury College.

Kaufmann, Daniel, Aart Kraay and Pablo Zoido-Lobaton (1999a), 'Governance matters', mimeo, The World Bank, Washington, DC.

Kaufmann, Daniel, Aart Kraay and Pablo Zoido-Lobaton (1999b), 'Aggregating governance indicators', mimeo, The World Bank, Washington, DC.

Kawachi, Ichiro and Lisa Berkman (2000), 'Social cohesion, social capital and health', in Lisa Berkman and Ichiro Kawachi (eds), *Social Epidemiology*, New York: Oxford University Press.

Kawachi, Ichiro, Lisa Berkman and R. Glass (1999), 'Social capital and self-rated health: A contextual analysis', *American Journal of Public Health*, **89**, 1187–93.

Kawachi, Ichiro, Lisa Berkman, Bruce Kennedy, Kimberley Lochner and Deborah Prothrow-Stith (1997), 'Social capital, income inequality and mortality', *American Journal of Public Health*, **87**, 1491–8.

Klitgaard, Robert (1994), ' Taking culture into account: from "let's" to "how"', in Ismail Serageldin and June Tabaroff (eds), *Culture and Development in Africa*, Washington, DC: The World Bank.

Klitgaard, Robert (1998), 'The changing world of policy analysis', mimeo, Santa Monica: RAND Graduate School.

Knack, Stephen (1999a), 'Social capital, growth and poverty: a survey of cross-country evidence', Working Paper no. 7, World Bank, Social Capital Initiative, Washington, DC.

Knack, Stephen (1999b), 'Economic applications of social capital: an economist's perspective', paper presented at the annual meeting of the American Agricultural Economists Association, Nashville, TN.

Knack, Stephen and Philip Keefer (1995), 'Institutions and economic performance: cross-country tests using alternative institutional measures', *Economics and Politics*, **7**, 207–27.

Knack, Stephen (1997), 'Does social capital have an economic pay-off? A cross-country investigation', *Quarterly Journal of Economics*, **112**, 1251–88.

Koo, Bon Ho and Dwight Perkins (eds) (1995), *Social Capability and Long-Term Economic Growth*, New York: St Martin's Press.

Kozel, Valerie and Barbara Parker (2000), 'Integrated approaches to poverty assessment in India', in Michael Bamberger (ed.), *Integrating Quantitative and Qualitative Research in Development Projects*, Washington, DC: The World Bank, pp. 59–68.

Krishna, Anirudh and Norman Uphoff (1999), 'Mapping and measuring social capital: a conceptual and empirical study of collective action for conserving and developing watersheds in Rajasthan, India', Working Paper no. 13, World Bank, Social Capital Initiative. Washington, DC.

La Porta, Rafael, Florencio Lopez-de-Silanes, Andrei Shleifer and Robert Vishney (1997), 'Trust in large organizations', *American Economic Review*, **87**, 333–8.

La Porta, Rafael, Florencio Lopez-de-Silanes, Andrei Shleifer and Robert Vishney (1998), 'The quality of government', *Journal of Law Economics and Organization*, **15**, 222–79.

Lesser, Eric (2000), 'Leveraging social capital in organizations', in Eric Lesser (ed.), *Knowledge and Social Capital: Foundations and Applications*, Boston: Butterworth–Heinemann.

Lin, Nan (2001), *Social Capital: A Theory of Social Structure and Action*, New York: Cambridge University Press.

Loury, Glen (1977), 'A dynamic theory of racial income differences', in P.A. Wallace and A. LeMund (eds), *Women, Minorities and Employment Discrimination*, Lexington, MA: Lexington Books.

Massey, Douglas and Karin Espinosa (1997), 'What's driving Mexico–U.S. migration? A theoretical, empirical and policy analysis', *American Journal of Sociology*, **102** (4), 939–99.

Mauro, Paulo (1995), 'Corruption and growth', *Quarterly Journal of Economics*, **110** (3), 681–712.

Meyerson, Eva (1994), 'Human capital, social capital and compensation: the relative contribution of social contacts to managers' incomes', *Acta Sociologica*, **37**, 383–99.

Moore, Mick (1997), 'Societies, polities and capitalists in developing countries: a literature survey', *Journal of Development Studies*, **33** (3), 287–363.

Morgan, Stephen and Aage Sorensen (1999), 'Parental networks, social closure and mathematics learning: a test of Coleman's social capital explanation of school effects', *American Sociological Review*, **64** (5), 661–81.

Moser, Caroline (1996), *Confronting Crisis: A Comparative Study of Household Responses to Poverty and Vulnerability in Four Poor Urban Communities*, Environmentally Sustainable Development Studies and Monograph Series 8, Washington, DC: The World Bank.

Narayan, Deepa (1997), 'Voices of the poor: poverty and social capital in Tanzania', Washington, DC: The World Bank (ESD Studies and Monographs Series, no. 20).

Narayan, Deepa (1999), 'Bonds and bridges: social capital and poverty', mimeo, The World Bank, Washington, DC.

Narayan, Deepa (2000), *Can Anyone Hear Us? Voices of the Poor*, New York: Oxford University Press.

Narayan, Deepa and Lant Pritchett (1999), 'Cents and sociability: household income and social capital in rural Tanzania', *Economic Development and Cultural Change*, **47** (4), 871–97.

North, Douglass (1990), *Institutions, Institutional Change and Economic Performance*, New York: Cambridge University Press.

Olson, Mansur (2000), *Power and Prosperity: Outgrowing Communist and Capitalist Dictatorship*, New York: Basic Books.

Ostrom, Elinor (1990), *Governing the Commons: The Evolution of Institutions for Collective Action*, New York: Cambridge University Press.

Portes, Alejandro (1998), 'Social capital: its origins and applications in contemporary sociology', *Annual Review of Sociology*, **24**, 1–24

Portes, Alejandro and Patricia Landolt (1996), 'The downside of social capital', *The American Prospect*, **26** (May–June), 18–21, 94.

Portes, Alejandro and Julia Sensenbrenner (1993), 'Embeddedness and immigration: notes on the social determinants of economic action', *American Journal of Sociology*, **98** (6), 1320–50.

Posner, Daniel (1999), 'Ethnic fractionalization: how (not) to measure it? What does (and doesn't) it explain?', paper presented at the annual meeting of the American Political Science Association, Atlanta, GA.

Putnam, Robert (1993), *Making Democracy Work: Civic Traditions in Modern Italy*, Princeton, NJ: Princeton University Press.

Putnam, Robert (2000), *Bowling Alone: The Collapse and Revival of American Community*, New York: Simon and Schuster.

Rauch, James and Peter Evans (1999), 'Bureaucratic structure and bureaucratic performance in developing countries', Working Paper no. 99-06, Department of Economics, University of California, San Diego.

Rist, Gilbert (1997), *The History of Development: From Western Origins to Global Faith*, London: Zed Books.

Rodrik, Dani (1999a), *The New Global Economy and Developing Countries: Making Openness Work*, Baltimore, MD: Johns Hopkins University Press.

Rodrik, Dani (1999b), 'Where did all the growth go? External shocks, social conflicts and growth collapses', *Journal of Economic Growth*, **4** (4), 385–412.

Rubio, Mauricio (1997), 'Perverse social capital – some evidence from Colombia', *Journal of Economic Issues*, **31** (3), 805–16.

Sampson, Robert, Jeffrey Morenhoff and Felton Earls (1999), 'Beyond social capital: spatial dynamics of collective efficacy for children', *American Sociological Review*, **64** (5), 633–60.

Schafft, Kai and David Brown (2000), 'Social capital and grassroots development: the case of Roma self-governance in Hungary', *Social Problems*, **47** (2), 201–19.

Sen, Amartya (1999), *Development as Freedom*, New York: Knopf.

Singerman, Diane (1995), *Avenues of Participation: Family, Politics and Networks in Urban Quarters of Cairo*, Princeton, NJ: Princeton University Press.

Smelser, Neil (1997), 'The interdisciplinary enterprise', *ASA Footnotes*, April.

Stiglitz, Joseph (1998), 'Towards a new paradigm for development: strategies, policies and processes', Prebish Lecture, UNCTAD, Geneva.

Temple, Jonathan (2000), 'Growth effects of education and social capital in the OECD', mimeo, Oxford University.

Temple, Jonathan and Paul Johnson (1998), 'Social capability and economic growth', *Quarterly Journal of Economics*, **113** (3), 965–90.

Tendler, Judith (1995), 'Social capital across the public–private divide', mimeo, MIT, Cambridge, MA.

Tendler, Judith (1997), *Good Government in the Tropics*, Baltimore, MD: Johns Hopkins University Press.

Townsend, Robert (1994), 'Risk and insurance in village India', *Econometrica*, **62** (3), 539–91.

Unger, Danny (1998), *Building Social Capital in Thailand: Fibers, Finance and Infrastructure*, New York: Cambridge University Press.

United Nations (1951), *Measures for the Economic Development of Underdeveloped Countries*, New York: Department of Social and Economic Affairs.

Varshney, Ashutosh (2001), 'Ethnic conflict and civil society: India and beyond', *World Politics*, **53** (April), 362–98

Wade, Robert (1988), *Governing the Market: Economic Theory and the Role of Government in East Asian Industrialization*, Princeton, NJ: Princeton University Press.

Wenger, Etienne and William Snyder (2000), 'Communities of practice: the organizational frontier', *Harvard Business Review*, **78** (1), 139–45.

Wilson, William Julius (1987), *The Truly Disadvantaged*, Chicago: University of Chicago Press.

Wilson, William Julius (1996), *When Work Disappears: The World of the New Urban Poor*, New York: Knopf.

Woolcock, Michael (1998), 'Social capital and economic development: toward a theoretical synthesis and policy framework', *Theory and Society*, **27** (2), 151–208.

Woolcock, Michael (1999), 'Managing risk and opportunity in developing countries: the role of social capital', in Gustav Ranis (ed.), *The Dimensions of Development*, Yale: Center for International and Area Studies, pp. 197–212.

Woolcock, Michael (2001), 'The place of social capital in understanding economic and social outcomes', *Canadian Journal of Policy Research*, **2** (1), 11–17.

Woolcock, Michael (forthcoming), *Using Social Capital: Getting the Social Relations Right in the Theory and Practice of Economic Development*, Princeton, NJ: Princeton University Press.

Woolcock, Michael and Deepa Narayan (2000), 'Social capital: implications for development theory, research and policy', *World Bank Research Observer*, **15** (2), 225–49.

World Bank (1992), *World Development Report, 1992*, New York: Oxford University Press.

World Bank (1997), *World Development Report, 1997*, New York: Oxford University Press.

World Bank (1998), *Assessing Aid*, New York: Oxford University Press.

World Bank (2000a), *The Quality of Growth*, New York: Oxford University Press.

World Bank (2000b), *World Development Report 2000/01*, New York: Oxford University Press.

3. Reflections on social and antisocial capital

Paul Streeten

Economists have not welcomed the concept of 'social capital'. Rising interest in it has been compared to the intellectual equivalent of a stock market bubble.[1] Steven Durlauf (1999) questions 'both the importance which some have attributed to social capital and whether it is ultimately as benign a phenomenon as its advocates assume'. A main complaint has been that its meaning is unclear and that different authors attach different meanings to it. Kenneth Arrow (2000) has urged 'abandonment of the metaphor of capital and the term "social capital" '. His main reason is that social networks are built up for reasons other than their economic value to the participants. Both building new and enjoying existing social relations have intrinsic value.

According to Robert Solow (2000), 'capital stands for a stock of produced or natural factors of production that can be expected to yield productive services for some time'. Solow goes on to ask several rhetorical questions, which 'is the quickest way to explain why I doubt that "social capital" is the right concept to use in discussing whatever it is we are discussing – the behavior patterns mentioned earlier, for instance'. If social capital had bite as a concept, it would show up in international time series as a residual.[2] There is also no determinate relation between expenditure or the devotion of resources and the resulting social capital, or between that capital and output. Mainstream economists tend to reject, or at least treat sceptically, the concept of 'social capital'.

But so do many dissenting, radical economists, though obviously for different reasons. Social capital by its very nature is part of the growth-and-productivity-centred approach to development. The idea is to demonstrate that social relations have a positive impact on growth and productivity. If poor people (or anyone else) want to advance their economic and political interests, they need to get organized. But this is not necessarily the organization found in traditional social or community groups. What is being concealed by the concept, according to these critics, is the essential issue of economic and political power.

Sociologists and political scientists have also been critical of the concept because they fear that it indicates the intellectual imperialism of economics, another invasion by economic thinking of their territory.

At the same time the concept of social capital provides common ground for those disappointed with laissez-faire and markets as well as those disillusioned with governments. It unites on a 'third way' those who are against interventions and regulations as well as those who dislike the free play of market forces. 'Like Mr. Blair's "third way", the very phrase "social capital" hints at the pleasingly communal but stirs in an invigorating dash of hard economics.'[3] It also promises common ground for economists, sociologists, political scientists, historians and anthropologists, and appeals to those who favour interdisciplinary approaches. It goes back to Aristotle, who regarded man as a political or social (rather than purely selfish) animal, and can be grounded in human nature. And it has common sense in its support. James Meade once said he would like to have written on his tombstone, 'He tried to be an economist, but common sense kept breaking in.' Those who like to operate with the concept 'social capital' without having made it palatable to economists or sociologists may sympathize with Meade's observation.

FIVE ASPECTS OF SOCIAL CAPITAL

There are many ways of classifying social capital: horizontal versus vertical, bonding versus bridging and so on. I should like to suggest another type of classification. We can distinguish five different aspects of social capital and social investment (additions to the stock of capital).

First, social investment or investment in social capital is (or can be) like a non-durable consumption good, like an apple. While we are forging networks, creating trust, we enjoy it. Investing in making new friends gives pleasure. If this is the whole story and the activity is wholly pleasurable, no costs are involved. But it also can have costs, especially of scarce time. Oscar Wilde said that the trouble with socialism is that it takes too many evenings. The same can be said about the activities called for by civil society, whether by parent–teacher associations or chess clubs. To that extent the creation of social capital shares with other forms of investment the fact of a present sacrifice for the sake of future benefits. It would come under the second aspect. Nevertheless, in moderation, some forms of building up social relations are enjoyed in their own right, or at any rate there is an excess of intrinsic enjoyment over costs.

Second, it is like a durable consumption good, like a television set or a well-stocked library, or a painting. The social relations, the interaction, the activities of the bowling club or the chess society are enjoyed in and for themselves. They give people recognition, identity, status, dignity, a sense of belonging, friendship, honour, social status and prestige. Indeed, the primary objective of having joined an association is often not material benefit; this is an incidental result of it.

Third, it is also like a non-durable production good, like coal that fires an engine. It is used up in the process of producing a durable product. We invest, particularly in the form of time, in joining a guild or an association or a firm in the hope of economic returns. Both the first and the second aspect are relevant to embarking on a marriage.

Fourth, the end product of creating social capital is like a durable capital good. It is like a machine tool or a knitting frame. It can yield good jobs and a stream of higher salaries, profits, rents and other forms of pecuniary benefits. This could be an intended effect or it could be the incidental, unanticipated result of the first aspect, of having entered the relationship initially for its own sake. But equally, the first aspect or the second aspect can be the unanticipated result of the intention of economic returns, when we make friends of people we initially joined only for economic reasons.[4]

Fifth, it is like a durable investment good for non-marketed activities, like a refrigerator or vacuum cleaner that is used inside the home. For example, housework can be done more efficiently when neighbours help, when you can trust them. Communities with much social capital tend to have better schools, less crime, fewer teenage pregnancies. (Some of these may also be counted as durable consumption goods.) Quite apart from its contribution to raising productivity, the whole of civil society can be a guarantee of liberty in a democracy. It can see that government does not neglect the interests of its citizens.

These five aspects are interdependent. We may enter a club for pleasure, companionship or self-interest, but in the process we acquire the trust and the skills that bring substantial economic benefits. Or we may have joined for economic reasons and in the process acquire friends. By allowing others to take responsibility for us we learn to take responsibility for them. Business is more easily and more quickly conducted between people who trust each other.

The characteristics pertaining to the likeness to an apple, a television set, a piece of coal, a machine tool, and a refrigerator can either all be combined in harmony or they can give rise to conflicts. Humanists, who insist on social relations as ends-in-themselves, and social capital developers, who see them as means to growth, may disagree. The form and content of the social capital, the groups who are included, the time horizon and the constituencies for its support will be different for the two schools of thought.

Social capital comprises several components. First, there is trust. It is well known that societies that can rely on trust can save on transaction costs. Not having to check other people's behaviour saves money and time. Secondly, there is an aggregate of behavioural norms. The norms are the regulative principles underlying trust and are strengthened by trust. Thirdly, there are social networks (horizontal and vertical) such as membership in choral societies, soccer clubs, cooperatives, bird-watching clubs, bowling leagues, charities, church study groups, book clubs, citizens' associations, churches, sports clubs, human rights chapters, jazz clubs, rotary clubs, Red Cross chapters, social workers' groups, parent–teacher associations and boy scouts. Networks yield externalities. It is not necessary to be a member of a network in order to derive a benefit from it, such as reduced crime rates in a neighbourhood. Finally, there is a combination of the above: trust, networks and norms or, for short, TNN.

The ability to associate depends on the degree to which communities share norms, and out of such shared norms grows trust. But social capital amalgamates incommensurable objects – beliefs, behavioural rules and such forms of capital assets as interpersonal networks – without telling us how to amalgamate them. It is useful to separate the following.

Trust promotes cooperation, especially in large organizations. Norms arise from trust and reinforce trust. Networks are groupings such as savings and credit associations, extended kinship, lobbying organizations and hierarchical relationships associated with patronage (that do not inevitably lead to betterment). According to Robert D. Putnam (2000) 'Social trust in modern social settings can arise from two related sources – norms of reciprocity and networks of civic engagement.' In a lecture he gave as an example of the norm of reciprocity a saying he attributed to Yogi Berra: 'I go to my friends' funerals so that they should come to mine.' (I have heard it attributed to Woody Allen.) Networks create trust among their members and sometimes with non-members. It is important to look not only at what goes on within these groups but also at the relations between groups. As we shall see, the positive effects of intra-group relations may be offset by the negative effects of inter-group relations.

Trust is the most difficult concept. Sociologists have tried to explain trust in terms of the notion of social capital: the fund of conventions, expectations and shared values that enable societies to renew themselves across the generations. But theorizing trust in these terms is not very enlightening. It does not tell us how trust waxes and wanes, or even what it consists in. If people trust one another more in some societies than in others, what accounts for such differences? How can degrees of trust be measured or compared? Should we attempt to measure it at all, or do such attempts imply falling victim to the fallacy that what cannot be counted does not count, or even exist? Can we even be sure that, when we talk of trust, we mean the same thing? Recent studies suggest that trust is shaped by experience, not native personal traits, and that it is fragile, prone to breaking down altogether.[5]

Some authors, such as Andrew M. Kamarck, want to broaden the concept of social capital to include the 'institutions and the customs and the traditions of the people'.

Social capital is the social infrastructure; the socially constructed reality – the mental architecture – within which we live. It is the institutions and the stored, largely unarticulated, information people acquire on the ways to live in their community, economy and society. It consists of the pattern of perception and thought that children acquire while growing up; the habits and human relationships that the people regard as natural and given. It is the accepted knowledge – the whole complex of shared assumptions, beliefs, attitudes, morals, customs, and traditions that characterize a society or social group. It can be thought of as the set of strategies that a society uses to organize and to explain to itself its way of existing. A society evolves its particular social capital to try to cope with its world and this human social capital identifies a group or people to itself and regulates its behaviour.[6]

NEGATIVE EFFECTS: ANTISOCIAL CAPITAL

Social capital is generally regarded as a good thing. Putnam, for example, looks at states in the USA with high social capital (Minnesota, North Dakota and Vermont) and those with low social capital (Louisiana and Mississippi) and finds that the former have better health, better education, less crime and violence and greater affluence. The question of the direction of causality remains. Do healthy people have more friends, or do friends keep you healthy? But, whatever the answer, there is also negative social capital.

There is, of course, nothing surprising in the fact that social capital, like all other factors of production, can be put to bad uses as well as to good ones. It would be possible to define social capital as only those forms of group allegiance that have positive, desirable effects, but this would not be a helpful definition. It would mean that, whenever we have good results, social capital is tautologically assumed to be present. It is preferable to define it by its characteristics rather than its desirable (or undesirable) effects. Networks and social interaction can cause illegitimacy, bribery, corruption, nepotism, cronyism and crime. These can involve vast inequities. Civil society cannot only mean membership of choral societies and football clubs, but can be another name for lobbyists and rent-seekers. The Ku Klux Klan, the Mafia, the Aryan Nations, urban gangs, militia movements, drug cartels, crime syndicates, are all part of civil society, or uncivil society. The purpose of some of these groups, such as the Ku Klux Klan, is to suppress other social groups. Some forms of social capital are more valuable than others. Card-playing clubs are less important than voter turnout or blood donation.

Mancur Olson (1982) told us that interest groups (part of civil society) slow down economic growth. He suggests that one of the reasons for British economic decline has been the internal and external peace and stability that permitted interest groups to destroy efficiency. Defeated Germany and Japan grew rapidly because their civil society had been destroyed. He showed how special interest groups impede economic growth. The negative effect of rent-seeking interest groups on economic growth contradicts the positive effect that Putnam postulates. Instead of making for social cohesion, they promote conflict.

There are organizations like the Mafia, the Camorra, protection rackets and gangs that make money by creating a nuisance or a danger or a climate of distrust and then charge the potential victims for the removal of that self-created nuisance. Far from delivering goods, they extort money for the removal of self-created 'bads'. The operation is like that of the blackmailer or the kidnapper or the hijacker. This kind of activity prevents the creation of the social capital that promotes economic growth. Francis Fukuyama (1995) suggests that such criminal organizations have appeared in places such as southern Italy, the American inner city, Russia and many sub-Saharan African cities where the natural impulse towards sociability is blocked from expressing itself through legitimate social structures. [*Editors' note*: see Chapter 12 by Colletta and Cullen in this volume.]

Even benign long-term relationships can be obstacles to economic betterment. They can form a sort of anti-social capital. Organizations are a means of achieving the benefits of collective action when the price system fails. But, conversely, organizations can prevent markets from coming into existence. Communitarian institutions can be a hindrance to development. For instance, the extended family can make financial demands that prevent business accumulation and success; or many husbands looking after children (as for example, in a Yoruba area of Nigeria) can prevent more efficient insurance and capital markets.[7] The progress from Ferdinand Tönnies's *Gemeinschaft* (community) to *Gesellschaft* (society) can mean a loss of social capital, though a gain in productivity. In the writings on development in the 1950s and 1960s, what we would nowadays call social capital was regarded as an obstacle to development that had to be eliminated before development could proceed. Religious, ethnic and racial ties were regarded as impeding development. Giving jobs to members of your family can prevent the best people from getting them and is regarded as nepotism by the new ethics. When people begin to move in search of jobs, and particularly from the country to the city, there is a loss of social capital (Schiff, 1999).

Networks and associations can lead to social exclusion. Think of the Indian caste system, Jim Crow laws in the old American South, apartheid in South Africa or any old boys' network or old school tie. Patronage networks are based on kinship, social class, friendship or love, where merit should prevail. The norms that dictate honest behaviour in one setting can be used to enforce discrimination and exclusion in another. Tight group consciousness and solidarity can be and often are accompanied by hostility to or exclusion of other groups. Even in associations that are not aiming at exclusion, the fact that they are ethnically or economically homogeneous can reinforce social stratification and inequality.

If civil society grows too strong relative to the state, the society can suffer or be destroyed, as was seen in pre-1989 Lebanon, the former Yugoslavia and Sri Lanka. When, on the other hand, the state is too strong, we get a situation like that in the old Soviet Union. Bad government, like Bangladesh's and Pakistan's, tends to encourage the formation of civic groups. Excessive arm's-length market transactions can, like excessive government, destroy social capital. Although up to a point government, markets and civil society can be substitutes for one another, what is needed is a balance between state, civil society, the private profit–seeking sector and the extended family. Without this balance, social links that are valuable both in themselves and for economic efficiency can be destroyed. Commerce and culture both depend on social (or cultural) capital. It is desirable to keep a balance between them. In the Renaissance such a balance existed. Today it seems to be shrinking. The need for a balance between government action and social capital applies also on a smaller scale. Cooperatives and community organizations require a set of laws, regulations and government interventions for their proper functioning. The wrong kinds of interventions, or too many, or the complete absence of them can destroy social capital.

PECULIARITIES OF SOCIAL CAPITAL

One of the peculiarities of social capital is that it does not wear out with use, but with disuse (Ostrom, 2000). In this respect it resembles what Dennis Robertson, a long time ago, called love and which can stand for morality, civic spirit, trust – in fact, for social capital. Robertson (1956) asked the question, 'What does the economist economize?' His answer was 'love', which he called 'that scarce resource'.

> Robertson explained, through a number of well-chosen illustrations from the contemporary economic scene, that it was the economist's job to create an institutional environment and pattern of motivation where as small a burden as possible would be placed, for the purposes of society's functioning, on this thing called 'love', a term he used as a shortcut for morality and civic spirit. In so arguing, he was of course at one with Adam Smith, who celebrated society's ability to do without 'benevolence' (of the butcher, brewer and baker) as long as individual 'interest' was given full scope.[8]

But, as Albert Hirschman points out, there is a flaw in this argument. Resources like love, like the ability to speak a foreign language or to play the piano, atrophy if not used, and their supply may increase rather than decrease through use. But too much reliance on them can also be counterproductive. There is a confusion between the practice of an ability and the use of a resource. But civic spirit is also unlike the practice of an ability that indefinitely improves with practice. We should set limits to how much we rely on it and this is where Robertson has a point. Unlike a skill, which grows with practice without impinging on other skills, civic spirit can be practised at the expense of self-interest. It is therefore important to have institutions (like the market) that economize in the need to exercise civic spirit. At the same time, it is true that human capital also deteriorates if the skills are not used and even physical capital can rust when not used. User cost can be negative, so that using the capital can improve it, while not using it can deteriorate it.

HYBRID INSTITUTIONS

When I was a student, the presumption was that government could do no wrong. Today nearly the opposite is true: the fashionable presumption is that government can do no right. At the same time, not everyone is happy to leave most things to the private, profit-seeking, non-accountable sector. NGOs, private, voluntary associations and the civil society have provided common ground for the critics of both government and the private sector. And they provide, of course, the basis for social capital. But a judicious combination of the private and the public sector can also produce valuable social capital. Institutions that incorporate the good features of each sector without suffering from some of the defects of voluntary associations can provide a sounder basis for social capital. It is doubtful whether the distinction between private and public ownership or management is relevant to efficiency or equity. Much of the discussion is conducted in binary terms: central planning versus free markets (which is not the same as private versus public ownership). Sometimes a spectrum between these two poles is considered, but the ideological values attached vary with the position on this spectrum. For example, Soviet-type planning is bad; therefore the nearer we are to free markets the better. But an intermediate position between the two ends of the spectrum may be preferable to either extreme.

Hybrid institutions that encourage initiative and enterprise, and are subject to covering their costs, but are at the same time accountable to the public, can harness the best of both sectors. The British Commonwealth Development Corporation (CDC), for example, is run autonomously on commercial lines, in the sense that it has to cover its costs (and to that extent is subjected to market discipline) and that its board consists of bankers and industrialists. It draws its funds mainly from the Exchequer (the British Treasury), and its objective is to maximize development, not profits. It does not only lend funds, withdrawing once a project is completed and participation becomes most important, like all other development agencies, but also manages firms and projects. In this respect it is unique.

The CDC is also a model for a symbiosis between large-scale and small-scale enterprise, between the private and public sector, and between foreign and domestic capital and entrepreneurship. And it is accountable to the public. It is an example illustrating the philosophy of both/and against either/or. It has pioneered these principles first in the Kulai oil palm project in Malaysia and then in the Kenya Tea Development Authority, and in other projects in Swaziland and Botswana and elsewhere. A modern nucleus estate does the management, the processing, the exporting, the marketing, and provides the extension services and the credit for a group of smallholders clustered around the estate. The activities best carried out on a large scale, with modern techniques, are done by the nucleus estate, while the growing of the crop is done by newly settled smallholders. This type of project has proved highly successful, although it is rather management-intensive and the calls on skilled professional management and extension services would have to be reduced if it were to be replicated on a large scale in labour surplus economies, such as those of South Asia.

Whereas the World Bank is criticized and disliked by both the Left and the Right, the CDC is loved by both. It is regarded as a splendid example both by British conservatives, businessmen and bankers (except that it does not attempt to maximize profits) and by Labour Party adherents, because it is a success story by a public sector company, is charged with maximizing its impact on development and is accountable to the public. At the same time it trains local counterparts and hands over to local people control, management and ownership as soon as they are ready, and starts on a new project with the money thus freed. Another model is the National Dairy Development Board in India. The production of milk remains traditional and informal, while processing, credit and marketing follow modern, formal sector lines.

A similar model has been followed by private foreign agribusinesses. It has been called the 'core-satellite' model, or contract farming or smallholder out-grower scheme. Companies like Heinz, Del Monte, United Brands, Nestlé and Shell provide marketing, equipment, technical assistance, credit, fertilizer and other inputs, as well as ancillary services, and smallholders grow fruit and vegetables. Here there is a danger of exploitation by the large firm of the smallholder. In order to balance bargaining power in drawing up contracts, the smallholders have to be organized. Then they can use their power both directly and indirectly on the government to give them political support. The high fixed costs of the processing plant make it important for the company to secure an even and certain flow of inputs which is ensured by the contract. It is preferable to either open market purchases or a plantation with hired labour, though contract farming is sometimes supplemented by these other forms. The smallholders, in turn, acquire an assured market, credit and inputs at low costs.

This type of an institutional arrangement can combine some of the advantages of plantation farming, such as quality control, coordination of interdependent stages of production and marketing, with those of smallholder production, such as autonomy, keener incentives and income generation for poor people. But the possibility of abuse of its monopsonistic power by the private company against the smallholders makes it necessary to have smallholder organizations with countervailing power or public regulation or, best of all, the kind of hybrid animal that the CDC represents. The CDC is a public sector institution whose objective is not to maximize profits. It presents a challenge and an invitation to exercise our institutional imagination, which has been rather inert compared with our scientific and technological imagination. Hybrid institutions that encourage trust, accountability and responsibility and at the same time draw on people's enterprise, initiative and sense of venture can form the best basis for social capital.

GLOBAL SOCIAL CAPITAL

While national social capital has received a good deal of attention, global social capital has been relatively neglected. Associations running across national frontiers include international NGOs, professional organizations, interest groups, churches, political alliances, Internet communities, international intergovernmental organizations such as the World Bank, the IMF, the United Nations and its agencies and profit-seeking multinational corporations. They owe their existence to the growing intensity of cross-border contacts and to the growing awareness of shared global, or at least transnational, problems. Do they contribute to global social, cultural or economic achievements? How are they related to national and subnational social capital; how to global public goods?

Globalization and the formation of global social capital can come from above (multinational firms, multilateral institutions, world markets, international capital flows) or it can come from below (Greenpeace efforts to prevent Shell from sinking an oil rig with toxic properties in the North Sea; the campaign in the South Pacific to protest against the resumption of French nuclear weapons tests).[9] The protesters against globalization at Seattle, Washington, Prague, Quebec and London (on 1 May 2001), Gothenburg (Goteborg, Sweden) and Genoa, such as Earth First! and the Ruckus Society, present, paradoxically, an example of globalization from below. With their mobile-phone coordination, web-based propaganda, cosmopolitan composition, transatlantic travel and Nike sneakers, the anti-globalization rebels protest against the system that created them. The end of the OECD's planned Multilateral Agreement on Investment in 1998 and of the Seattle meeting of the World Trade Organization were two of the movement's successes. The

UNDP has a board of NGOs to advise the administrator on issues involving firms, governments and civil society.[10]

Several global conferences organized by the United Nations on women, population, the environment, development and social priorities, with their parallel events organized by NGOs, balancing and counteracting the intergovernmental aspects, have begun to show new styles of participation, accountability and representation (Falk, 1996, p. 59). Though rudimentary, these beginnings may present a form of education for world citizenship. Institutions such as the regional banks, various United Nations bodies and international NGOs can contribute to this process. The aim would be to produce patriotic cosmopolitans, people who combine loyalty to their families, communities and countries with solidarity to humanity as a whole.

The IMF, the World Bank and orthodox economists argue for full integration of the developing countries into the global economy. But, in order to achieve a human world order, this must be accompanied by policies that guarantee the satisfaction of basic needs, that correct for highly unequal asset and income distribution, and that prevent the growth of insecurity and social exclusion. To bring 1.3 billion people now below the poverty line up to minimum level would call for a fourfold increase in current aid. We know that this is not likely to happen. The aid prospects look gloomy. [*Editors' note*: see the discussion in Chapter 10 by Daniere *et al.*]

In addition to markets and states, there are three influential actors on the global stage: transnational corporations, international organizations and the global civil society. (The family or household no longer plays an important part on the global scene.) Transnational corporations have been praised for making the most valuable contributions to development and condemned as not, perhaps, the devil incarnate, but at any rate the devil incorporated. No doubt, they wield considerable power and are not under global control. And different corporations behave very differently. Their economic power is often greater than that of many states and their activities can affect the politics of governments and people. Ideally and eventually, a system of global incorporation, global taxation and global accountability should match the global reach of these corporations. Meanwhile international (that is, intergovernmental) cooperation will have to limit the abuse of their power and attempt to steer its use to the public good.

The United Nations and its agencies and other worldwide international and regional public agencies and organizations are specifically charged with promoting the general interest, including economic and social well-being, in different spheres. Here again, a greater degree of public control, accountability, transparency and, more particularly, wider participation by voluntary societies, religious congregations, trade unions, private firms, professional organizations, women's and youth organizations, and so on, would be desirable. It is these international agencies, together with the fledgling global civil society, that are the seat of the global conscience of the world.

Last but not least, there is the global civil society in the making, the material for global social capital, neither private nor public. The bonds of global non-governmental, non-profit organizations that draw on the voluntary energies of their members contribute, often highly efficiently, not only to the gross national product but to a flourishing civil society and the social capital, essential for a democracy. They include voluntary societies, advocacy groups, hobby groups, grassroots organizations, churches and other religious associations, action groups, professional societies, colleges, universities, Oxfam, Bread for the World, Greenpeace, *Médicins sans Frontières*, orchestras, hospitals, museums, the International Red Cross, Friends of the Earth, Amnesty International, charities, cooperatives, the Grameen Bank, neighbourhood organizations, local action committees, and many other and similar institutions. They stretch across national frontiers and forge links that bypass national frontiers and loyalties. They have put issues on the agenda of governments and of public debate that might otherwise have been neglected: poverty, the environment, women's (and children's) rights and human rights generally, political freedom and governance, empowerment, corruption, the role of women (and children), population, habitation, the waste of military expenditure and the 'peace dividend', debt relief for the poorest countries, and others. They lobby governments, bargain with international organizations and propagate different ways of living. They constitute the core of any future world citizenship, even though their loyalties may be confined to quite narrow issues or special interests. Their number has increased enormously in the last few decades. There are now about 40 000 non-profit international non-governmental organizations.

They can mobilize world opinion in order to draw attention to global problems, such as some environmental and human rights groups have done so successfully. Greenpeace on some environmental issues, Amnesty International on human rights or Oxfam on public education in development issues, as well as the execution of projects, can serve as examples. Other organizations provide humanitarian relief or engage in cooperation beyond state frontiers, for example by establishing links with local self-help groups and supporting their health, education or community projects.

Undeniably, non-state agents differ vastly in their capabilities and some of them appear to have hardly any influence at all. This seems to exempt them from any role in shaping a global civil society. Still, to the extent that they do have leverage within their specialized sphere of activity, they have a responsibility, and they must strive to make their own specific contribution to the realization of a global civil society.

Before the Prague meeting of the World Bank and the International Monetary Fund in the year 2000, the Bank's president, James Wolfensohn, spent some time with non-governmental organizations including the Bolivian Episcopal Conference, the Coalition for Democracy and Civil Society of the Kyrgyz Republic, and a representative from World Vision from Uganda. The discussion ranged from corruption to the control of multinational corporations, to the equitable distribution of the gains from the Chad–Cameroon oil pipeline. It was the first time that such a meeting took place. It is the beginning of the politics of a global economy.

Globalization has so far applied mainly to the free flow of trade, finance, technology and some educational and cultural impulses in accordance with free market principles. The movement of people has been much less free. And the growth of institutions to protect the poor and the weak, to promote civil and human rights, to provide educational and health facilities and social safety nets has lagged behind the drive of market forces. The result has been growing international inequality.

How can the United Nations agencies and other international and regional organizations become more responsive to the demands and needs of the global civil society and more participatory? We hear a lot about the need for greater participation, but the international organizations preaching this gospel have not been outstanding in practising what they preach. It has something to do with the blind spot of autoprofessionalism, a subject on which I keep a secret file. It contains facts and reflections about dentists' children having bad teeth, marriage guidance counsellors suffering from broken marriages, management experts being unable to manage their own affairs, evaluators never evaluating their own activities, and the auditors of the Royal Economic Society having to refuse to audit its books.

We have also recently heard a good deal about the need to decentralize government and to draw more on participatory organizations in the political arena. The world has found unworkable and has rejected the process of centralized decision making in centrally planned economies. But the very same process governs the relations between management and labour within both capitalist and public sector firms. We know that, under regimentation, people do not give their best. Democracy and participation should be introduced not only in politics but also in the private sector; and not only in government and in profit-seeking firms, but also in private voluntary societies and non-governmental organizations such as trade unions and churches; even in some families there is a need for greater participation, or at least better access to those in power, particularly by women and in some areas by children. This might be called vertical participation: to make the membership of these agencies more responsive to the needs of all its members through a higher degree of participation and access to power. By horizontal participation I mean the inclusion in the international organizations of some representatives of the civil society.

With the end of the Cold War, the role of the United Nations and its agencies can once again become what it was intended to be at its foundation, but with adaptation to the new power constellations and the new technologies of the present world. Japan and Germany must be given bigger roles. They should be encouraged to take positive initiatives in raising resources, and in the many activities surrounding various aspects of human security. Peace keeping and peace making applies to military and territorial security; ex-President Clinton talks of personal security (from conflicts, poverty- and drug-related crimes, violence against women and children, terrorism) and health security; food security is the mandate of the Food and Agriculture Organization (FAO); health security that of the World Health Organization; financial security that of the International Monetary Fund, the World Bank and the regional development banks; environmental security that of the United Nations Environment Programme; and job and income security that of the International Labor Office (ILO). Community security against ethnic and religious clashes and political security against the violation of human rights should be added to the list. The creation of secure, productive, remunerative, satisfying, freely chosen livelihoods should be top priority for policy makers.[11]

Human security can often be increased, not by increasing, but by reducing defence expenditure. Ethnic conflicts, civil wars, external aggression and genocide frequently have economic and social roots in the extreme human insecurity that arises from hunger, poverty, unemployment, discrimination, social exclusion and cultural disintegration. Tackling the root causes of poverty, exclusion and racial and religious conflicts by preventive action (rather than by intervention after conflicts have broken out into open wars) can be much more effective and save many lives.

There is also global antisocial capital at work. Sophisticated, well-connected networks of criminals are a real and growing national security threat. There is a rise of transnational syndicates that know no boundaries to their illicit activities. The Clinton administration produced a report, released by the National Security Council in December 2000, that describes how Russian, Chinese, Nigerian, Middle Eastern and Italian gangs have enthusiastically embraced globalization and technology to expand their domains and escape the police. Among their activities are terrorism, the illegal drug trade, alien smuggling, trafficking in women and children, copyright violations, money laundering, car theft, paedophilia, and others. Diversified organized crime has become intertwined with the political elites in some countries. Some of these organizations are simultaneously engaged in legitimate activities such as building highways while trading heroin. They may, of course, be regarded as negative aspects of the private profit-seeking sector rather than as antisocial capital. But the loyalties, bonds and honour among thieves resemble those that are evident in social capital. 'All the wondrous developments of the new economy – falling costs, fewer borders, easy communications – help international terrorists and criminals as much as they do businessmen.'[12] In December 2000, a high-level conference was convened in Palermo, at which a Convention against Transnational Organized Crime was opened for signature. Military, economic and political power will have to meet the new threat.

Some libertarians (such as Margaret Thatcher) are eager to destroy the civil society, both local and global, while reformers (such as Mikhail Gorbachev) in societies in which it has been destroyed have tried to rebuild it. Russia and some of the East European countries are still suffering from the absence of the trust and the institutions that a flourishing civil society creates. But here again, as in the case of the complementarity of private and public activities, the strength of the civil society and of NGOs in particular often lies, not in opposing the public sector, but in cooperating with it, whether for finance, or for replication of successful ventures, or for support in opposing exploitative local power elites. In this way the state can contribute to the formation of social capital. In other circumstances, for example when faced with a predatory state, which would, unhindered, detract from social capital, their function is to combat it. But at the global level there are no corresponding governmental institutions to cooperate with (or oppose) the fledgling global civil society. Apart from international (not global) institutions, there are only global corporations and global NGOs.

SUGGESTIONS FOR FUTURE WORK

It would be interesting to explore the relation between the size of a country, its social capital and its economic growth. How do we explain the success of so many small countries, when all the economic arguments are against it? They enjoy no economies of scale, the uncertainties of foreign trade are greater, and so on. Could it be that social cohesion is more easily achieved in a small society, that trust and its social capital are greater? Could it be that concessions and sacrifice for the common good are more readily made when it is known and seen that your turn to benefit and for others to make sacrifices will come later?

What is the right balance between civil society, the state and the private sector to produce good social capital? The commonly accepted model is that of the 'rational individual', maximizing his/her self-interest. If social capital were important, this would have to be revised to incorporate altruistic motivations. These can contribute to better economic performance, as well as being valuable in their own right.

Does the Internet strengthen community spirit and social capital formation or weaken them? Robert Putnam has argued in his book *Bowling Alone* (2000) that television is one of the main causes that has weakened American civic spirit and social capital. The emphasis on individual choice and autonomy has dominated recent living conditions. Individual choice, however, can be in conflict with social cohesion. The growth in divorce rates and the easing of divorce law can be counted as a gain if we measure progress in human welfare as the widening of choices or as a loss if we regard the breakdown of the family, an important social institution, as social disintegration. Suicide is a matter of choice and therefore good, or a form of dysfunction, to be counted as negative social capital. Free choice can itself become a burden, as the little girl testifies who asked her mother plaintively, 'Mummy, must I always do as I like?'

As William A. Galston (1999, pp. 1–8) has reminded us, the desire for individual choice has been in conflict with another strong desire: the longing to be tied to others in a community. And it seems that the combination of these apparently conflicting desires can be approximated on the Internet. What Galston calls 'voluntary community' has three conditions: low barriers to entry, low barriers to exit and interpersonal relations shaped by mutual adjustment rather than hierarchical authority or coercion. The Internet clearly contributes to the formation of groups based on common interests. These groups of shared interests either are ends in themselves (rock groups, sports teams, choral societies) or they can serve personal or professional objectives: for example, information about specific diseases. But are these groups communities? Galston, following Thomas Bender (1982), suggests four characteristics of community: limited membership, shared norms, affective ties and a sense of mutual obligation.

Are these present in computer-mediated communications? Limited membership is not common among on-line groups because entry and exit are relatively easy. Albert Hirschman's exercise of voice, as opposed to exit, will not be a regular practice among them. Shared norms, on the other hand, are common among on-line groups. Moral persuasion and group disapproval of violators tend to establish them. In spite of the libertarian philosophy of many Internet users, affective ties can be established, although the Internet is also open to simulation, deception and invention. Finally, the development of a sense of mutual obligation among members would imply a willingness to accept sacrifices for other members. Neither among interest-based groups nor outside the Internet is such a willingness to make sacrifices common today. Arthur J. Tanney, who has placed reminiscences of his visits to the bungalows in the Catskills on a website, said:

> We're more connected than we've ever been in history, with the Internet, cell phones and cable TV. As connected as we are we're more disconnected than we've ever been. And that sense of community that I experienced in the bungalows, of belonging, of being in the same place together is gone.[13]

The conclusion is that it is too early to know how on-line groups will affect the tensions between autonomy and connection. William Galston (1999, p. 8) concludes:

> Because [the voluntary communities] emphasize exit as a response to discontent and dissatisfaction, they do not promote the development of voice; because they emphasize personal choice, they do not acknowledge the need for authority; because they are brought together and held together by converging individual interest, they neither foster mutual obligation nor lay the basis for sacrifice.

NOTES

1. Steven N. Durlauf (1999).
2. Partha Dasgupta argues that, for social capital to play a role, it is not necessary for a residual to appear. See Dasgupta (2000).
3. 'The strange persistence of politics', *The Economist*, 31 March 2001, p. 54.
4. Partha Dasgupta (2000, pp. 380–81).
5. 'A matter of trust', *The Economist*, 17 February 2001. Also see Glaeser *et al.* (2000).
6. Andrew M. Kamarck (2001) and personal communication.
7. See Dasgupta (2000, p. 389).
8. Albert O. Hirschman (1986, p. 154).
9. See Richard Falk (1996, p. 58).
10. This is not to say that the greater influence of unelected, unaccountable and unrepresentative NGOs is necessarily good. See Paul Streeten (1997, pp. 193–210).
11. It should be noted that, what some regard as benefits, others regard as threats to competitiveness and therefore welfare. For instance, job security, guaranteed old age pensions and a comprehensive welfare programme may be regarded as contributing to human security, but also as adding to 'inflexibility' and hence to social costs.
12. Fareed Zakaria (2000, p. 9).
13. Joseph Berger (2000, p. 5).

REFERENCES

Arrow, Kenneth (2000), 'Observations on social capital', in Partha Dasgupta and Ismail Serageldin (eds), *Social Capital: A Multifaceted Perspective*, Washington, DC: The World Bank, p. 4.

Bender, Thomas (1982), *Community and Social Change in America*, Baltimore, MD: Johns Hopkins University Press.

Berger, Joseph (2000), 'Yesterday's borscht and knishes return as today's reading list', *The New York Times*, Arts Section E1, 31 August.

Dasgupta, Partha (2000), 'Economic progress and the idea of social capital', in Partha Dasgupta and Ismail Serageldin (eds), *Social Capital; A Multifaceted Perspective*, Washington, DC: The World Bank, pp. 325–424.

Durlauf, Steven N. (1999), 'The case against social capital', *Focus* **20** (Fall), 3.

The Economist (2001), 'A matter of trust', 17 February.

The Economist (2001), 'The strange persistence of politics', 29 March.

Falk, Richard (1996), 'Revisioning cosmopolitanism', in Martha Nussbaum and Joshu Cohen (eds), *For Love of Country: Debating the Limits of Patriotism*, Boston: Beacon Press, pp. 53–60.

Fukuyama, Francis (1995), *Trust: The Social Virtues and the Creation of Prosperity*, New York: The Free Press.

Galston, William A. (1999), 'Does the Internet strengthen community?', *Philosophy & Public Policy*, **19** (Fall), 4.

Glaeser, Edward L., David Laibson, José A. Scheinkman and Christine L. Soutter (2000), 'Measuring Trust', *Quarterly Journal of Economics*, **65**, 811–46.

Hirschman, Albert O. (1986), 'Against parsimony: three easy ways of complicating some categories of economic discourse', in *Rival Views of Market Society*, New York and London: Viking.

Kamarck, Andrew M. (2001), *Economics for the Twenty-first Century*, Aldershot: Ashgate Publishing.

Olson, Mancur (1982), *The Rise and Decline of Nations: Economic Growth, Stagflation and Social Rigidities*, New Haven, CT: Yale University Press.

Ostrom, Elinor (2000), 'Social capital: a fad or a fundamental concept?', in Partha Dasgupta and Ismail Serageldin (eds), *Social Capital: A Multifaceted Perspective*, Washington, DC: The World Bank.

Putnam, Robert D. (2000), *Bowling Alone. The Collapse and Revival of American Community*, New York: Simon & Schuster.

Robertson, Dennis H. (1956), 'What does the economist economize?', in *Economic Commentaries*, London: Staples Press.

Schiff, Maurice (1999), 'Labor market integration in the presence of social capital', Development Research Group, World Bank, Washington, DC.

Solow, Robert M. (2000), 'Notes on social capital and economic performance', in Partha Dasgupta and Ismail Serageldin (eds), *Social Capital: A Multifaceted Perspective*, Washington, DC: The World Bank, p. 6.

Streeten, Paul (1997), 'Nongovernmental organizations and development', in *The Annals of the American Academy of Political and Social Science: The Role of NGOs, Charity and Empowerment*, special editors Jude L. Fernando and Alan W. Heston, 5 November.

Zakaria, Fareed (2000), 'Globalization grows up and gets political', *The New York Times*, Op-Ed, Section 4, 31 December.

4. Bonds and bridges: social capital and poverty

Deepa Narayan[1]

The development community is increasingly paying attention to the social aspects of development. A country's economic development is embedded in its social organization, and addressing structural inequities requires not only economic changes but also societal transformation (Stiglitz, 1998). But social phenomena are so all-pervasive, and often so vaguely defined, that taking them into account in a systematic way is very difficult. One approach to untangling and analysing some of the social forces at work in development is through the concept of social capital. The term refers in general to the glue that holds groups and societies together: bonds of shared values, norms and institutions. In this chapter, I concentrate on two aspects of social capital in particular, 'cross-cutting ties' or 'bonds and bridges' and the interaction between informal and formal institutions. This interaction is one of complementarity or substitution. Although the focus is narrow, the chapter argues that these elements of social capital and their interrelationship help explain a number of puzzles and have important implications for policy. The section immediately following this introduction, 'What is social capital?', provides the view of social capital used in this chapter. 'The analytical framework' then presents the analytic framework, while 'The empirical evidence' reviews the empirical evidence supporting it. The chapter concludes with 'Policy implications'.

WHAT IS SOCIAL CAPITAL?

The debate on social capital has brought together sociologists, anthropologists, political scientists and economists. While differences remain, there is agreement that, in contrast to all other concepts of capital central to the development debate, social capital is unique in that it is *relational*. 'Whereas economic capital is in people's bank accounts and human capital is inside their heads, social capital inheres in the structure of their relationships. To possess social capital, a person must be related to others, and it is these others, not himself, who are

58

the actual source of his or her advantage' (Portes, 1998). 'As an attribute of the social structure in which a person is embedded, social capital is not the private property of any of the persons who benefit from it' (Coleman, 1990). It exists only when it is shared. 'Social capital is embedded in social structure and has public good characteristics' (Narayan, 1997).

While the debate is vigorous as to whether social capital is truly capital, whether it should be widely or narrowly defined, and whether it can be constructed or is an endowment, the active engagement of scholars and practitioners has moved the field forward in terms of conceptual development and empirical results;[2] hence the value of this term. For the purposes of this chapter, social capital is viewed as the norms and social relations embedded in the social structures of society that enable people to coordinate action and to achieve desired goals.

The following section presents a simple framework for exploring the effect of social capital. Its central thesis is that all societies and all social groups have social capital. However, for societal well-being or the collective good, a transition has to occur from exclusive loyalty to primary social groups (bonding) to networks of secondary associations whose most important characteristic is that they bring together people who in some ways are different from the self (bridging). Social relations underlie all social institutions and in turn feed back and reinforce the organization and functioning of a country's formal and informal institutions. [*Editors' note*: see the discussion by Molinas in this volume, Chapter 6.]

THE ANALYTICAL FRAMEWORK

This section presents a simple analytic framework of relationships growing out of the concepts and theories discussed above. The framework, sketched in Figure 4.1 below, highlights the interaction between two key dimensions, cross-cutting ties and state functioning. The framework permits a structured examination of the way different combinations along these two dimensions affect the social and economic performance of countries, or regions or communities within countries.

Cross-cutting Ties

The underlying dynamic reflected in the framework is that voluntary cross-cutting networks, associations and related norms based in everyday social interactions lead to the collective good of citizens, whereas networks and associations consisting of primary social groups without cross-cutting ties lead to the betterment of only those groups. Primary social group solidarity is the

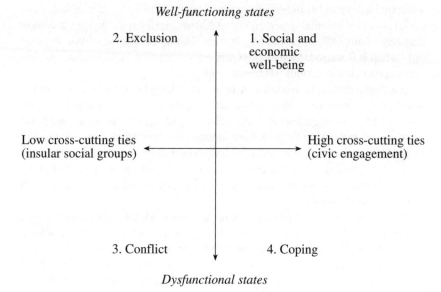

Figure 4.1   Relationship between cross-cutting ties and governance

foundation on which societies are built. The impact of primary social groups depends on their resources and power. But when power between groups is asymmetrically distributed, it is cross-cutting ties between social groups that become critical to both economic opportunity and social cohesion.

While primary groups and networks undoubtedly provide opportunities to those who belong, they also reinforce pre-existing social stratification, prevent mobility of excluded groups, minorities or poor people, and become the bases of corruption and cooption of power by the dominant social groups. Cross-cutting ties which are dense and voluntary, though not necessarily strong (as in the right-hand half of Figure 4.1) help connect people with access to different information, resources and opportunities. In addition, as people get to know others who are different from themselves, there is less likelihood that social differences will grow into divisive social cleavages.

On the other hand, the social fabric of a country may consist of primary social groups with few interconnections between groups, or consist of groups with inherent power asymmetries such as the caste system in India, as in the left-hand half of Figure 4.1. These societies are likely to be characterized by social exclusion and polarization at best, and at worst by corruption, violence and economic stagnation, where the disadvantaged cope by depending on informal social mechanisms for livelihood, security and insurance.

Functioning of the State

The functioning of government institutions can be described in various ways, but most authors focus on two aspects that determine government performance. First is the overall governance environment which fosters the rule of law, citizen rights and freedom to associate, since these create the societal norms which influence the emergence, and subsequent performance, of a range of societal institutions.[3] The second aspect is the competence, authority, resources and accountability of government organizations working within the overall governance environment.[4]

The vertical axis in the framework depicted in Figure 4.1 indicates the level of state functioning. In the top half are states which function effectively, maintain order, collect taxes and so on, while in the bottom half are states where institutions are ineffective, or at the extreme have collapsed altogether.

Complementarity and Substitution

The framework is especially helpful in capturing some of the dynamic aspects of the relationship between social capital and the formal institutions of the state. Social capital has an impact on the overall governance environment and the efficacy of government institutions. Under conditions of good governance, the functioning state *complements* the functions of the informal social groups. In societies in which primary social groups are connected through cross-cutting ties, economic prosperity and social order are likely. But when a society's social capital inheres mainly in primary social groups that are disconnected from one another, the more powerful groups dominate the governance structures to the exclusion of other groups. Such societies are characterized by latent conflict. As the efficacy of government deteriorates, informal social groups become *substitutes* for the state. In societies with isolated social groups, people try to earn their livelihood in economically stagnant situations or struggle merely to survive in the context of violence, crime and war. The following paragraphs use Figure 4.1 to explore this broad dynamic further.

The two critical dimensions along which countries (or regions or communities within a country) vary are in the level of functioning of the state and the extent of cross-cutting ties among social groups. In the ideal scenario (Quadrant 1, well-being), good governance and high levels of government functioning are complemented by high levels of cross-cutting ties among social groups and lead to positive economic and social outcomes. Countries that belong in this quadrant include the Scandinavian countries and the Netherlands. All have historically been characterized by high economic development, social cohesion and the relative absence of crime, violence, conflict and exclusion.

In Quadrant 2 (exclusion) are countries (or regions or communities) with governments that function well, but that have been taken over or excessively influenced by the dominant primary social groups. They are characterized by relatively few cross-cutting ties across social groups, leading to exclusion of the non-dominant groups. The chief characteristic of Quadrant 2 is latent conflict. Countries in this quadrant might include South Africa under apartheid; Latin American countries like Peru and Mexico, with large indigenous populations; some well-performing Indian states which exclude lower caste and tribal groups; some parts of the United States; Germany and many of the countries in Eastern Europe with high exclusion of minority groups. Excluded groups may eventually organize across communities, leading to social movements that challenge the status quo and the power of the state. If these societies open up to the excluded and explicitly build bridges across social groups, they may progress and eventually move into Quadrant 1.

Alternatively, they may degenerate into Quadrant 3 (conflict), becoming embroiled in prolonged conflict, violence, civil war or anarchy, with gradual dissolution of the functioning state. As the state ceases to fulfil its functions, the primary social groups become informal substitutes for the state, and power and authority are taken over by 'warlords', the Mafia, guerrilla movements and other groups which use violence and coercion.

When societies are characterized by social groups with abundant cross-cutting ties and poorly functioning governments, as in Quadrant 4 (coping), the informal networks become substitutes for the failed state and form the basis for coping strategies. These include informal credit, informal contractual arrangements, increased informal activities and self-employment, barter and 'grey' economies, community-run basic schools and health clinics, and so on. In Kenya, a participatory poverty assessment in six districts documented approximately 30 000 self-help groups in rural areas, with little or no contact with any government agencies (Narayan and Nyamwaya, 1996). In Russia, Richard Rose (1995) has documented the informal coping networks that emerged with the collapse of the communist state. With increasing conflict and lawlessness, Russia moved into Quadrant 3, and is struggling to move into Quadrant 1.

The current development paradigm has focused on reforming the state or markets to help countries prosper and has had mixed success at best. The framework outlined above suggests that interventions aimed at economic prosperity need to take into account underlying social organization and actively facilitate cross-cutting social interactions of previously isolated and even warring groups. This does not mean government mandating heterogeneity of membership in formal groups and associations, but it does mean creating economic, political, institutional and social incentives to help build physical and social space in which cross-cutting, or bridging linkages among people from different social groups, can begin to emerge.

Table 4.1 lists a number of important factors that contribute to well-being and the role of informal and formal institutions. It underlines the relationships of substitution and complementarity between institutions. In the ideal, complementary relationship, there will be close collaboration between informal and formal institutions. Conversely, when the corresponding institutions are far apart, substitution will predominate. Suppose, for example, that trust were the contributing factor in question. In the best of circumstances, informal institutions regulate trust through social mechanisms, rewarding trustworthy behaviour and applying social sanctions such as ostracism and shame to those who violate the norms. Formal institutions strengthen the overall environment of trust through equitable access to justice, the rule of law, enforceable contracts and a police force that protects citizens. Values of trust and mutual respect can also be reinforced through appropriate school curricula. When the formal system fails, vigilante groups or gangs accountable to no one may emerge.

In addition, Table 4.1 reminds us that not all forms of traditional social capital are benign, and that some state actions are required to negate the effects of exclusionary or conflictual forms of social capital. For example, gender differentials in feeding and taking care of sick children are widely biased against girls. Public policy interventions that increase the status of girls, for instance through scholarship programmes, could, over time, change local norms about the respective values of boy and girl children.

THE EMPIRICAL EVIDENCE

As traditional growth models have failed to explain satisfactorily differences in economic performance between countries, researchers have increasingly turned to non-economic variables for explanations (for example, Knack and Keefer, 1997). However, this extension of interest to social characteristics has been limited by extremely weak data sets. Despite data problems, the pattern of findings that emerges from the recent literature supports the picture emerging from the four quadrants of Figure 4.1, and also the underlying relationships posited between associationalism, government performance and socioeconomic outcomes.

Quadrant 1: Well-being – Well-functioning Government, Abundant Cross-cutting Ties

Several authors have examined the relationship among economic development, government quality and social capital. Given the limited quality of existing social capital measures, all authors use proxy indicators. Fedderke and Klitgaard (1998) examined the relationship between the level of per capita

Table 4.1 Role of formal and informal institutions in promoting well-being

Mechanisms	Informal institutions	Formal institutions
1. Information sharing	Families, friends, peers, neighbours, kin, ethnic networks, informal groups, work-related networks Festivals, rituals, sports events, story telling, religious activities	Newspapers, trade journals, magazines, books, radios, television, Internet Roads, post offices, electricity, telephones Schools, colleges, vocational centres, literacy programmes, extension programmes Political competition, citizenship rights, freedom to associate, independent audits, freedom of press, information disclosure laws, civil society participation and other accountability mechanisms
2. Risk mitigation	Differential health care spending, selective feeding strategies, home-based preventive care Revolving credit societies within family diversification, kin or social group network, intergenerational transfer work-related networks	Health insurance policies, subsidized healthcare for the poor, health education Investment in human capability, unemployment insurance, social security, safety net schemes; pensions; laws enforced for open and fair hiring based on merit; investment incentives for private sector; financial intermediaries; insurance; Credit Rating Bureau
3. Local public goods, basic services and common property resources	Community groups	Coproduction with local groups through direct or indirect representation
4. Transaction costs	Family, extended kin, ethnic network, traditional council, community groups, neighbourhood or social groups-based security systems	Courts, tribunals, dispute resolution bodies, mediation centres, police, security forces, social services, alternative dispute resolution mechanisms, zoning laws

GDP in 1960 and 1985, as well as the average growth of per capita GDP and an exhaustive list of political and social institutional indicators. They found that higher levels of GDP were associated with greater civil and political rights, including protection of human rights, tolerance for diversity and compromise in conflict. They also found that higher levels of GDP were associated with lower levels of political instability and higher levels of efficiency in public institutions, as measured by the efficiency of the judiciary and civil service bureaucracy and lower corruption.

Making creative use of the Adelman–Taft index (AT) of socioeconomic development (Adelman and Morris, 1967), Temple and Johnson (1998) demonstrate that social capability measured in the 1960s predicted, more accurately than conventional indicators, which countries would grow in the 1980s. For example, their model predicts that, for India to achieve the same level of socioeconomic development as South Korea by 1960, then annual growth of income per capita would have been 3 per cent instead of 1.3 per cent. Under this scenario, India's income per capita in 1985 would then have been almost 60 per cent higher.

These findings that relate economic growth to the AM index have been criticized because the index includes some economic indicators. To address this criticism for further analysis, Temple and Johnson test the same model using only four social indicators: kinship (dominance of the immediate family over the extended family or clan and tribal allegiances); the extent of mass communications (newspaper circulation and number of radios per capita); the importance of an indigenous middle class (proportion of men employed in the professions, in contrast to number of expatriates in these professions); and modernization of outlook (which includes an assessment of social and political participation through voluntary associations and also the support for political and economic modernization). The first three have statistically significant relations to growth. The relationship between mass communications and growth remains robust even after controlling for a range of human capital, trade policy, political stability and ethnic fragmentation. The authors conclude by suggesting that the extent of mass communication may be a good proxy for the strength of civic communities, as reflected in trust and membership of associations.

La Porta *et al.* (1997) used trust data from the World Values Survey to examine the thesis that trust or social capital determines the performance of society's institutions. (Trust is the propensity to cooperate.) They find the effects of trust on government performance (as measured by efficiency of the judiciary, corruption, bureaucratic quality, tax compliance and civic participation) to be both statistically significant and quantitatively large. In addition, they test Fukuyama's thesis (1995) that family loyalty is detrimental to the growth of large corporations, and that trust beyond the family has to become the basis for cooperation for this transition to occur. La Porta *et al.* find a positive coefficient between the relative share of the top 20 firms and trust in people (0.65), and a negative coefficient with trust in family (–0.56). This appears to confirm Fukuyama's thesis that, for the development of large corporations, trust has to transcend the primary group of the family.

Expanding the argument of Putnam *et al.* (1993) that the Roman Catholic church lowers trust in society by imposing a hierarchical structure on society, La Porta *et al.* include two other hierarchical religions, the Eastern Orthodox church and Islam. They find a strong negative correlation between hierarchical religions and trust (–0.61). Holding per capita income constant, they find that countries with more dominant hierarchical religions have less efficient judiciaries, greater corruption, lower-quality bureaucracies, higher rates of tax evasion, lower rates of participation in civic activities, lower importance of large firms in the economy, inferior infrastructure and higher inflation.

Finally, Knack and Keefer (1997), also using the same World Values data set for 29 market economies, conclude that trust and civic cooperation are associated with stronger economic performance. However, associational activity is not correlated with economic performance, contrary to Putnam's findings about Italy. They speculate that any positive effects of groups may be balanced by the damage done by distributional coalitions – the Olson (1982) thesis. This speculation is not borne out by their analysis, however, since the measure of associations is weak and does not include intensity of participation in groups or the nature of groups. Knack and Keefer also conclude that trust and civic cooperation are stronger in countries with formal institutions that effectively protect property and contract rights, and in countries that are less polarized along lines of class and ethnicity.[5]

Quadrant 2: Exclusion – Well-functioning Government, Poor Cross-cutting Ties

This discussion examines the relationship between income inequality which, in the absence of more direct measures, is used as a proxy for exclusion, growth, ethnic heterogeneity and government performance. Despite limitations of proxy indicators for social capital, the patterns of results which emerge point to the importance of cross-cutting ties across social groups for engendering cooperation, trust, better government performance and well-being.

Dani Rodrik broke new ground in a 1997 paper, 'Where did all the growth go? External shocks, social conflict and growth collapses'. In it, he examines econometrically the interactions between social conflict and external shocks on the one hand and the domestic conflict-mediating institutions on the other to explain the persistence of growth and the magnitude of the collapse in growth in the 1970s. Rodrik argues that, when social divisions run deep and the institutions of conflict management are weak, exogenous shocks trigger distributional conflicts. Such conflicts diminish the productivity with which a society's resources are utilized and divert activities from the entrepreneurial sphere to the political sphere. He concludes that the countries that experienced the sharpest drops in growth after 1975 were those with socially divided societies as measured by indicators of income inequality, ethnic and linguistic fragmentation and/or conflict and social trust. These countries also had weak institutions of conflict management measured by the quality of governmental institutions, honest and non-corrupt bureaucracy, rule of law, democratic rights and institutionalized modes of social safety nets.

Rodrik found that ethnolinguistic fragmentation was a significant determinant of income inequality even after controlling for institutional quality, a result that survived a range of robustness tests.

Knack and Keefer (1997) demonstrate that the Gini coefficient for income inequality is strongly associated with lower trust and civic cooperation. When income inequality is considered as a proxy (albeit imperfect) of social cleavages and social exclusion, two findings are worth noting. First is the fact that measures of income inequality are quite stable, even during periods of rapid growth. A possible interpretation is that, since the dominant social groups make policy and resource allocation decisions, these decisions reinforce their power and prosperity, and hence policy interventions do not result in major changes for those excluded. The second consistent finding is that countries with initial unequal income distributions experience slower growth.[6] Birdsall and Sabot (1994) come to similar conclusions in comparing high inequality and low growth in Latin America and low inequality and high growth in East Asia, but they turn to political economy considerations to explain the different strategies in the two regions. In Latin America, the political elite has little incentive to invest in the well-being of the poor, but in East Asia the threat of communist insurgency led to government investment in the rural poor, in education and health and in rural infrastructure. Larraín and Vergara (1997), using data for 45 developed and developing countries, conclude that distributive inequalities give rise to social pressures and conflict, and these in turn generate greater instability in economic policies and lower investment. Rodrik also concludes, on the basis of cross-country regressions, that severe income inequality is a threat to political and economic stability. When people see some living in luxury while others are impoverished, it creates social unrest that typically culminates in the overthrow of government, disruption of the local economy and collapse of foreign investor confidence.

Negative associations between the ethnic diversity of societies and growth have been reported by Easterly and Levine (1995) and Mauro (1995). Collier and Gunning (1997) demonstrate that ethnic fractionalization negatively affects policy and reduces productivity more directly. They also show that the correlations are stronger with the delivery of public services such as schools and telephones and weaker for macroeconomic policy. The wide use of the ethnolinguistic fragmentation indicator has created a mindset which equates ethnic diversity with economic and political disaster, particularly in Africa. In an important study, Collier and Hoeffler (1998) establish that the relationship between civil war and ethnic fractionalization is not linear. The most unstable societies are those with two fairly equal ethnic groups. On the other hand, highly fractionalized societies, such as are found in many countries in Africa, are as stable as the most homogeneous societies.

In Latin America, by contrast, if one groups all the non-Spanish indigenous people together and all the Spanish speakers together, many countries then consist of two large groups with little interaction among groups, a situation rife with latent conflict. A poverty study in Peru found that the overall poverty levels had declined (Hentschel *et al.*, 1998). However, the non-Spanish speaking population had not been integrated politically, socially or economically. In fact it had fallen further behind in income terms even after controlling for education, location, access to services and land and/or house ownership.

Using Tarrow's (1998) concepts of contentious politics and political opportunity, Fox (1996) shows how some indigenous groups can successfully organize to challenge the power of a repressive state. Mexico has the largest population of indigenous groups in Latin America: 10 million people comprising 56 officially recognized ethnolinguistic groups. Fox demonstrates that indigenous communities are high in social solidarity and horizontal decision making, that is bonding social capital, but still among the poorest in Mexico. He shows that these communities of scattered population can be successful when they network with other geographically spread-out communities, find allies in political elites, or are supported by other non-political elites, such as the Catholic Church. Only then do they have sufficient bargaining power to challenge local power structures successfully, overcome the repression imposed by authoritarian regimes, and acquire the power and resources of the state to meet their basic needs.

Quadrant 3: Conflict – Dysfunctional or State, Limited Cross-cutting Ties

Income inequality, isolated primary groups and a governance structure which is coopted by a few, unaccountable to the majority, can lead to violence, conflict and high levels of crime. [*Editors' note*: see discussion by Colletta and Cullen in this volume, Chapter 12.] The effective power of the state can be taken over by those who exercise the most force and coercion, and in effect run parallel economies and substitute governance structures. When the state authority, law and order extend irregularly across territory and functional relations (including class, ethnic and gender relations), power centres shift away from the state to extralegal authorities that coexist with the state but remain autonomous within it. In many countries emerging from war, the authority of the state remains limited to the centre, with loss of control and legitimacy over the periphery. Power gets usurped from a weak state and used for personal rule and control. The impunity of drug trade, unlawful treatment of the poor by the police or local Mafia, high crime rates and rich communities behind high-security fences are all examples of the crisis of such a state.

Haiti provides ample evidence of the degeneration into violence and civil war when social cleavages deepen, and formal institutions become instruments for control and private riches for one social group while others live in poverty and personal insecurity. White and Smucker (1998) trace today's social cleavages and failure of the state back to the country's colonial days. In 1804, when Haiti gained its independence, two social groups emerged with different interests. One group was composed of a large number of newly freed slaves, who fought for personal freedom from bondage, and the other group was composed of a small class of freed people of colour (which included the wealthy), who fought for economic and political freedom. 'These sharply defined social distinctions where neither class assumed responsibility for providing the national public good set the stage for Haiti's evolution as an independent but deeply divided society.' White and Smucker describe social capital as 'truncated', rich at the local level but weak at regional and national levels. In the presence of an oppressive state and the absence of state-provided services, these informal social relations become substitutes and serve as the primary social safety nets for the poor. The Haitian state, despite recent changes, is marked by political intolerance, patronage, extraction of wealth and lack of protection for the majority of its citizens.

Mauricio Rubio (1997) shows how, in Colombia, the existence of a large and growing illegal and underground economy run by powerful criminal organizations has resulted in parallel institutional environments that reward and favour opportunistic and criminal behaviours. Rubio shows how high levels of social capital within 'criminal' organizations are directed to extralegal activities, rent seeking and high returns exclusively for those involved in such activities. The organizations that run in parallel with government institutions actually provide higher returns to those who participate than a regular career would offer. Rubio estimates that, between 1980 and 1993, the average remuneration for minor criminal activities, excluding drug trafficking and kidnapping, tripled in real terms, while returns for formal work remained stagnant. Currently, the annual income of a petty criminal in Colombia is around $20 000 per year, about 10 times the per capita GDP.

On the basis of a study of persistent intercommunal violence in India in particular cities, Varshney (1998) argues that there is an integral link between the structure of civic life in a multiethnic society and ethnic conflict. Interethnic networks become agents of peace because they build bridges and manage tensions, but if communities are organized only on intraethnic lines and the interconnections with other communities do not exist, ethnic violence is quite likely. He divides both interethnic and intraethnic networks into formal associational forms of engagement and everyday forms of engagement. Associational networks include professional organizations, reading clubs, cadre-based political parties, film clubs and NGOs. Everyday forms of engagement consist of simple, routine interactions such as families visiting each other, children playing together, joint participation in festivals or eating together. Varshney concludes that, while both forms of social interaction are important, in large cities associational forms are sturdier than everyday forms of engagement, especially when confronted with attempts by politicians to polarize people on ethnic lines.

Quadrant 4: Coping – Poorly Functioning State, Abundant Cross-cutting Ties

Societies with higher levels of cross-cutting ties rather than deep social cleavages and ineffective or coopted states are characterized by the replacement of the formal system by informal systems. If the state is not totalitarian or coercive, societies may not disintegrate into widespread crime, violence or war, but large segments of society are left to their own devices to cope in the best ways they can.

Rose (1995) uses the term 'hour-glass society' to describe such societies, like Russia during the transition. There is a rich social life at the base, consisting of strong informal networks relying on trust between friends, relatives and other face-to-face groups and which may include friends of friends. At the top of the hour glass, there is rich political and social life, as elites compete for power, wealth and prestige. There is cooperation within and between elites and formal institutions as the elites use the resources of the state for their own betterment. The narrow mid-point of the hour-glass insulates individuals from the influence of the state, and citizens can be described as 'negatively integrated' from the demands of a potentially oppressive state. The state, on the other hand, tolerates small-scale 'rogue' organizations as long as they do not interfere with the affairs of the state.

Using data from the New Russia Barometer, a nationwide survey, Rose notes that only one in eight respondents reported that they earned enough from their official jobs to meet their basic needs. The majority get by because, in addition to the official economy, they rely on a multiplicity of unofficial economic activities such as growing food, exchanging help and services with friends, having a second job or depending on tips and bribes. There is a vast disconnection between the rich social mechanisms and exchanges at the bottom and local formal institutions. Three-quarters of the people also said that they never participated in local-level formal institutions. The same proportion said that most people could not be trusted and that one had to be careful in dealing with people. The level of distrust in political parties, parliament, police, court and civil servants ranged from 71 per cent to 83 per cent. When asked if they expected fair treatment from the local police and government, 70 per cent reported that they did not. Distrust in the formal institutions combined with high inflationary pressures in Russia results in 'a hundred friends being worth more than ten million rubles'.

This hour glass metaphor fits many developing countries in which formal institutions are marked by high levels of corruption and the informal systems of coping become the primary sources for safety, insurance and livelihood for the majority of their people. These networks can become overextended, and unless there are strong allies outside the communities the informal groups remain isolated and economically stagnant. It is in these environments, when there is political space to organize, that civil society emerges and often begins to function as a shadow government, providing services that the state is incapable of providing. Civil society movements may be crushed by the political regime, or may alternatively become forces for transformation of the state. In effect, this means moving from a role of substitution to one of complementarity with the state. The case of the Bangladesh Rural Advancement Committee (BRAC) is an example of the latter. As a Bangladeshi NGO, BRAC provided an extensive network of schools for the poor without any state involvement, and was initially perceived to be a competitor and threat to the power of the state. In fact, it was a substitute for the failure of the state to provide basic education services for poor children. Over time, however, the state has become a partner with BRAC in reaching the poor with these services.

POLICY IMPLICATIONS

Two sets of policy implications flow from the foregoing analysis. The first set deals with the way countries (or communities within countries) can strengthen cross-cutting ties and governance to improve economic and social well-being (movements towards Quadrant 1 in the framework). The second set includes practical social policy interventions that are likely to be helpful.

Movement Towards Well-being

Cohesive family, clan or tribal groups lay the foundation for social and economic well-being, but it is only when these groups develop bridging ties (both weak and dense) with other social groups that societies can build cohesive webs of cross-cutting social relations at all levels. Societies in western Europe, particularly the Scandinavian countries and the Netherlands, have achieved high levels of social inclusion, peace and economic prosperity, which would place them in Quadrant 1 of the framework presented in Figure 4.1.

Power is unequally distributed in all societies, but societies differ markedly in the degree, extent and permanence of power asymmetries and social exclusion. When the networks of those excluded or disempowered consist primarily of 'people like themselves', and are not linked to outside groups, information, power and resources, the networks serve an important insurance and solidarity function. However, they do not become *agents for transformation* into high-return production groups or into powerful social movements that challenge the powers of the state. In Latin America, it is only when indigenous groups become included in local governance structures, or when they form alliances with other indigenous groups, that they are able to claim attention and resources from the state. The same is true for lower-caste groups in India or for the inclusion of African Americans in US society. Similarly, successful strategies for the provision of services to excluded groups, such as micro-credit schemes, initially take advantage of social solidarity among small groups of the poor in order to extend credit to those without formal collateral. But over time, as a deliberate strategy, they socialize poor clients in the methods of formal institutions and actively help connect the poor to the formal banking systems.

Latent conflict between the dominant groups and those excluded is a characteristic of Quadrant 2 (exclusion) in Figure 4.1. To move towards economic and social well-being, states must (a) develop mechanisms for including the excluded in the formal systems of finance, education and governance, (b) promote change in values and norms to support inclusion, (c) create economic opportunities, and (d) encourage social connectivity between the excluded and those in power in different spheres of activity.

When the web of cross-cutting linkages among primary social groups is weak or non-existent, and interests of the excluded groups cannot be channelled through formal institutions of the state, then conflict and violence between groups based on religion, caste, race or ethnicity may escalate. Dominant or militant groups coopt the power of the state to their own ends and become substitutes for the state. A militarized or collapsed state characterizes Quadrant 3 (conflict) in Figure 4.1. Because of the absence of cross-cutting ties, the reconstruction of society and state (movement from Quadrant 3 to Quadrant 1) must include participatory processes to create social cohesion, reconciliation and peace between former enemies and reintegration of former soldiers into society. Particular attention needs to be paid to mechanisms for power sharing, consultation, justice, governance and provision of security for all. Equally important is equitable distribution of resources among former enemy groups for reconstruction of infrastructure, education, economy and governance across territories inhabited by different groups. Mass media that portray mutual respect, reconciliation and tolerance among previously warring groups can help provide the support needed to heal wounds and increase the probability of knitting society together again.

Widespread economic stagnation and use of coping strategies characterize Quadrant 4 (coping) in Figure 4.1. These are societies with dense cross-cutting ties, but where the formal institutions are coopted by special interest groups, the informal networks and connections between those excluded become overloaded by the burden of trying to offer services previously (or possibly never) provided by the state. The result of such overloading is that networks of association are reduced to coping strategies. Because of weak reciprocal connections among many different social groups, the collapse of the state need not degenerate into widespread violence and crime. But in this regressive environment, the informal institutions become poor *substitutes* for formal institutions, whether in provision of credit, education, infrastructure, legal protection, security or other basic services. To make progress in this environment, civil society must move beyond the delivery of services and take on the role of mobilizing social movements to demand changes in governance.

Policy Interventions

To design the right policy intervention, it is vital to understand the nature of a society's formal and informal institutions. Moving from a relationship of substitution to complementarity between informal and formal institutions may involve interventions by the state, the private sector, civil society groups or all three. Interventions may be at the community level or at the level of national laws, or changes in rules and regulations. Expansion of cross-cutting ties may be promoted through incentive schemes for the private sector or civil society groups supported by the government, or directly through improved communication channels such as roads, telephones, the Internet and media. Policies need to be tailored to take into account both the level of functioning of the state and the current strength of cross-cutting ties.

It is important to note that the role played by civil society, and the contribution it makes, will differ in the different quadrants of the framework. In Quadrant 1 (well-being), the key role for civil society groups is to keep the state accountable and support processes that balance the power of various interest and social groups in society. In Quadrant 2 (exclusion), the key role is in facilitating the organization and mobilization of excluded groups, identifying potential allies in powerful groups to challenge the state's exclusionary practices. In Quadrant 3 (conflict), the key roles shift to peace mediation, reconciliation and reintegration of previously warring and possibly armed groups into society. Finally, in Quadrant 4 (coping), in the absence of an effective state, civil society groups have important roles in service delivery, while at the same time mobilizing society to demand better governance. This means, of course, that civil society organizations will sometimes face the need to transform themselves (for example, from service delivery to advocacy), a task fully as difficult as transforming states.

In practical terms, the most promising interventions are likely to be of two kinds. First, *investments in the organizational capacity of the poor* are crucial, both at the micro level in direct support of poor people and at the macro level through changes in laws and rules so as to support associational activity. For example, in Bolivia the Law of Popular Participation established a framework for decentralization with two important components. One was the devolution of fiscal resources and authority to the municipal level; the other was assignment of an oversight role to local communities. The government recruited NGOs to mobilize local communities to fulfil their new role. The NGOs provide training to community groups in participatory needs assessments, formulating priorities, collaborating across communities and monitoring municipal decision making and expenditures (Faguet, 1998).

Second, *cross-cutting ties can be fostered directly*, through a variety of mechanisms that fall under seven broad headings: information, inclusive participation, conflict management mechanisms, education and values, economic restructuring, governance and decentralization, and demand-driven service delivery.

Information

Whether one views social capital through a sociological, political or economic lens, all perspectives lead one to the conclusion that a free information flow is essential for equal opportunity, consensus building, keeping the state accountable and challenging the state when necessary. Making access to information about employment or investment opportunities widely available helps to offset the information isolation of excluded groups. Information is a public good that can be fostered through easy and equal access to communication channels and public information disclosure laws. Civil society organizations have an important role in informing people about their rights to information.

Perhaps the biggest revolution in the past century was the information revolution. The power of newspapers, books, post offices, telephones, cellular telephones, faxes and the Internet to disseminate information quickly is immense. In 1997, the Nobel Prize was won by Jody Williams and her group, who organized a campaign for the signing of an international treaty on land mines largely from a cabin in the woods of Vermont, USA. Poor, landless women in

Bangladesh have become the ones with cellular telephones and the power to connect people to relatives, friends or businesses anywhere in the world, through a programme sponsored by Grameen Telecom. Telephones already link poor buyers and sellers to daily market prices for commodities in cities, thus changing their negotiating power with middlemen in fundamental ways, and the Internet has the potential to bring about far more such changes. It is clear that government investment in physical infrastructure can play a critical role in supporting connectivity across space and social groups. Examples include roads, power supply, telephones, post offices and community halls that ease communication and movement of people and information, and provide space for different social groups to come together. Civil society organizations may not be much involved in infrastructure investment, but they have an obvious part to play in promoting connectivity, and in educating people about their rights to information.

Inclusive Participation

Citizen voice, participation and representation of all social groups in state decision making generate consensus, trust and social learning. Citizen and civil society participation challenges the state, and at the same time keeps the state accountable. It is essential for citizens and civil society groups to have access to timely and reasonably independent information about state action and performance, for example through citizen-led audits of government. A good recent example is the independent report produced by citizen groups in India on the state of primary education in that country. The findings of the report have been made widely available, with issues and findings reported and debated in the national media. In some areas in Rajasthan, India, civil society pressure for information disclosure has led to village governments posting in a public space information on all government funds received and detailed accounts of expenditures. This has led to widespread knowledge of fraudulence, and in many cases to corrective action.

Freedom to associate is a prerequisite for open participation and shapes the emergence of civil society organizations. In many countries, restrictive and regressive civil society laws and regulations prevent the emergence of such groups and restrict the mobilization of local resources to support civil society action. Tax exemptions and other incentives for the private sector to invest in and connect with local communities, invest in poor areas and support local initiatives and leadership development all nurture civil society development and action without loss of independence.

State accountability and citizen choice are supported by political pluralism and competition at all levels. When citizen groups have the right to elect local and national officials, they have the potential power to have their interests represented in local governance. The interests of excluded groups rarely get represented without contentious politics and collective action by those excluded. But without political pluralism there is rarely any opportunity for recourse. In this area, action by civil society organizations to help excluded groups organize and mobilize is especially important.

Conflict Management Mechanisms

Every society has conflict resolution mechanisms to protect human and property rights. These are critical to create societies that are socially cohesive, in which people feel secure and are willing to invest. Laws, regulations and fair treatment of all social groups are critical in generating trust and social and economic stability. Access to the judiciary and expectations of quick and 'cheap' justice help promote trust and use of the formal system. Alternative dispute resolution mechanisms are also important, so that disputes can be resolved quickly and less formally.

It is obvious that conflict prevention is better than conflict resolution. The problem, as diplomats and mediators attest, is that there is very little incentive to invest in conflict prevention. The best strategy is to increase social interaction among those social groups that have little do with one another. This could involve use of public space in ways that encourage people from different social and ethnic groups to live, work or engage more frequently together, particularly in multiethnic societies. Providing high-quality public transport which all social groups use, and safe public parks, places of worship, community halls and recreational and sports facilities which encourage common civic life will lead to much needed 'weak ties' across social groups. Inclusion of excluded groups in local governance structures is a powerful way of creating new social ties.

The family (however defined) lays the social foundation of societies. But the state has an important role to play in providing social and economic safety nets to protect families from breaking apart, particularly in the face of violent conflict and as they adjust to transitions from violence to peace. These measures might include childcare, health care, counselling, demilitarization and reintegration of soldiers into community life, retraining and economic cushions for men and women to cope with the transition into new lives. Civil society groups can obviously play a key role in such programmes.

Education and Values

Many children and young people in rich societies spend the ages between four and 22 years in educational institutions. And in all countries the goal includes at least free primary education for everyone. It is clear from the literature on social capital, as well as that on development, that education and literacy matter for economic development. But schools are also critical for the socialization function they perform. Together with families, schools instil values that promote nationhood, citizenship and ethics, and that recreate societies. While education is important for livelihood issues, its importance in generating social cohesion has been underestimated and overlooked. The language of instruction, the extent of segregation (official or unofficial) of social groups in schools, the extent to which the school curriculum portrays different social groups fairly so as to promote mutual respect and tolerance – all these affect the probability of inter-group harmony, even while each group maintains its distinctive identity. The state usually takes primary responsibility for education, but civil society organizations can have a major influence on curricula and in ensuring adequate performance.

Economic Restructuring

Economic restructuring, like civil service reform or the construction of large dams, displaces large numbers of people. Depending on the pre-existing distribution of power and connectivity among social groups, access to new opportunities will also be unequally distributed. Unless careful attention is paid to the existing social institutions, even nominally redistributive programmes may reinforce current – or create new – social and economic cleavages. To create opportunities for the inclusion of previously excluded groups means achieving a new alignment of social actors, and requires an investment in understanding the existing social structures, processes and values. Civil society organizations, including social research institutes, can be valuable partners in understanding the political and economic context within which reform has to be shaped.

Governance and Decentralization

The impetus behind current decentralization efforts in more than 70 countries is to bring governance and government resources closer to people. The goal is governments that are responsive to local needs and accountable to local citizens. However, this will only work if two types of institutional mechanisms exist to connect ordinary citizens and their local governments in a two-way flow of information. First, mechanisms are needed for channelling information about government resources, programmes and performance to ordinary citizens. Second, mechanisms are needed through which local people can channel their preferences while maintaining their independence of government, so that they can voice dissent without repercussions for their families or social group. The interests of the poor and other marginal groups are not represented unless such groups mobilize and organize.

Few countries embarking on decentralization programmes have such mechanisms in place, and even fewer invest resources to educate and mobilize local people to perform their new roles as informed citizens asserting their new rights. The focus is usually on the creation of devolved state structures rather than on the structure of the society in which these new organizational forms have to function. The Law of Popular Participation in Bolivia is one of the few cases where these institutional mechanisms have been thought through. Bolivian civil society organizations are mobilizing efforts to build strong people's organizations, so as to ensure that the participation law works for the benefit of indigenous groups. Limited community capacity continues to be a constraint.

Demand-driven Service Delivery

Coproduction between the state and community groups creates synergy and complementarity in the management of local public resources. It also creates local ownership, an essential ingredient of sustainable projects. Collective action for the provision of local public goods, in partnership with agencies external to the community, is important at all levels of development, even though the form of participation may change over time. For example, a person's involvement in a water supply scheme might evolve over the years from collective labour to dig trenches and lay pipes, through membership of a committee, through belonging to a cooperative venture and eventually to being a paying customer.

Introducing participation and collective action in the management of local resources usually requires fundamental shifts in agency mission, roles, values and indicators of success. Instead of seeing themselves as suppliers of inputs (pipes, sewers, seedlings, electricity), agencies have to become supporters of inclusive local organizations and enablers of resource flows. The necessary shifts in culture and the incentives facing agencies are difficult to bring about, but essential if changes are to be sustained over time. Civil society organizations have a long history of helping communities to obtain and maintain services that were theoretically provided by state agencies. They can be helpful to state agencies as the latter feel their way in their new roles.

In summary, using the lens of social capital, and especially the concepts of cross-cutting ties among social groups and governance, leads to some interesting new insights for policy design. Interventions can stem from civil society, the private sector or the state, and can cover a wide range of fields, including changes in rules so as to include those previously excluded in formal governance structures, at local, regional and national levels; political pluralism and citizenship rights; fairness for all social groups before the law; public access to mediation, conflict resolution or negotiation councils; availability of public spaces that bring social groups together; infrastructure that eases communication; and education, media and public information policies that reinforce the norms and values supporting tolerance and respect for diversity. But whatever the sector or topic, interventions need to be designed explicitly to enhance *complementarity*. That is, they need to take into account not only their immediate impact on a particular sector, but also their contribution to fostering a rich network of cross-cutting ties within society and between society's informal and formal institutions.

NOTES

1. The framework for this chapter was discussed at a two-day research workshop held at the World Bank in June 1998. Veronica Nyhan and Magdalena Syposz provided valuable research assistance.
2. See also Collier and Hoeffler (1998) and Woolcock and Narayan (2000).
3. See, for example, Rodrik (1997), and Fedderke and Klitgaard (1998).
4. See, for example, Stern and Stiglitz (1996), and Knack and Keefer (1997).
5. It is important to note that ethnic diversity does not necessarily mean polarization. The 'ethnic polarization' measure the authors use, the percentage belonging to the largest ethnic group, is different from the ethnolinguistic fractionation measure used by Easterly and Levine (1995) in their study of the 'tragedy of growth' in Africa. The latter measures the probability that two randomly selected persons from a given country will not belong to the same ethnolinguistic group.
6. This finding is even stronger for initial unequal distribution of land in developing countries (Deininger and Squire, 1997).

REFERENCES

Adelman, Irma and Cynthia Taft Morris (1967), *Society, Politics and Economic Development: A Quantative Approach*, Baltimore, MD: Johns Hopkins University Press.

Birdsall, Nancy and Richard Sabot (1994), 'Inequality as a constraint on growth in Latin America', draft, International Forum on Latin American Perspectives, Inter-American Development Bank, Washington, DC.

Coleman, James S. (1990), *Foundations of Social Theory*, Cambridge, MA: Belknap Press of Harvard University Press.

Collier, Paul and J.W. Gunning (1997), 'Explaining African economic performance', *Journal of Economic Literature*, 64–111.

Collier, Paul and A. Hoeffler (1998), *On Economic Causes of Civil War*, Oxford: Oxford Economic Papers.

Deininger, Klaus and Lyn Squire (1997), 'Economic growth and income inequality: reexamining the links', *Finance and Development*, **34**, 38–41.

Easterly, William and Ross Levine (1995), 'Africa's growth tragedy: a retrospective, 1960–89', Policy Research Working Paper 1503, Policy Research Department, Macroeconomics and Growth Division, Finance and Private Sector Development Division, World Bank, Washington, DC.

Faguet, Jean-Paul (1998), 'Decentralization and Local Government Performance: Improving Public Service Provision in Bolivia', mimeo, Centre for Economic Performance, London School of Economics.

Fedderke, Johannes and Robert Klitgaard (1998), 'Economic growth and social indicators: an exploratory analysis', *Economic Development and Cultural Change*, **46** (3), 455–89.

Fox, Jonathan (1996), 'How does civil society thicken? The political construction of social capital in rural Mexico', *World Development*, **24** (6), 1089–1103.

Fukuyama, Francis (1995), *Trust: The Social Virtues and the Creation of Prosperity*, New York: The Free Press.

Hentschel, Jesko *et al.* (1998), *Peru: Poverty Comparisons, Latin America and the Caribbean Region*, Washington, DC: World Bank.

Knack, Stephen and Philip Keefer (1997), 'Does social capital have an economic payoff? A cross-country investigation', *Quarterly Journal of Economics*, **112**, 1251–88.

La Porta, Rafael, Florenci López-de-Silanes, Andrei Shleifer and Robert Vishny (1997), 'Trust in large organizations', *American Economic Association, Papers and Proceedings*, **87** (2), 333–8.

Larraín, Felipe B. and Rodrigo M. Vergara (1997), 'Income distribution, investment and growth', Harvard International Institute for Development Discussion Paper Series 596, Harvard International Institute for Development, Cambridge, MA.

Mauro, Paulo (1995), 'Corruption and growth', *Quarterly Journal of Economics*, **110** (3), 681–712.

Narayan, Deepa (1997), 'Voices of the poor: poverty and social capital in Tanzania', Environmentally and Socially Sustainable Development Network, Studies and Monographs Series 20, World Bank, Washington, DC.

Narayan, Deepa and David Nyamwaya (1996), 'Learning from the poor: a participatory poverty assessment in Kenya', Environment Department Papers 034, Environment Department, Social Policy & Resettlement Division, World Bank, Washington, DC.

Olson, Mancur (1982), *The Rise and Decline of Nations: Economic Growth, Stagnation and Social Rigidities*, New Haven, CT: Yale University Press.

Portes, Alejandro (1998), 'Social capital: its origins and applications in contemporary sociology', *Annual Review of Sociology*, **24**, 1–24.

Putnam, Robert (1993), *Making Democracy Work: Civic Traditions in Modern Italy*, Princeton, NJ: Princeton University Press.

Rodrik, Dani (1997), 'Where did all the growth go? External shocks, social conflict and growth collapses', Working Paper 6350, NBER, Cambridge, MA.

Rose, Richard (1995), 'Russia as an hour-glass society: a constitution without citizens', *East European Constitutional Review*, **4** (3).

Rubio, Mauricio (1997), 'Perverse social capital – some evidence from Colombia', *Journal of Economic Issues*, **31** (3), 805–16.

Stern, Nicholas and Joseph Stiglitz (1996), 'Development strategy in a market economy: objectives, scope, institutions and instruments', European Bank for Reconstruction and Development, London.

Stiglitz, Joseph (1998), 'Towards a new paradigm for development strategies, policies and processes', Prebisch Lecture presented 19 October at UNCTAD, Geneva, Switzerland.

Tarrow, Sidney (1998), *Power in Movement: Social Movements and Contentious Politics*, 2nd edn, Cambridge: Cambridge University Press.

Temple, Jonathan and Paul Johnson (1998), 'Social capability and economic growth', *Quarterly Journal of Economics*, **113** (3), 965–90.
Varshney, Ashutosh (1998), 'Ethnic conflict and the structure of civic life', paper presented at the annual meeting of the American Political Science Association, Boston, MA.
White, Anderson and Glenn Smucker (1998), 'Social capital and governance in Haiti: traditions and trends', *The Challenges of Poverty Reduction*, Washington, DC: World Bank.
Woolcock, Michael and Deepa Narayan (2000), 'Social capital implications for development theory, research, and policy', *World Bank Research Observer*, **2** (15), World Bank, Washington, DC.

PART II

Empirical and Experimental Evidence on
Social Capital and Well-being

5. Social capital, education and credit markets: empirical evidence from Burkina Faso

Christiaan Grootaert, Gi-Taik Oh and Anand Swamy

This chapter tests empirically the central idea that, given available resources, technology and formal institutional structures, economic outcomes can vary depending on the nature of social norms and relationships. For example, consider a set of communities in a typical developing country. All else being equal, communities with inactive parent–teacher associations might be expected to have schools of little value. Likewise, communities with lenders and borrowers that trust each other might be expected to have credit markets that function more smoothly.

This chapter examines the role of social capital in affecting well-being through these two specific channels: the performance of educational institutions and the functioning of credit markets. Using data collected from households in Burkina Faso, this study uses indicators of membership in associations and characteristics of communities to assess the impact of social capital on school attendance and distress sales. The main findings are that (a) community participation in parent–teacher associations is associated with substantially higher rates of school attendance, and (b) the incidence of consumption crises, as indicated by distress sales, is substantially lower in villages in which community lending institutions are active.

The chapter is organized as follows: The next section describes the survey on which this chapter is based. The third section focuses on education and the fourth on consumption crises. The final section concludes with summary observations.

ANALYSING AND MEASURING SOCIAL CAPITAL AT THE HOUSEHOLD LEVEL: HOW CAN THE OVERALL IMPACTS OF SOCIAL CAPITAL ON WELL-BEING BE EVALUATED?

One can adopt a general approach that aims to assess, in principle, the contribution of all types of social capital to economic welfare. For example, Narayan and Pritchett (1999) and Grootaert (1999) use the log of per capita consumption expenditure as a measure of economic welfare and show that, while controlling for a large set of individual and community characteristics, social capital leads to higher welfare among households in Tanzania and Indonesia, respectively. Alternatively, one can look more narrowly at the specific channels through which particular types of social capital operate. This approach has been used to study the role of norms and networks in maintaining irrigation projects (Wade, 1988), increasing access to credit (Fafchamps, 1997), diffusing technical knowledge (Isham, forthcoming) and improving the delivery of community-based water systems (Isham and Kähkönen 2002; forthcoming).

We follow the second approach. We analyse the role of social capital in affecting two outcomes that are of central importance among households in Burkina Faso: school attendance by children and consumption crises as indicated by the incidence of asset sales. At the household level, how should social capital be measured? The approach pioneered by Putnam (1993) focuses on membership of associations. Association membership can affect economic outcomes in two ways. First, the association may be formed to further a specific economic objective, such as a credit cooperative. However, there can also be indirect benefits of association membership. For example, two members of a recreational group may develop mutual trust that then enables them to share valuable information or credit.

A second approach to measuring social capital focuses on membership of ethnic groups, neighbourhoods or communities. Borjas (1995) shows the importance of 'ethnic capital' among immigrant groups in the United States. He finds that even after controlling for individual, parental and neighbourhood characteristics, the average skill level of the ethnic group to which the individual belongs has a large impact on his or her skill acquisition. Unlike associations, individuals cannot choose to have this type of social capital (except perhaps via migration decisions). In this chapter, both the association membership approach and the community characteristics-based approach are used.

Until recently, the typical household survey did not have information on the types of variables that might reflect social capital. An important step towards addressing this problem has been taken at the World Bank, which has sponsored surveys to collect detailed information on social relationships in addition to traditional economic variables. As part of this effort, the Local Level Institutions (LLI) project of the World Bank has conducted large-scale household surveys in Bolivia, Burkina Faso and Indonesia.

The data set for this chapter comes from the LLI survey of households in Burkina Faso. Data were collected at the community, district and household levels. The data are from a household survey that aimed to capture households' actual participation in local institutions, their use of services, the welfare levels of households and their coping strategies.

The data collection covered the rural areas of four provinces in Burkina Faso: Houet, Sanmatenga, Sissili and Yatenga. Within each of the four provinces, one administrative department was selected for the data collection; in Houet two departments were selected. In each province, 12 villages were chosen on the basis of four criteria: organizational level, economic situation, cultural diversity and proximity of services. Within each village 20 households were selected randomly to participate in the survey, leading to a total sample of 960 households.[1]

SOCIAL CAPITAL AND EDUCATIONAL OUTCOMES IN BURKINA FASO

This section provides a survey of the literature on the relationship between education and economic development in Burkina Faso and the potential role of social capital in improving educational outcomes.

To recent observers like Kevane and Englebert (1997), Burkina Faso's recent economic history poses a paradox. Growth has been slow, averaging 3.64 per cent per annum from 1970 to 1995, leading to only a small increase in per capita income. This is despite a number of favourable conditions: a development-oriented state, good macroeconomic management and, because of the low per capita income, opportunities for rapid 'catch-up growth'. The quality of the bureaucracy also appears to be relatively high. Englebert (1996) quotes a World Bank economic memorandum on Burkina: 'Wherever they may come from, foreign missions visiting Burkina invariably report being favourably impressed by the quality of public sector management.' Burkina-Faso also ranks fairly high in terms of measures of quality of governance developed by political risk services. These measures have been shown to be positively correlated with economic growth (Keefer and Knack, 1995). Kevane and Englebert (1997) argue that, despite all these factors, the prospects for growth are being undermined by a shortage of entrepreneurs, which in turn is partly due to shortages of human capital. Some entrepreneurs are on occasion unable to prevent embezzlement owing to their inability to write or keep accounts.

A glance at the data reveals that adult literacy rates in Burkina Faso are much lower than the average for sub-Saharan Africa, with adult male and female literacy rates of 28 per cent and 9 per cent in 1990. Equally disquieting is the fact that current school enrolment rates remain low. In 1988–9 the World Bank estimated that the primary and secondary enrolment ratios were 31 per cent and 6 per cent, respectively (World Bank, 1991). Our survey covers 960 households in the provinces of Houet, Sanmatenga, Sissili and Yatenga, of which 815 have children. The households were asked whether all the children aged five to 14 'regularly attended school'. Only 10 per cent answered in the affirmative.

Why is school attendance so low? The expansion of education has been a priority for the government of Burkina Faso and the supporting international organizations such as the World Bank for some time now. Typically, between 10 and 15 per cent of government expenditure in Burkina Faso is allocated to education (Englebert, 1996). Still, according to a World Bank's report on education in Burkina Faso (World Bank, 1991), numerous problems remain, including poor quality of teaching, inadequate supplies of textbooks, and high pupil–teacher ratios. Interestingly, the report identified 'limited community participation in education' as a significant problem and proposed that communities be involved to a greater extent in construction and management of schools. At first sight this lack of community participation may not seem surprising. Economists like Mancur Olson (1982) and others have long emphasized the difficulties associated with organizing such collective action. However, in Burkina Faso there is a rich tradition of socioeconomic cooperation and a relative lack of tension among ethnic groups.[2] The most documented ethnic group in Burkina Faso, the Mossi, who comprise close to half of the population, are said to place a very high value on sharing and mutual support. In his study of the structures of social life, anthropologist Alan Fiske (1991), describes extensive cooperation among the Mossi (also referred to as 'Moose') with regard to allocation of land, water, mutual insurance and pooling of labour. He emphasizes that common good, rather than individual benefit, is affirmed in such activities: 'That the Moose pool their labour collectively, and share their food, often in the face of incentives to do otherwise, demonstrates that a critical motivational orientation is toward corporate participation and belonging, and that their paramount goals concern mutual solidarity, a sense of common identity and belonging, unity and kindness' (ibid., p. 268).

Our survey data suggest that the population itself feels that cooperation is at a high level. When asked whether they felt that other households in the village made a fair contribution to collective action at the village level, 89 per cent of households answered in the affirmative.

However, while acknowledging traditions of reciprocity and interdependence in Burkina Faso, some critics have argued that it is unrealistic to expect active community participation in school management. Citing Olson (1982) and Axelrod (1984), Maclure (1994) argues that collective action can be sustained only if the temptation to free-ride is overcome by a system of incentives and sanctions. He argues that it is difficult to ensure accountability in environments in which resources are limited and literacy levels are low. He also suggests that, in Burkina Faso, governmental institutions and resources tend to be dominated by elites and that 'the majority of the rural populace in

Burkina Faso is restricted from participating actively in decision-making' (p. 249).

We believe that ultimately this is an empirical question: do parents in Burkina Faso participate actively in school management? We explore this question below, and then turn to our central issue: does community involvement in schools increase school attendance?

The Determinants of School Attendance

We have data on 2534 children aged five to 14. Of these, 22 per cent of girls and 36 per cent of boys attend school. In the villages that have a primary school (29 out of 48), 38 per cent of children attend school, and in villages which do not have a primary school 16 per cent attend. This suggests that living in close proximity to a school increases the likelihood that a child will attend school, but it is by no means sufficient to ensure attendance.

Tables 5.1a, 5.1b, 5.1c, and 5.1d provide summary statistics for school attendance. In Table 5.1a we break down school attendance by household wealth, measured by per capita land-ownership.[3] No clear correlation seems to exist between wealth and school attendance.

In Table 5.1b we break down school attendance by province and language group/ethnicity. Percentages are reported only in the cells where the number of observations is more than 15. Large differences exist between provinces, with relatively high rates of attendance in Sissili and Houet. The most striking

Table 5.1a Percentage school attendance, by province and land ownership quartile (number of children in parentheses)

	1st quartile	2nd quartile	3rd quartile	4th quartile	All
Yatenga	14.6	29.6	21.9	21.0	21.8
	(150)	(152)	(196)	(133)	(631)
Houet	33.7	46.7	35.7	31.6	36.9
	(246)	(122)	(95)	(57)	(520)
Sissili	41.1	37.3	39.6	39.7	38.7
	(151)	(142)	(120)	(83)	(496)
Sanmatenga	23.1	17.6	21.9	18.6	20.7
	(177)	(136)	(132)	(75)	(520)
Total	28.7	32.4	27.6	26.7	29.1
	(724)	(552)	(543)	(348)	(2 167)

Table 5.1b   Percentage school attendance, by province and language group
ethnicity (number of observations in parentheses)

	Moore	Dioula	Fulfunde	Gourounsi	Other	All
Yatenga	23.4		0.0			22.4
	(630)		(24)			(660)
Houet		49.2	14.1		39.6	38.3
		(177)	(78)		(394)	(681)
Sissili	26.1			45.3		35.5
	(318)			(333)		(669)
Sanmatenga	21.2		0.0			20.6
	(509)		(15)			(524)
All*	23.5	48.2	8.7	45.3	37.6	29.5
	(1 466)	(189)	(126)	(333)	(420)	(2 534)

Note: * The number of observations in the 'All' row exceeds the sum in the other rows because
of the empty boxes (cells with too few observations). Moore is the language spoken by the
Mossi.

element here is the relatively low school attendance rates among the Fulfunde
in Yatenga and Houet, and relatively high rates of attendance among the
Gourounsi, compared to Moore-speakers, in Sissili.

Table 5.1c breaks down school attendance by province along religious
lines. There is some indication that attendance rates are higher among
Catholics, especially in Houet, although this pattern is not observed in

Table 5.1c   Percentage school attendance, by province and religion (number
of observations in parentheses)

	Muslim	Catholic	Animist
Yatenga	22.5		
	(645)		
Houet	35.2	61.8	31.7
	(384)	(76)	(208)
Sissili	34.9	46.2	32.6
	(393)	(65)	(196)
Sanmatenga	23.1	19.1	16.6
	(290)	(63)	(156)
All	28.3	42.2	27.8
	(1 712)	(218)	(561)

Table 5.1d   Percentage school attendance, by gender and religion (number of observations in parentheses)

	Muslim	Catholic	Animist	All*
Male	36.9	43.5	31.1	36.4
	(880)	(124)	(306)	(1 338)
Female	19.1	40.4	23.9	22.4
	(832)	(94)	(255)	(1 196)

Note: * The number of observations in 'All' column exceeds the sum of numbers of observations in the rows because of omission of an 'other' category.

Sanmatenga. As mentioned above, attendance rates of girls are substantially lower than for boys.

Table 5.1d suggests that gender differentials are lower among Catholics than among members of other religions.[4] Our main purpose in this section, however, is to evaluate whether social capital affects school attendance. As mentioned earlier, there has been an effort in Burkina Faso to increase parental participation in order to improve school performance. Our measure of parental participation is based on the number of times a household that sends at least one child to school attends a PTA meeting during the year. Table 5.2 provides the average for this variable and the percentage of children who attend school, by province. At this level of aggregation we do not see a correlation between parental involvement and school attendance. However, in comparing school attendance and parental involvement across provinces, we are not controlling for other factors.

We now turn to a more detailed regression analysis of school attendance. In Table 5.3 the dependent variable takes the value 1 if the child attends school, and zero otherwise. The coefficient of greatest interest is on the village average of the number of PTA meetings attended during the year, by households that send at least one child to school.[5] We see that one extra PTA attendance per household is associated with an increase of 3.5 percentage points in the probability that the child attends school. With a *t*-statistic of 3.69, the coefficient is significant at any reasonable level. We get a very similar result if we exclude the household to which the child belongs in the computation of our PTA attendance variable. Given that attendance rates in Burkina Faso are so low, this is a substantial effect.

It is important that we note one qualification. A common problem in cross-sectional regressions in general, and especially in the social capital literature, is potential omitted variable bias. Here any omitted village-level variable that affects PTA attendance as well as school attendance by children is likely to

Table 5.2   PTA visits and school attendance, by province

Province	Average number of PTA attendances in previous year among households which send at least one child to school (number of observations in parentheses)	Percentage of children aged 5–14 who attend school (number of observations in parentheses)
Yatenga	2.85	22.42
	(92)	(660)
Houet	2.14	38.33
	(105)	(681)
Sissili	4.64	35.58
	(133)	(669)
Sanmatenga	3.58	20.61
	(67)	(524)
Total	3.39	29.80
	(397)	(2 534)

bias upwards the coefficient on our PTA variable. Suppose, for instance, the school in a particular village has an especially devoted and capable teacher. This may motivate children to go to school. It may also encourage the parents of the children who go to school to attend PTA meetings.[6]

Our findings were arrived at after controlling for a large number of characteristics of the child, the household and the village, and dummies for provinces. We discuss these below. Older children are more likely to be sent to school; an extra year increases the probability of school attendance by 0.026. We interact the gender dummy with religion dummies, with the excluded religion being animist. Among animists the probability of attending school is 0.089 higher for a male child than for a female child. Among Muslims the additional probability of school attendance for a male is 0.214 (0.089 + 0.125). Christians, especially Protestants, seem more prone to send their children to school and there are no significant differences according to the gender of the child. Among the ethnic groups, consistent with the summary statistics we saw earlier, the Gourounsi, Dioula and Mossi are more likely to send their children to school than the excluded category ('other'), whilst the Fulfunde are less likely to send their children to school than the excluded category. Farmers are more prone to send their children to school than non-farmers.

One interesting result showing the intergenerational transmission of human capital characteristics is that the child is less likely to go to school if the head

Table 5.3   Determinants of school attendance (probit model, dependent var = 1 if child went to school)

Variable	Marginal effect*	
Village av. no. PTA meetings attended per year by HHs sending at least one child to school	0.035	(3.69)
Land per capita	−0.063	(1.71)
Number of livestock owned	0.001	(1.23)
Number of farming equipment owned	0.025	(1.25)
Log av. per capita income of other village HHs	−0.053	(1.33)
No primary school in village	−0.180	(6.50)
Head has no education	−0.056	(1.75)
Male household head	0.022	(0.36)
Age of household head	0.000	(0.15)
Farmer household head	0.081	(1.76)
Catholic	0.105	(1.61)
Protestant	0.277	(1.83)
Muslim	−0.021	(0.48)
Male child	0.089	(1.93)
Muslim × male	0.125	(2.36)
Catholic × male	0.025	(0.30)
Protestant × male	−0.274	(1.52)
Number of children in HH	0.003	(0.57)
Age of child	0.026	(6.31)
Moore	0.302	(1.88)
Bobo	−0.258	(1.51)
Gourounsi	0.494	(2.98)
Fulfunde	−0.333	(3.13)
Dioula	0.11	(2.08)
Yatenga	0.086	(2.57)
Sissili	0.010	(0.25)
Houet	0.572	(3.55)
Number of observations	2 032	
Log likelihood	−1 076.52	
Chi-squared	355.05	
Probability > chi-squared	0.00	

Note: * Probability derivatives at mean of each explanatory variable; the reported z-scores are those associated with the underlying probit coefficients, based on robust standard errors.

of the household has no education. We also tested whether there were spillovers from the education of other household heads in the village, along the lines of Borjas (1995), by including the proportion of other household heads in the village who have no education. This variable did not enter significantly and was dropped. The age and gender of the household head do not have a statistically significant impact. Household wealth as embodied in ownership of livestock and the number of farming assets owned by the household also have no statistically significant effect. Per capita land ownership of the household enters negatively, which may reflect a higher need for children to work on the land in households that own more land, which in turn may negatively affect the probability of going to school. The number of children, which we include to reflect any 'crowding-out' possibilities, does not enter significantly.

We included a dummy that took the value 1 if there was no primary school in the village. This has a large negative coefficient of –0.18. This finding has the straightforward implication that opening a school in each village is one way to increase school attendance. We also controlled for village wealth by including the log of the average per capita consumption expenditure of other households in the village, which does not have a statistically significant impact.

The coefficients on the province dummies show some interesting patterns. The excluded province is Sanmatenga. We had seen earlier, in the summary statistics, that Sissili has much higher attendance rates than Sanmatenga. Once we control for other variables (especially the presence of a school in the village) this effect disappears. However, the fact that the dummies for Yatenga and Houet are positive and significant suggests that the other explanatory variables in our model cannot entirely explain why attendance rates in these provinces are higher than in Sanmatenga.

SOCIAL CAPITAL AND 'DISTRESS SALES'

We now turn our attention to the other aspect that we wished to test empirically. As in the previous section, we begin with an overview of the issues and the existing literature, which guides us towards specific testable propositions.

In many poor agrarian economies, including that of Burkina Faso, earnings are not only low, but also highly variable. Crop yields can be variable owing to (say) drought or to localized production shocks. Other personal factors such as illness can also reduce incomes by reducing earning capacity. There are several possible responses to this uncertainty. The first is to take steps to reduce the variability of income by diversifying in various dimensions: choosing a risk-reducing crop mix, cultivating multiple non-adjacent plots with different soil qualities, or having family members enter different occupations (say, having one family member migrate to the city). Reardon *et al.* (1992) have demonstrated the effectiveness of income diversification as a means of smoothing consumption in Burkina Faso. A second widely used approach to smoothing consumption in the face of income variability is personal savings. Given very low mean incomes and large variability, however, a household can face substantial risk despite taking such measures. An additional method for reducing consumption variability is also common: risk pooling with neighbours, relatives or friends. A household that receives an income shock may receive loans, cash gifts, gifts of labour or other forms of assistance to help tide it over during an emergency, with the expectation of reciprocity.

The potential role of risk pooling in smoothing consumption fluctuations in Burkina Faso has been convincingly outlined by Carter (1997), using a detailed household-level data set put together by the International Crop Research Institute for the Semi-Arid Tropics. The potential for risk pooling only exists if a significant proportion of income shocks are idiosyncratic, that is, not common across households. Carter (1997) points out that, although Burkinabe agriculture is vulnerable to large aggregate shocks, households are also subject to many idiosyncratic shocks.[7] Rainfall can vary not only across agroclimatic regions but also between villages in a region, or even between fields in a village. Household-specific shocks can also occur as a result of damage by animals, sickness and so on. Based on his estimates of the relative importance of aggregate and idiosyncratic risk, Carter's simulation exercise suggests that, in a given year, a typical household in the Sahel that is entirely dependent on self-insurance will face a subsistence crisis with probability 0.21.[8] However, if ten households form a network and agree to donate all of their income above the subsistence level to a household that is falling below subsistence, this probability falls to 0.16.

The fact that mutual insurance is advantageous is no guarantee that it will emerge. In many parts of the developing world, especially in the rural areas, legal institutions for enforcing financial contracts are, at best, in the process of being developed. Third-party enforcement is often not available even for relatively simple debt contracts, let alone complicated arrangements involving state-contingent payments. Mutual insurance then depends either on altruism, enlightened long-term self-interest or social norms that favour cooperation.[9] The importance of social capital in such contexts hardly needs to be emphasized. Below we measure social capital as it pertains to mutual insurance by looking at the role of community lending institutions. We will evaluate the extent to which the presence of community lending institutions reduces the incidence of distress sales.

Some anthropologists have argued that risk pooling takes place mostly within ethnic groups. We have earlier discussed Fiske's (1991) comments regarding the extent of cooperation among the Mossi. He emphasizes that cooperation is not driven by self-interest (as, for example, in the repeated game models of economists), but is an intrinsic value, practised even when it is not individually beneficial. Describing labour and consumption-pooling arrangements, Fiske writes:

> In such cases the younger and stronger members of a communal group apparently would be much better off from a material standpoint if they worked alone, retaining personal control over the products of their labour, and selling or investing the surplus. . . . Phenomenally it appears that the Moose [Mossi] enjoy working, eating, and living together for its own sake. (Ibid., p. 266)

Other evidence that support in crisis comes from within the ethnic group, in particular from within the extended family in the village, comes from Veirech (1986, p. 156). Veirech describes how villages are divided into compounds consisting of a cluster of families belonging to the same lineage.[10] The compound leader has many privileges in terms of access to land and other resources but also has many social obligations. Veirech writes:

> The compound head was under greater pressure than the ordinary household to have abundant grain on hand to meet his extra social obligations. These included the obligations to share, to provide hospitality, to provide for the less fortunate. . . . It was the compound head who usually took responsibility for the handicapped, infirm and aged family members. (Ibid., p. 162)

If the members of one's own ethnic group are most likely to provide support in crisis, a household should be more likely to receive assistance in a disaster if there are more members of its ethnic group in close proximity. We will test this proposition below.

Given this background, we now address the following question: to what extent does social capital reduce the probability that a household will engage in a distress sale?

Determinants of the Incidence of Distress Sales

Even if financial markets work very smoothly, in any economy some households will be selling assets. A household is said to engage in a distress sale if, when faced with an income shock, it is forced to sell an asset because it cannot borrow to tide it over the emergency. We conclude that a household has engaged in a distress sale if it answers the following question in the affirmative: in the past year did your household have to sell any land, livestock or equipment in order to have money to buy enough food or clothing, or to pay for health care?

A word of clarification regarding the notion of a distress sale may be helpful. The sale of livestock in order to smooth consumption is fairly common in

Africa, and it can be questioned whether this is necessarily a sign of 'distress'. Even fairly wealthy households may engage in this practice when they receive an income shock, though they are not facing a crisis, in the form of (say) the threat of starvation.[11] However, so long as there are transactions costs (dead-weight losses) associated with distress sales, in most cases it will be economically more efficient for the household to borrow or receive a gift of cash in response to an income shock. Below we show that social capital reduces the probability that in order to smooth consumption the household will sell a productive asset and likely generate deadweight losses.

Our measure of social capital, as it pertains to distress sales, is based on the answer to the following question: which type of organization is most likely to help when your household is either short of money or suffering illness? The seven possible answers were community organization, district government, central government, religious organization, NGO, businessman–trader and other. We constructed the 'community organization index', which is the proportion of households in the village that reported 'community organization' among these seven possible measures. One way for a household to gain from the presence of such an organization is via its own membership. However, to the extent that the household has links with others that belong to such a group, there can be spillovers as well.

Column 1 of Table 5.4 shows the proportion of households reporting distress sales by province; we see an exceptionally high figure for Sanmatenga, 0.82. Column 2 shows the proportion of households in the province that rely primarily on community lending institutions. Again the outlier is Sanmatenga, with the lowest figure, 0.16. We also computed these proportions separately for each village (48 villages) and found a strong correlation of −0.55, with p-value 0.0001. Prima facie, we have a case for thinking that the presence of community lending institutions lowers the incidence of distress sales.

Table 5.4   Distress sales and community lending, by province

Province	Proportion of households engaging in distress sales	Proportion of households relying on community lending institutions
Yatenga	0.39	0.50
Houet	0.44	0.32
Sissili	0.54	0.46
Sanmatenga	0.82	0.16
All	0.55	0.36

Table 5.5   Determination of distress sales

Variable	Marginal effect*	Absolute value of *t*-statistic
'Community organization index' = proportion of village households dependent on community lending organizations	−0.424	(3.53)
Household head is male	0.129	(1.38)
Age of household head	−0.004	(2.50)
Number of children	0.019	(1.74)
Farming household	−0.057	(0.70)
Household has no toilet	0.126	(2.50)
Household depends on river water	−0.110	(1.11)
Household head has no education	0.005	(0.08)
Log average per capita income of other village households	0.234	(2.49)
Proportion of other households which dissaved in year	−0.173	(0.92)
Proportion of irrigated area in village	−0.534	(2.04)
Land owned per capita by other households in village (hectares)	−0.536	(1.98)
Average number of farming equipment owned by other village households	−0.428	(2.77)
Average number of cattle owned by other village households	0.007	(2.63)
Catholic	−0.069	(0.76)
Protestant	0.380	(1.43)
Muslim	0.041	(0.66)
Moore	0.077	(0.45)
Bobo	−0.394	(1.52)
Dioula	−0.007	(0.07)
Fulfunde	0.058	(0.32)
Gourounsi	0.101	(0.54)
Yatenga	−0.386	(4.04)
Sissili	−0.340	(3.35)
Houet	−0.452	(2.54)
Number of observations	662	
Log likelihood	−360.74	
Chi-squared	190.44	
Probability > chi-squared	0.000	

Note: * Probability derivatives at mean of each explanatory variable and *z*-scores based on robust standard errors.

Table 5.5 explores this hypothesis more systematically. The dependent variable takes the value 1 is the household has engaged in a distress sale in the last year, and zero otherwise. The explanatory variable of greatest interest is 'community organization index'. Our central finding is that a household which is in a village where the index takes the value 1 is 42 per cent less likely to have a distress sale than if it is in a village where it takes the value 0. This result is not sensitive to whether the household itself is included when defining the index.

We have controlled for a large number of other potential determinants of the incidence of distress sales. Controlling for household wealth poses a challenge. Since a distress sale is a consumption crisis in which assets are sold, using measures of household consumption expenditure, or household ownership of land, livestock or equipment, as explanatory variables would create the possibility of simultaneity bias. Therefore we included a set of variables that should be correlated with household wealth but should not change in response to a distress sale. These variables included a dummy for whether the household is dependent on river water, a dummy for whether it has a toilet, a dummy for whether the household head is a farmer, and his/her age. The dummy for 'no toilet' comes in positive and significant, which is not surprising, since these are poorer households. If we include per capita land owned by the household, number of livestock owned and number of types of farming assets owned (results not reported) we obtain qualitatively similar results. Thus our main result is not sensitive to the way in which household wealth is measured. We also included dummies for the household's language group and religion and for whether the head of household is male, since, in principle, these can affect the households' access to networks. These do not enter significantly.

We include province dummies to reflect climatic or other unobserved factors common to villages in a province. The excluded province is Sanmatenga. The dummies for Yatenga, Sissili and Houet are negative, large and statistically significant. This suggests that factors other than those in our model account for some of the higher probability of distress sales in Sanmatenga.

As mentioned earlier, a particular concern in an exercise like this is that some omitted village-level variable may bias the coefficient on 'community organization index'. For example, it is possible that, if the household lives in a wealthy village, it can borrow money from its neighbours and avoid a distress sale. If such villages tend to set up community lending institutions, we will overestimate the impact of 'community organization index' if we do not control for village wealth. To minimize this possibility, we constructed a set of measures meant to reflect the wealth of other households in the village: the average land ownership per capita, average number of livestock owned, average number of pieces of farm equipment owned, and log of average per capita consumption expenditure. The land and equipment ownership variables come in negative and significant. If the other households in the village own one more hectare per person, the probability that the household has a distress sale falls by 0.54. Note that average land ownership per person is only 0.56 hectares, so a one-hectare increase is very large. If the other households in the village on average own one extra item of farming equipment, the probability of a distress sale is reduced by 0.43. It should be noted that the average number of items of farming equipment owned is 0.52, so a one-unit change is large. Two findings are puzzling: if others in the village own one extra farm animal, this increases the probability of a distress sale by 0.007. One explanation could be that, if maintaining and selling livestock is an important means of livelihood in the village, large stocks might be kept, and sold in response to an income shock. The per capita consumption expenditure of the other households in the village enters with the 'wrong' (that is, positive) sign, which is hard to explain.

It could also be the case that villages that have more community lending institutions happen, by sheer chance, to be less vulnerable to income shocks. If this were the case we might again overestimate the impact of community lending institutions, if we failed to control for the village's vulnerability to aggregate shocks. To avoid this problem we constructed two measures of the vulnerability of the village as a whole to income shocks: the proportion of irrigated area and the proportion of other households in the village who said they reduced their savings during the year. While the latter variable is not significant, the fraction of irrigated land has a large impact: all else being equal, a household in a completely unirrigated village would be 53 per cent more likely to suffer a distress sale than a household in a village in which all the land was irrigated. The reader might be concerned that the fraction of irrigated area in the village might just be picking up the effect of the fraction of irrigated area of the household, which we have not included. We checked that this is not the case by adding, in another regression model, the household's fraction of irrigated area. It does not enter significantly, and we obtain similar results.

Finally, in another regression model (not reported) we tested whether the presence of members of one's own ethnic group reduces the incidence of distress sales. This exercise requires the construction of a variable, which is the fraction of the village that belongs to the household's ethnic group. Given the small sample size per village (around 20 households) this can be done reasonably only for the largest ethnic group, Mossi. We estimated the distress sales equation over the sample of Mossi households, and included the fraction of Mossi in the village as an explanatory variable. The fraction of Mossi entered with a negative sign, consistent with the hypothesis that members of one's ethnic group are more likely to provide crisis support, but failed to be statistically significant.

CONCLUSIONS

One of the most urgent tasks faced by the government of Burkina Faso, and many others in Africa, is the expansion of education. Despite decades of effort by governments, with the support of international donors, school attendance and literacy rates remain very low. Part of the problem is on the 'supply' side. Indeed, of the 48 villages in our data set only 29 have a primary school. This implies that, in many cases, the building of school facilities will be an important part of a primary education strategy.

However, attendance in existing schools is also very low. Many observers have suggested that this is in part because rural communities are remote from the management and functioning of these institutions. A potential solution to this problem is the development of parent–teacher associations. We found that a child is more likely to go to school if he or she lives in a village in which parents are more active in PTAs; one extra PTA attendance per household (among households which send at least one child to school) increases the probability of school attendance by 3.5 per cent. Given that only 24 per cent of girls and 36 per cent of boys attend school, this is a substantial effect.

We believe that this is a potentially important finding at both the conceptual and policy levels. In terms of policy it has the straightforward implication that there is likely to be a large pay-off to efforts to increase parental involvement in parent–teacher associations. At the conceptual level it points to the importance of the linking social capital: to the extent that in many developing economies crucial inputs are provided by the state, social capital within communities may not be enough if community–state relations are poor. Our analysis of educational outcomes highlights this fact.

Mutual insurance is an area in which social capital's potential importance is easy to see. On this issue we have a strong and intuitively plausible result. The presence of active community lending institutions substantially reduces the incidence of distress sales. In further research it would be interesting to explore the nature of community lending institutions in Burkina Faso and compare them to other successful community-based institutions, such as the Grameen Bank in Bangladesh.

NOTES

1. The survey and the provinces are discussed in detail in CND (1998) and Donnelly-Roark *et al.* (1999).
2. See Maclure (1994) and citations therein. For a discussion of the relative absence of ethnic tensions, see Englebert (1996, p. 125).
3. Because rented land is typically secure in the possession of the renters in Burkina Faso, we count it as part of the 'owned' land.

4. We do not present figures for Protestants because there are too few Protestant households (13).
5. If there are five households in the village that send at least one child to school and, taken together, they attend PTA meetings a total of 20 times, this variable takes the value $20/5 = 4$.
6. To address this problem, ideally we would like to find an instrument, that is, a variable, that affects PTA attendance that does not directly affect school attendance.
7. For example, in the Sahel region, mean annual millet yield per hectare was 504 kilograms in 1981 and 205 kilograms in 1980 (Carter, 1997, p. 562).
8. Carter (1997) defines a subsistence crisis as consuming less than 200 kilograms of grain per capita during a year.
9. For a convincing account of credit as a means of risk sharing, and of the role of social norms in enforcing such arrangements, see Udry (1994). Platteau (1991) surveys an array of risk-sharing arrangements across the developing world.
10. Each ethnic group consists of a number of lineages.
11. Fafchamps *et al.* (1998) calculate that livestock sales compensate up to 30 per cent of the income shortfalls resulting from drought.

REFERENCES

Axelrod, Robert (1984), *The Evolution of Cooperation*, New York: Basic Books.
Borjas, George (1995), 'Ethnicity, neighborhoods and human capital externalities', *American Economic Review*, **85** (3), 365–90.
Carter, Michael (1997), 'Environment, technology and the social articulation of risk in West African agriculture', *Economic Development and Cultural Change*, **46**, 557–90.
CND (Commission Nationale de la Décentralisation) (1998), 'Décentralisation rurale et institutions locales au Burkina Faso', Ouagadougou, Burkina Faso.
Donnelly-Roark, Paula, Xiao Ye and Karim Ouedraogo (1999), 'Burkina Faso local level institutions: preliminary research analysis: local level institutions and rural decentralization in Burkina Faso', mimeo, Institutional and Social Policy Unit, Africa Region, The World Bank, Washington, DC.
Englebert, Pierre (1996), *Burkina Faso: Unsteady Statehood in West Africa*, Boulder, CO: Westview Press.
Fafchamps, Marcel (1997), 'Trade credit in Zimbabwean manufacturing', *World Development*, **25**, 795–815.
Fafchamps, Marcel, Chris Udry and Katherine Czukas (1998), 'Drought and saving in West Africa: are livestock a buffer stock?', *Journal of Development Economics*, **55**, 273–305.
Fiske, Alan P. (1991), *Structures of Social Life: The Four Elementary Forms of Human Relations*, New York: The Free Press.
Grootaert, Christiaan (1999), 'Social capital, household welfare and poverty in Indonesia', Local Level Institutions Study, Working Paper no. 6, Social Development Department, The World Bank, Washington, DC.
Isham, Jonathan (forthcoming), 'The effect of social capital on technology adoption: evidence from rural Tanzania', *The Journal of African Economics*.
Isham, Jonathan and Satu Kähkönen (2002), 'How do participation and social capital affect community-based water projects? Evidence from central Java, Indonesia', in Christiaan Grootaert and Thierry Van Bastelaer (eds), *Social Capital and Development*, Cambridge: Cambridge University Press.

Isham, Jonathan and Satu Kähkönen (forthcoming), 'Institutional determinants of the impact of community-based water projects: evidence frm Sri Lanka and India', *Economic Development and Cultural Change*.

Keefer, Philip and Stephen Knack (1995), 'Institutions and economic performance: cross-country tests using alternative institutional measures', *Economics and Politics*, **7** (3), 207–27.

Kevane, Michael and Pierre Englebert (1997), 'A developmental state without growth? Explaining the paradox of Burkina Faso in a comparative perspective', mimeo, Santa Clara, CA: Santa Clara University.

Maclure, Richard (1994), 'Misplaced assumptions of decentralization and participation in rural communities: primary school reform in Burkina Faso', *Comparative Education*, **30** (3), 239–54.

Narayan, Deepa and Lant Pritchett. (1999), 'Cents and sociability: household income and social capital in rural Tanzania', *Economic Development and Cultural Change*, **47** (4), 871–97.

Olson, Mancur (1982), *The Rise and Decline of Nations*, New Haven: Yale University Press.

Platteau, Jean-Philippe (1991), 'Traditional systems of social security and hunger insurance: past achievements and modern challenges', in E. Ahmed, J. Drèze, J. Hills and A. Sen (eds), *Social Security in Developing Countries*, Oxford: Clarendon Press.

Putnam, Robert (1993), *Making Democracy Work: Civic Traditions in Modern Italy*, Princeton, NJ: Princeton University Press.

Reardon, Thomas, Christopher Delgado and Peter Matlon (1992), 'Determinants of income diversification amongst farm households in Burkina Faso', *Journal of Development Studies*, **28** (2), 264–96.

Udry, Chris (1994), 'Risk and insurance in a rural credit market: an empirical investigation in northern Nigeria', *Review of Economic Studies*, **61**, 495–526.

Veirech, H. (1986), 'Agricultural production, social status and intra-compound relationships', in Joyce Lowinger Moock (ed.), *Understanding Africa's Rural Households and Farming Systems*, Boulder, CO and London: Westview Press.

Wade, Robert (1988), *Village Republics*, New York: Cambridge University Press.

World Bank (1991), 'Burkina Faso: Fourth Education Project', Population and Human Resources, Operations Division, Sahelian Department, Africa Region.

6. The interactions of bonding, bridging and linking dimensions of social capital: evidence from rural Paraguay

José Molinas[1]

In the first part of this volume, Woolcock (Chapter 2) and Narayan (Chapter 4) detail how three dimensions of social capital can significantly affect economic and environmental outcomes. 'Bonding' social capital refers to relations among family members, close friends and neighbours; 'bridging' social capital refers to relations among more distant associates and colleagues who have somewhat different demographic characteristics irrespective of how well they know one another; 'linking' social capital refers to alliances with sym-pathetic individuals in positions of power.

This chapter considers the determinants and interactions of selected forms of bonding, bridging and linking social capital among individual peasants, community groups and peasant federations in Paraguay. In particular, it poses the question whether two alternative path-dependent processes, rural poverty alleviation or rural poverty acceleration, partially depend on the nature of bonding, bridging and linking relationships within a community.

The path-dependent properties that we explore can be illustrated with two hypothetical communities. In the first, a flood forces neighbours collectively to rebuild a bridge. This increases the number of informal, open community events within the community, such as maintenance of the local feeder road, which in turn leads to an increase in the effectiveness of the local peasant committee (as members build on the solidarity established by this incident and the subsequent expansion of community activities). This encourages other community members to join the local committee. The larger number of organized peasants then generates more resources to finance linking activities, owing to the presence of increasing returns to scope. With more resources, the larger peasant organization is in a better position to identify and incorporate best practices from the committee, leading to an improvement in the organization's linking strategy. The better linking strategy then has a positive effect on committee performance: the committee is better able to improve its collective resources for joint commercialization of agricultural products, rotating loan funds and improving the local school. A virtuous circle of increasing social capital has resulted, which has led to long-term poverty alleviation.

In the second community, a major crop failure leads to a large amount of unexpected migration to the nearest city. This decreases the number of informal, open events: the leaders of the annual community festival are no longer in the community. The effectiveness of the local peasant committee falls, as the remaining community members feel less solidarity based on common experiences. The smaller number of organized peasants then begins to lose its ability to gain resources to finance linking activities: the rotating loan funds and the community store are closed down. A vicious circle of decreasing social capital has resulted, which has led to long-term poverty acceleration.

There are two main results from the empirical analysis of these Paraguayan rural organizations. First, it shows that there are important feedbacks taking place among the different dimensions of social capital. Second, it implies that a better understanding of the mutually determining relationships among dimensions of social capital may enable policy makers to catalyse potential virtuous circles of rural poverty alleviation.

The remainder of this chapter is organized as follows. The second section describes the data sources. The third and fourth sections model the determinants of successful peasant committee performance, committee attendance and peasants' decisions to join a local committee. The final section illustrates how a better understanding of these dimensions of social capital may enable policy makers to catalyse potential virtuous circles of rural poverty alleviation.

HOUSEHOLDS, PEASANT COMMITTEES AND HIGHER-LEVEL ORGANIZATIONS IN RURAL PARAGUAY

The data come from surveys in the departments of Concepción, San Pedro and Caaguazú in Paraguay. These departments, which comprise 13 per cent of the national territory and 19 per cent of the total rural population, belong to the relatively poor 'intermediate region' of Paraguay. This region contains less than half of the total rural population but 95 per cent of rural families living in extreme poverty (IFAD, 1992; DGEEC, 1992). More than 90 per cent of farms in this region are peasant farms,[2] accounting for about one-third of all peasant farms in the nation.

Peasants in this part of rural Paraguay have three types of social alliances that may lead to improvements in well-being: within their own households, within local peasant committees and within 'higher-level organizations' (HLOs), which are federations of local peasant committees. To identify the interaction of bonding, bridging and linking social capital that is formed by these alliances, this chapter uses individual-, community- and national-level data from surveys of 374 peasant households and of 104 peasant committees.

Bonding social capital can be measured by the individual decision whether to join with one's neighbours in a peasant organization: this is one indicator that an individual has strong social connections with close friends and neighbours. This information is found in the household survey, carried out in 1995 by the *Centro Paraguayo de Estudios Sociológicos* (CPES), which contains data on demographic characteristics; production and income; housing and sanitary conditions; and membership of local organizations.

Bridging social capital can be measured by the performance of the community's peasant organization. This is one indicator that peasants from one community are effectively interacting with peasants from other communities within a peasant federation. This information is found in the committee survey, which was carried out simultaneously with the household survey in most villages and contains information on committee activities, membership, degree of participation in each committee, the history of the committee and aggregate characteristics of the village.

In Paraguay, what are the specific mechanisms through which a successful committee creates bridges with its neighbours? Within their HLOs, local peasant committees formally interact with neighbouring communities. For example, a committee delegate is expected to attend regular HLO meetings, to exchange information and to mobilize economic or political resources with other delegates. It follows that a strong, effective committee is more likely to play a productive role for its neighbours by increasing information sharing, lowering transactions costs and reducing collective action dilemmas (Molinas, 1997).

Linking social capital can be measured by the organizational strategies of peasant federation. Each of the 104 peasant committees belongs to an HLO: 41 belong to cooperatives and 63 belong to peasant organizations. Cooperatives are economically oriented HLOs that are registered and monitored by a specialized government agency and receive tax subsidies, technical assistance and credit. Peasant organizations are economically and politically oriented HLOs that are independent of the government.

These two types of HLOs have different organizational strategies, which imply differing forms of linking social capital. Peasant organizations depend more on local committees than do cooperatives. To become a member of a peasant organization, a person must belong to the local committee; cooperatives accept individual members as direct members; in addition, the regional leaders of peasant organizations belong to local committees. By contrast, the regional leaders of cooperatives are often urban managers and agronomists. This difference implies that the process of linking in peasant organizations is generated from within, which is not necessarily true of cooperatives.

THE DETERMINANTS OF SUCCESSFUL PEASANT COMMITTEE PERFORMANCE AND ATTENDANCE

What determines if a peasant committee in Paraguay is successful, thereby providing a productive bridge to neighbouring communities? What determines whether peasants regularly attend their committee meetings, thereby leading to more formal bonding within their own communities? This section explores whether two specific characteristics of committees are important for these outcomes: the type of HLO affiliation and the level of informal interaction among villagers.

First, as noted in the previous section, cooperatives and peasant organizations have different organizational strategies, which are directly related to their abilities to link with individuals in positions of power. The independent peasant organizations, which identify with popular movements, are more politically active than the government-supported cooperatives[3] and also focus on a wider rage of economic and political activities. This is likely to facilitate higher degrees of mutual interdependence and cooperation among members (Hechter, 1990). Second, as detailed in Molinas (1998a, 1998b), peasants in some villages regularly interact in informal, open community events such as road maintenance and festivals. This is likely to facilitate higher degrees of mutual trust among community members.

Accordingly, the empirical analysis in this section tests whether the differing linking strategies of peasant organizations and the differing levels of informal interaction have a positive effect on strengthening the bridging and bonding dimensions of peasant social capital, as measured by committee performance and membership attendance. First, indicators of six committee-specific characteristics related to committee performance are developed. Using principal components, an 'index of successful performance' is then created from these six indicators.[4] Regression analysis then identifies the factors that are associated with this index, as an indicator of bridging social capital, and with a measure of membership attendance, as a related indicator of bonding social capital.

Successful peasant committees in Paraguay have the following characteristics. Members regularly attend committee meetings, delegates regularly attend HLO meetings, the committee conducts a large number of activities, the committee's organizational experience is copied by neighbouring committees, members are satisfied with the overall performance of the committee, and leaders (including delegates) are satisfied with the overall performance of the committee.

How can one measure each of these characteristics? The first column in Table 6.1 lists the mean and standard deviations of six variables created from the committee surveys that measure each of these characteristics.

- 'committee attendance' is the average share of committee members who attended the last four meetings of the committee;
- 'HLO attendance' is the attendance at the last three meetings of the HLO by the committee's delegates;
- 'poverty alleviation activities' are the number of poverty alleviation activities undertaken by the committee;[5]
- 'organizational emulation' is a dummy variable that indicates whether the organizational experience of the committee was copied in the area;
- 'members' satisfaction' is a measure of the members' satisfaction with overall performance of the committee (ranging from 1 = extremely dissatisfied to 5 = very satisfied);[6]
- 'leader's satisfaction' is a measure of the leader's satisfaction with organizational performance of the committee (ranging from 1 = very serious difficulties to 4 = excellent).

Using principal component analysis, these variables have been integrated into an 'index of successful performance' for the 104 surveyed committees. The second column of Table 6.1 lists the correlations of each of the six indicators with this index (the first factor from the principal component analysis).[7]

What committee- and village-level characteristics are likely to affect committee performance, and thereby increase the probability that local peasants are effectively connected to peasants beyond their community's borders? The identification of these potential determinants is based on related work in Paraguay (Molinas, 1997, 1998a, 1998b). They include demographic characteristics of the committees, including age of the committee and composition of membership, as well as socioeconomic characteristics of the community, including well-being and inequality.

Table 6.1   Indicators of successful performance of peasant committees

Variable name	Mean (and standard deviation)		Correlation with 'index of successful performance'
Committee attendance	70.7	(30.2)	0.78
HLO attendance	2.2	(1.1)	0.65
Poverty alleviation activities	3.3	(1.9)	0.85
Organizational emulation	0.34	(0.47)	0.45
Members' satisfaction	3.0	(0.8)	0.71
Leader's satisfaction	2.2	(0.66)	0.70

Note: See text for description of each variable.

The potential determinants of committee performance are the following:

- 'peasant organization', a dummy variable that indicates whether the peasant committee belongs to a peasant organization (as opposed to a cooperative);
- 'index of informal interactions', formed by counting the number of informal, open community events per year, based on the responses of committee leaders about the periodicity of these informal events;
- 'index of women's participation', created by principal components, combines two sub-indices: the ratio of female members to male members and a dummy variable if a woman is a member of the executive committee;
- 'membership share', the households in the peasant community that are committee members;
- 'organization × membership', an interaction term ('peasant organization' × 'membership share');
- 'land wealth', the value of the median community land holdings adjusted by the mean price of community land per hectare to make comparison possible among communities that differ in land quality, location and other characteristics;
- 'number of training courses', measuring how many training courses were organized for the local committee directly or indirectly by its HLO during 1995;
- 'land Gini', the Gini coefficient of land possession in the community;
- community initiative,' a dummy variable which indicates whether the committee was formed by community initiative (as opposed to outside initiative);
- 'leadership tenure', the tenure of the current leadership (in months);
- 'age of committee', the age of the committee (in years) since it was formed.

The econometric strategy using these variables is as follows. First, they were tested as potential determinants of the 'index of successful performance'. As discussed above, this variable is considered as a proxy for the degree of linking social capital among members of the peasant committee. Second, they were tested as potential determinants of one of the six components of the index: 'committee attendance', the average share of committee members who attended the last four meetings of the committee. This variable is considered as a proxy for the degree of bonding social capital among members of the peasant committee.[8]

Table 6.2 presents results for these two different specifications.[9] Specification 1 presents the determinants of the 'index of successful performance'; specification 2 presents the determinants of 'committee attendance'.

Table 6.2   The determinants of successful performance and attendance

Specification	(1)	(2)
Peasant organization	0.77***	0.77***
	(4.7)	(4.0)
Index of informal interactions	0.24***	0.15*
	(3.1)	(1.7)
Index of women's participation	0.21**	0.16*
	(2.52)	(1.7)
Membership share	0.50***	0.65***
	(3.14)	(3.4)
Organization × membership	−0.66***	
	(−3.03)	
Land wealth	−0.19**	−0.10
	(−2.44)	(−0.97)
Number of training courses	0.58***	0.38**
	(3.32)	(1.9)
Square of number of training courses	−0.52***	−0.41**
	(−2.96)	(−2.0)
Land Gini	0.58*	0.64*
	(1.96)	(1.8)
Square of land Gini	−0.61**	−0.71**
	(−2.08)	(2.1)
Community initiative	−0.0075	
	(−0.097)	
Leadership tenure	−0.048	
	(−0.64)	
Age	0.103	
	(1.33)	
N =	104	104
R2 =	0.53	0.32
R2-adjusted =	0.46	0.25
F =	7.76	4.4

Note: See text for explanation of variables; standardized coefficients and *t*-statistics in parentheses. *Statistically significant at the 10% level; **Statistically significant at the 5% level; ***Statistically significant at the 1% level.

The first row shows that the coefficient for 'peasant organization' is positive and statistically significant in both specifications of the model: committees from peasant organizations are more successful than the ones from cooperatives, and the attendance level at meetings of the local committee is also higher in committees from peasant organizations.[10]

The second row of Table 6.2 shows that the indicator of informal interactions among community members is a significant determinant of the 'index of successful performance' (at the 0.01 level) and 'committee attendance' (at the 0.10 level). Informal social interactions such as sports activities, parties and festivals are associated with more successful and better attended committees.

Overall, these specifications provide partial evidence that the strategies of HLOs and informal social interactions of community members are significant determinants of the performance and attendance of local committees. These results have been obtained while controlling for the impact of the gender composition of the membership, the age of the committee since it was founded, the way the committee was formed, the tenure of the leadership, the share of community members, the level of outside intervention, the degree of inequality within the community and the level of well-being in the community. A deeper discussion of these controlling variables can be found in Molinas (1998a). However, we should notice here that in both specifications (1) and (2), women's effective participation improves the committee's performance. The positive impact of women's participation on committee performance and on committee attendance level is consistent with the hypothesis of women being more cooperative than men (Folbre, 1994).

In addition, there is a quadratic relationship (an inverted U-shape) between the level of inequality and both the dependent variables. In the Paraguayan countryside, it is often observed that in equal communities a coordination problem arises among peasants because nobody has an overarching incentive to be the committee's organizer (Molinas, 1998a). With a group of people who benefit more from the peasant committee, the coordination problem stated above may be easier to overcome. The community may agree that those who will benefit more should be the entrepreneurs for the collective good. At the other end, acute levels of inequality may increase conflict level in the community and exacerbate seasonal migration, deterring the well functioning of peasant committees (ibid.).

THE DETERMINANTS OF INDIVIDUALS' DECISIONS TO JOIN LOCAL PEASANT COMMITTEES

This section examines empirically the impact of the committee's performance on individual peasant's decisions to join a local committee. The individual household's decision to join a peasant committee is modelled as a function of the committee's performance, controlling for a set of other potential determinants of membership.

What motivates us to discuss the determinants of a peasant's decision to join local committees? Consider first a peasant family with substantial financial and time constraints. Membership of a local committee may entail substantial costs, including the time commitment of attending meetings, and benefits, including the potential diffusion of information from other peasant committees in the HLO.

In considering whether to become a member, the family weighs the expected costs and benefits of this potential investment in its own social capital, conditional on its outside options. These outside options include its access to physical and human capital and to other sources of information: a well-educated, wealthy family with alternative sources of income may have few incentives to join the local peasant committee.

The family must also assess the potential benefits of free-riding: if the local committee performs services that benefit all families in the community, regardless of their membership status, the incentive to join the group will also be low. Finally, the family is likely to have a 'subjective cost of cooperation', based on their previous experience in other local organizations: have they found membership to be useful in the past?

Controlling, then, for outside options, the temptation to free-ride, subjective cost of cooperation, and other household- and village-level characteristics, one would expect that a peasant family will be more likely to join a successful committee than an unsuccessful committee. Or, put another way, the family will be more likely to bond formally with other families in a committee when the committee itself has successfully bridged with other committees within an HLO.

This hypothesis is modelled in this section, using data on committee membership from the household surveys. The dependent variable in this model is a binary variable (with mean of 0.56 and standard deviation of 0.5) that indicates whether the household head belongs to a peasant organization.[11] In a logit regression, the model tests whether the 'index of successful performance' is a significant determinant of this variable, controlling for outside options, the temptation to free-ride, the subjective cost of cooperation and household- and community-level household characteristics.

The following variables measure these characteristics:

- 'outside options', the percentage of the household income from non-farm sources (such as wages, remittances and commercial activities);
- 'free ride', a control for the degree of excludability of the peasant committees' activities, which is a measure of the temptation to free-ride;[12]
- 'subjective cost of operation', a proxy for the subjective costs of cooperation of each individual peasant household, a dummy variable that indicates if the peasant household has not engaged in labour exchange arrangements or other community organizations;
- 'land size', the land size of the peasant farm (in hectares);

- 'land title', a dummy variable that indicates whether the peasant household has a land title;
- 'expected income', an instrumental variable for the expected income of the non-organized household in US$/year. The method of estimation is the following: (1) an income regression is performed using only non-organized households, and (2) the coefficients of the regression are applied to the whole sample. The income regression contains as predictors: measure of labour, land, proxies for productive infrastructure, household head characteristics, demographic characteristics of the household, and regional indicators, among other variables;
- 'family labour', the number of household members of working age (which, according to Paraguayan statistics, includes ages from 12 to 65);
- 'adult education', the average level of education of adult household members (measured in years of schooling);
- 'women's household', the percentage of women at least 12 years old in the household;
- 'Caaguazu', a dummy variable that indicates if the peasant household is located in the department of Caaguazu;
- 'San Pedro', a dummy variable that indicates if the peasant household is located in the department of San Pedro.

The 'index of successful performance' and 'land wealth' are the same as in the previous regression model presented in Table 6.2.

Table 6.3 presents results for this specification. The results for the model indicate that the performance level of the committee has a positive and statistically significant effect on the likelihood that a peasant household will join its neighbours in a local committee. Using the marginal probabilities that can be generated from these results, a one-standard deviation increase in 'index of successful performance' is associated with an increase of 0.12 in the probability of joining the local peasant organization.

Unfortunately, this model is not able to test for the likelihood of simultaneity: in each community, one would expect that, as more members joined a committee, it would tend to be more successful. Nevertheless, the model does suggest that the household decision to join a committee in any period is dependent on the success of the committee – and that the magnitude of this effect is relatively large. Controlling for outside options, the temptation to free-ride, the subjective cost of cooperation, and household- and community-level household characteristics, families are more likely to join a local group when it successfully achieves its goals. Successful committees, with bridging strategies that provide mutual assistance across neighbourhoods, lead to more formal bonding within communities.

The variables 'outside options' and 'land title' are proxies, to some extent,

Table 6.3   The potential determinants of peasants' decisions to join a local committee

Performance	0.49***
	(7.60)
Outside options	−4.97***
	(6.32)
Free-ride	0.26
	(0.59)
Subjective cost of operation	−1.03***
	(8.27)
Land size	−0.04
	(0.43)
Land title	−1.52***
	(11.32)
Expected income	0.0013***
	(11.54)
Family labour	−0.05
	(0.28)
Adult education	−0.23**
	(3.98)
Women's household	0.01
	(2.07)
Land wealth	−0.0001
	(1.12)
Caaguazu	−2.32***
	(15.58)
San Pedro	−1.74**
	(5.34)
Constant	0.75
	(0.60)
−2 Log likelihood	306.47
χ^2	50.09
% of right predictions	68.97
N =	261

Notes: See text for explanation of variables; logit coefficients and *t*-stats in parentheses. Statistically significant at *10% level; **5% level, and ***1% level.

for the gains from cooperation in these peasant organizations.[13] The gains for members in these peasant committees are expected to be inversely related to the outside options (outside the organization) that the peasant household has in generating income. Outside options to increase net income compete with the options offered by the peasant organization. Therefore the higher the relative returns of outside options, the lower the potential gain from cooperation for a given peasant household. Probably the best proxy for outside options is the percentage of household income from non-farm-related sources ('outside options'). Since peasant organizations focus mainly on farm-related activities, the smaller the share of this type of activity in the household income, the higher the dependency on outside options of this particular household. The coefficient associated with outside options is negative, as expected, and statistically significant at the 1 per cent level in the model of Table 6.3. Additionally, the possession of land title ('land title') is positively related to access to institutionalized credit by the peasant household. Access to formal financial institutions could be an alternative to the loan funds administered by the peasant organizations. Therefore having land title is also associated with greater outside options. The coefficient associated with 'land title' is also negative and statistically significant at the 1 per cent level in the model of Table 6.3.

Participation in cooperative informal labour exchange arrangements and other community organizations signals the 'willingness to cooperate' of a particular peasant. These signals are used as a proxy for the subjective costs of cooperation of each individual household. The proxy for the subjective costs of cooperation ('subjective cost of operation') is negative and statistically significant at the 1 per cent level in the model of Table 6.3.

The results in this section – that household membership in peasant committees is more likely with a more successful committee – raise a further question: how does the larger size of a successful peasant committee affect its linking activities within a peasant federation? Specifically, does a significant increase in membership significantly increase the local resources that are available to a larger federation?

Econometric testing of this question is not possible, since only 16 peasant federations were surveyed. However, some qualitative evidence of this relationship may be observed by examining the range of activities carried out by the 104 peasant committees that were surveyed. These activities include demonstrations for better agricultural policies, joint commercialization of agricultural products, collective production, rotating loan funds and improving local schools and roads.

Most of these activities are subject to some degree of increasing returns to scope. This implies a positive effect of the membership size on the potential resources available to the HLO for linking activities. That is, with increasing returns to scope, the activities of peasants of larger HLOs have a higher productivity. A portion of the extra gains generated by the larger membership could be charged as a fee by the HLO. These extra resources could be used, for example, in financing some leaders' time to engage in lobbying, or to pay for technical assistance to elaborate their demands better.

The sources of increasing returns to scope in peasant organizations include the presence of fixed costs, the existence of a minimum group size (to capture the benefits), increasing productivity from specialization and learning by doing, and spreading of risks. In the context of these Paraguayan organizations, a larger membership may imply lower per capita fixed costs of administrative tasks associated with joint commercialization, higher capabilities to influence the design of agricultural policies, and better risk-managing possibilities that would enhance the sustainability of both rotating loan funds and social insurance mechanisms. Put another way, a larger membership, with higher productivity of activities, is likely to increase the potential linking resources of a federation.

CONCLUSION: FEEDBACK EFFECTS AND THE POTENTIAL VIRTUOUS CIRCLE OF RURAL POVERTY ALLEVIATION

This chapter has explored the determinants of different dimensions of social capital in rural Paraguay. The third section showed that HLOs with locally based, peasant leadership (a linking strategy) and communities with a dense network of interactions (a form of bonding social capital) are associated with better committee performance (a form of bridging social capital). The fourth section showed, in turn, that committee performance is a relatively large and significant determinant of a peasant's decision to join a local committee (an indicator of formal bonding). It also suggested that larger committees may, by taking advantage of economies of scope, be able to increase the potential linking resources of a federation.

These feedbacks among the bonding, bridging and linking dimensions of social capital are consistent with the generation of virtuous (vicious) circles of increasing (decreasing) stocks of social capital, which are likely to improve well-being. The deterministic models explored here suggest that policy makers may be able to catalyse virtuous circles of rural poverty alleviation. An exogenous increase in the level of local committees' performance, the prospects of joining local peasant committees, the density of interactions among the community population or the effectiveness of peasant federations' linking strategies may be motivated by a virtuous circle of increasing social capital. In the Paraguayan context, policy makers may be able to catalyse virtuous circles of social capital with policies that include (a) promotion of women's effective participation in peasant committees, (b) improvements of peer-monitoring systems of selected organization, (c) generation of small grants that encourage recreational and other informal activities in the community, and (d), channelling a larger share of public assistance (for example, public credit or agricultural extension) through peasant organizations.

NOTES

1. The author would like to thank Samuel Bowles and Carmen Diana Deere, Sunder Ramaswamy, Thomas Kelly, Jon Isham and Merrilee Mardon, as well as participants at the Twenty-first Middlebury Annual Middlebury Economic Conference (8–9 April 2000), for many useful comments and suggestions.
2. Peasant farms are defined as those family farms consisting of one to 20 hectares.
3. This difference in political commitment is manifested in their rent-seeking strategies. While the cooperatives rely on a more institutionalized bargaining with the government, supported by their special status, the peasant organizations rely on the type of actions typically associated with social movements (for example, demonstrations, appeals to the public opinion and strategic alliances with the labour movement).
4. Use of principal components is a statistical technique that, in many cases, is used to generate a single variable which captures the common variance of a set of related variables.
5. The range of these activities includes demonstrations for better agricultural practices (62 of 104 committees); joint commercialization of agricultural products (54); collective production (42); rotating loan funds (36); improving the local school (30) and local roads (22): administration of a village health centre (20) and community store (20); and seven other minor community activities (six committees or fewer).
6. Specifically, it is the average evaluation of three members who were selected randomly.
7. The mean and standard deviations of this index are 0 and 1, respectively. As the first factor from the principal component analysis, this index explains 50 per cent of the total common variance among the six indicators. Similar results to those reported below can be generated with indices that are built with smaller combinations of the six sub-indicators – and that therefore explain more of the total common variance
8. Admittedly, the use of 'committee attendance' as one of the six sub-components of the 'index of successful performance' raises the question: how can an indicator of bonding social capital contribute to an indicator of bridging social capital? Fortunately, the results presented in Table 6.2 and discussed below hold when 'committee attendance' is eliminated from the generation of the 'index of successful performance'. The complete index is used here because previous work by the author (Molinas, 1997, 1998a) suggests that all six of these characteristics capture adequately different aspects of the success of peasant committees.
9. A range of econometric tests was used to check for specification errors in these models. In the first specification, a Chow test rejected the null hypothesis of equality of coefficients and the intercept across two sub-sets of data: from the cooperatives and peasant organizations. After allowing different intercepts and coefficients for the fraction variable (by including 'organization × membership'), the Chow test failed to reject the null hypothesis of equality of the other parameters. In addition, no evidence of heteroscedasticity was found; the null hypothesis of normality of residuals (with the Jarque-Bera asymptotic LM normality tests) cannot be rejected; and Hausman specification tests did not show evidence of endogeneity of selected independent variables including ('index of informal interactions', 'number of training courses', 'index of women's participation' and 'membership share').
10. The use of standardized coefficients in this table facilitates the comparison of two related specifications with different dependent variables. For example, since 'peasant organization' is a dummy variable, the values of the coefficients in the first row of Table 6.2 indicate that

being part of a peasant organization is associated with an increase of 0.77 times the standard deviation of each dependent variable.
11. In many cases, more than one family member actively participates. Unfortunately, information on individual participation by household members is not available.
12. This was calculated as (number of non-excludable activities – number of excludable activities)/number of total activities. This variable ranges from 1 to –1, with 1 representing the highest temptation to free-ride and –1 representing the lowest.
13. A more complete discussion of the determinants of a peasant's decision to join a peasant organization is offered in Molinas (1998b).

REFERENCES

DGEEC (*Dirección General de Estadísticas, Encuestas y Censos*) (1992), *Censo Nacional de Poblacion y Viviendas*, Asunción, Paraguay.
Folbre, Nancy (1994), *Who Pays for the Kids? Gender and the Structures of Constraint*, New York: Routledge.
Hechter, Michael (1990), 'The attainment of solidarity in intentional communities', *Rationality and Society*, **2** (2), 142–55.
IFAD (International Fund for Agricultural Development) (1992), 'Fondo de desarrollo campesino. Proyecto de crédito en la región nordoriental del Paraguay', mimeo, Misión de evaluación ex-ante.
Molinas, José (1997), 'Rethinking rural development: making peasant organizations work. The case of Paraguay', PhD dissertation, University of Massachusetts, Amherst.
Molinas, José (1998a), 'The impact of inequality, external assistance, gender and social capital on local-level cooperation', *World Development*, **26** (3), 413–31.
Molinas, José (1998b), 'Who cooperates? A study of membership in peasant cooperatives', paper presented to the XXI International Conference of the Latin American Studies Association, Chicago.

7. Measuring social capital: adding field experimental methods to the analytical toolbox

Jeffrey P. Carpenter[*]

This chapter discusses the measurement of social capital using the method most often employed, standard survey techniques, and also using an underutilized method, economic experiments. The basic argument of the chapter is that investigators interested in social capital might increase the analytical power of their research by conducting experiments. More specifically, there are a number of experiments that, while designed by economists for other purposes, can also be usefully adapted for the field to validate survey results and measure social capital when one suspects that surveys may be biased by incentive and other problems.

The primitives of the concept of social capital are those characteristics of individuals including trust, trustworthiness, reciprocity, generosity and the propensity to cooperate in social dilemmas that make economic activity possible when contracts are hard to enforce. Presumably through some evolutionary process, behavioural conventions (for example, punishing free-riders or peer pressure) arise, allowing societies to accumulate social capital and steering them to more efficient outcomes. While social capital appears to be easily conceived of as a kind of interpersonal grease lubricating economic transactions, it is hard to measure and therefore the concept has not been widely adopted by policy makers.

The remainder of this chapter is organized as follows. The next section presents an argument for the use of economic experiments to measure social capital. The third section introduces four experiments that can be used to measure social capital (as defined above), while the fourth section reviews the results of the few studies that have used both methods to measure and study social capital. A final section concludes.

THE LINK BETWEEN SURVEY AND EXPERIMENTAL MEASURES OF SOCIAL CAPITAL

The conventional approach to empirically studying social capital is to analyse survey data. Examples of this approach include Putnam (1995), Fukuyama

(1995), Molinas (1999), Glaeser *et al.* (2000), Isham and Kähkönen (2002, forthcoming), Grootaert *et al.* (Chapter 5 of the present volume) and Daniere *et al.* (Chapter 10, this volume). These studies typically test hypotheses concerning the effect of social networks or behavioural characteristics of individuals on economic outcomes using self-reported responses to survey questions. At the same time, there is also a smaller, but growing, literature interpreting the behavioural responses elicited in economic experiments as measures of social capital within a population (Fehr *et al.*, 1997; Berg *et al.*, 1995; Eckel and Grossman, 1996a) and between populations (Ockenfels and Weimann, 1999; Croson and Buchan, 1999; Roth *et al.*, 1991; Fershtman and Gneezy, 1998). Very few studies employ both methods to study the same population. As a result, complementarities between these two methods – such as the ease of gathering demographic data in a survey and the incentive compatibility of experiments – are rarely exploited. Further, any interesting relationships that may exist between the two types of data remain largely unexamined.

There are methodological reasons for simultaneously employing both methods. Survey-based research and experiments face a common fundamental methodological criticism: to what extent are the research methods used valid ways to answer important questions about economic behaviour? Research using self-reported survey techniques may be problematic because surveys do not use incentive-compatible mechanisms to ensure the truthful revelation of behaviour and, in some cases, respondents may perceive an incentive to lie (for example, 'Do you pay your taxes?'). Experiments are criti-cized because their external validity is open to question (for example, to what extent can we generalize the results of experiments conducted with students in a context-free laboratory setting?). As detailed below, this chapter argues that the weaknesses of each method may be largely offset by the strength of the other. The potential for complementarities between the two research methods suggests that a more complete understanding of social capital can be gained by combining experiments and surveys in field sites of particular interest.

Some Problems with Surveys

Surveys are, probably, the best way to collect behavioural data when incentives are not an issue. There is no clear reason why the average respondent would misrepresent the truth when responding to questions such as 'How many social organizations do you actively belong to?' As such, demographic questions about behaviour are probably good measures of the depth of social networks. However, three concerns arise when using survey data based on behavioural questions: the 'hypothetical bias', the 'idealized persona bias' and 'incentive compatibility'.

To illustrate the hypothetical bias, consider the following survey responses to a question about adhering to a critical societial norm.[1] Of the survey respondents (all from the United States) 77 per cent said that they would intervene if a group of teenagers were harassing an elderly person. This seems plausible, but 35 per cent said they would intervene when a man threatened someone else with a weapon. This number seems high and we can easily understand why. Saying you would help in a hypothetical situtation is costless; actually doing so is not.[2]

The idealized persona bias can also be illustrated by an example. Consider the following phrases, often used to measure trust: 'When dealing with strangers, one is better off using caution before trusting them', or 'How often do you lend personal possessions to friends?' The data resulting from these questions may be problematic because people often reply as the person they think the researcher would like them to be or as the person they would like to be.

Finally, survey results may suffer from the lack of incentive compatability when participants do not feel the need to take a survey seriously (Bertrand and Mullainathan, 2001). Although respondents are often paid for the completion of a survey, there is no way to control if they paid attention while responding. Without giving respondents an incentive to take the survey seriously, even well designed questions may elicit 'noisy' responses. In contrast, in economic experiments, participants are given an incentive to pay attention because the decisions they make determine how much they are paid; not taking the experiment seriously will be costly.

There is growing evidence from experimental economics that survey-based measures of social capital may indeed lead to misleading results. Glaeser *et al.* (1999) compare the results of two trust experiments – a letter drop experiment designed by the authors and a version of the trust game developed in Berg *et al.* (1995) – with the responses to a social capital questionnaire that had been administered among the same subjects. The standard trust game has two phases. First, a player, the sender, decides how much of their show-up fee they would like to pass to another participant, the recipient, who is anonymous. The experimenter triples any money sent before it reaches the second mover. Second, the recipient then decides how much of the tripled amount to send back to the sender. The theoretic prediction of this game is straightforward: because any money sent to the recipient will be kept for sure, senders should send nothing. When this experiment is conducted in the laboratory settings, participants tend to send about half of their show-up fee and recipients send back, on average, the amount that they were sent. The amount sent by the 'sender' can be understood as a measure of trust and the amount sent back as a measure of reciprocity.

Glaeser *et al.* (1999, 2000) suggest that trust and reciprocity are not correlated with participants' reponses to survey questions designed to measure social capital, controlling for other possible factors. Consider the following question: 'Generally speaking, would you say that most people can be trusted or that you can't be too careful in dealing with people?' One's response to this question does not predict trusting behaviour in experiments where real money is a stake.[3]

Similar results have been found in studies conducted by Ben-Ner and Putterman (1999) who design an experimental two-sided dictator game experiment to examine and measure reciprocity between participants. In the dictator game, a 'sender' is given a sum of money to split with 'a recipient' who has no say in how the money will be divided. If the sender allocates anything to the recipient, the amount can be understood as a measure of generosity. Ben-Ner and Putterman add a second stage to this game: recipients are given a sum of money that they can share with the sender. The authors argue that any money given back during this stage is a measure of reciprocity. They then compare responses to survey questions with experimental behaviour. They find that established social capital indicators (for example, number of times the individual and his/her family entertains guests, the past charitable giving of the individual and his/her family) have little predictive power. Moreoever, the marginal effects have counterintuitive signs (for example, they find that the more a person's family volunteers or gives to charity, the less the recipient sends back to the sender controlling for how much was sent to her).

Burks *et al.* (2000) also find little correlation between participants' demonstrated trust and reciprocity and their responses to survey questions designed to measure social capital. Most notably, the authors find no relationship between how much participants actually trust 'strangers' in experiments and how much they say they trust strangers in general; how much they trust when there is little or a lot at stake; or how often they lend possessions or money to friends. As for reciprocity, the results also suggest no relationship between behaviour and self-reported measures of trust.

The comparisons of survey data and controlled experiments summarized here demonstrate the usefulness of running experiments to supplement surveys conducted in the field. Experimental methods will provide measures of social capital that are more representative of actual behaviour and therefore be a better basis for policy. At the same time, we stress that results from experiments in controlled laboratory settings do not provide definitive measures of social capital. Experimental economists are careful not to extrapolate from the behaviour they witness in the lab and do not assert that it can explain how things work in the more complicated real world.[4]

EXPERIMENTAL MEASURES OF SOCIAL CAPITAL

In this section we introduce four economic experiments which, while designed primarily for other purposes (for example, testing the predictive nature of game theory), can also be used to measure aspects of social capital.

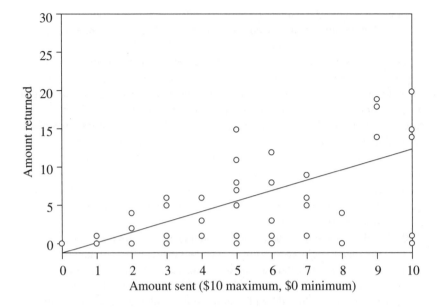

Figure 7.1   Student trust game results

Trust Game

We begin with the 'trust' game mentioned above and developed first in Berg *et al.* (1995).[5] Remember that the theoretical prediction of this game is that the sender should send nothing, because the receiver, acting rationally, has no incentive to reciprocate. By contrast, in most laboratory settings, senders do send part of their money and recipients reciprocate by sending back about the same amount.[6]

For example, Figure 7.1 illustrates the results from an experimental study trust, among students at the University of Minnesota and Middlebury College.[7] Here, 91 per cent of the observations deviate from the game-theoretic prediction. In general, trust – the amount one sends – is rewarded by reciprocity – the amount that one receives. Each dollar sent is matched one to one, as illustrated by the slope of the linear regression line. This dynamic allows most of the participants to earn amounts that are significantly higher than predicted earnings. Hence the results of this experiment demonstrate how trust and reciprocity enhance efficiency.

Ultimatum Game

The second game we will consider is the 'ultimatum game' first analysed in Gueth *et al.* (1982).[8] Like the trust game, the ultimatum game is also a two-person, sequential game; however, the ultimatum game concerns the division of a set amount of money and therefore is well suited for measuring fairness norms.

The game proceeds as follows. The first mover, 'the proposer', is given the opportunity to propose a division of a set amount of money ('the pie'), and the second mover, 'the responder', then either accepts the proposal or rejects it. If the proposal is accepted, the pie is divided accordingly; if it is rejected, neither receives anything. This game also has a straightforward theoretic prediction. Assuming, again, that the responder is non-satiated in money, he should accept any proposal because rejecting a proposal yields a pay-off of zero. Anticipating this, the proposer should offer the smallest unit of account to the responder, being confident that he will then accept. The final theoretical division of the pie is 'ε' for the responder and 'pie-ε' for the proposer, where 'ε' is the smallest unit of account.

Roth (1995) finds, in a study among students, that the modal offer is for half the pie (the mean is closer to 40 per cent), and offers of less than a quarter of the pie are routinely rejected. These results differ dramatically from the theoretical prediction, and it is reasonable to conjecture that the distance between the distribution of proposals and ε is a measure of the strength of fairness norms operating in a population. The highest rejected offer may be seen as a measure of negative reciprocity.

Table 7.1 illustrates how the ultimatum game can be used to quantify differences in forms of social capital (in this case, fairness and negative reciprocity) between populations. The table is created by gathering data from four studies of the ultimatum game that used seven different participant populations. The first column reports the results of Gueth *et al.* (1982) who played the game with German students; the next four columns come from Roth *et al.* (1991). This experiment was conducted with students from Israel, Japan, Slovenia and the USA. The final two columns list data from non-student experiments done by Carpenter *et al.* (2001) with workers at a distribution centre in Kansas and by Henrich (2000) with Amazonian horticulturalists in Peru.[9]

There are a number of interesting contrasts across these studies. Note, in the first row, the differences in the mean offers. American, Japanese and Slovenian proposers make noticeably higher offers than German, Israeli and Peruvian proposers. The particularly low offer made by the Peruvians is notable: this set of participants, from the indigenous *Macheguenga*, who have the least contact with modern market society of the groups surveyed, behave the most like *homo economicus*! A plausible explanation for this result is that these Macheguenga, one-time nomadic people, have recently been resettled into villages; since they have been accustomed to dealing only with kin, they may not have developed fairness norms to deal with people outside of their

Table 7.1 A comparison of ultimatum game results

Study	Gueth et al. (1982)	Roth et al. (1991)	Roth et al. (1991)	Roth et al. (1991)	Roth et al. (1991)	Carpenter et al. (2001)	Henrich (2000)
Subjects	German students	US students	Slovenian students	Israeli students	Japanese students	US workers	Peruvian horticulturalists
Mean offer	35%	45%	44%	36%	45%	45%	26%
Number 50/50 offers	7 of 21	14 of 27	12 of 30	8 of 30	10 of 29	22 of 30	4 of 21
Highest rejected offer	20%	60%	50%	50%	55%	10%	10%
Pr(offer <% rejected)	29%	50%	67%	60%	57%	50%	10%

extended family (see Henrich, 2000). These results are consistent with suspicions that resettlements or other dislocating influences can dramatically alter forms of social capital.[10]

The frequency of fair offers (50/50) in each population is tallied in the second row. There are two outliers: the Peruvian horticulturalists on the low end and American workers on the high end. We have already discussed the low offers of the horticulturalists. About three-quarters of the proposals from the workers were for half of a $100 pie. This mode is considerably higher than in the other studies. There are a number of contributing factors, which might explain this result. One explanation is that the workers deal intimately with each other on a daily basis; hence the social network existing among them is bound to be denser than those existing among anonymous students. As a result, the workers form a more cohesive 'in-group' which may contribute to a stronger fairness norm (Carpenter *et al.*, 2001).

Lastly, one can also compare the highest offers rejected, and probability of rejecting low offers to analyse differences in the propensity towards negative reciprocity across the populations. Beginning with the German students, American workers and the Peruvian horticulturalists, we see similarities in the highest rejected offer, but marked differences in the propensity to reject low offers. While the workers are quick to reject low offers, German students are more likely to accept low offers and the Peruvians accept almost all offers. Again, these differences might be explained by differences in the density of the social networks linking individuals. Members of a salient in-group are much more likely to reprimand other members and are less likely to be bothered by the transgressions of outsiders (Bornstein *et al.* 1996; Brewer, 1979; Kollock, 1996). Hence, from a social capital point of view, Table 7.1 can be viewed as summary statistics comparing the density of non-kin social networks in different societies. In this sample, workers in the USA appear to have very dense networks illustrated by the group sense of fairness and the propensity to punish deviations from fairness, while the Macheguenga, who have not internalized group fairness norms and do not punish greedy individuals, demonstrate weak social ties with others outside their kin group. An interesting analysis would include behavioural measures such as these as right-hand side variables in the standard social capital regression. On the evidence of Table 7.1, we might expect workers from the USA to go bowling with each other, but not the Macheguenga.

Dictator Game

The 'dictator game' was originally developed by Forsythe *et al.* (1994) to test whether people made modal offers for half the pie in the ultimatum game because of fairness considerations or fear of negative reciprocity. However, the dictator game has been frequently used to measure the altruism of participants. The game is run as follows. As in the ultimatum game, there is a first mover who decides on a split of some fixed pie. However, in this game the second mover simply gets whatever is allocated to her by the first mover – the dictator – and is not given the chance to accept or reject. Hence whatever the dictator allocates to the anonymous second player is a measure of his altruism.

In the dictator game the theoretical prediction is clear: if the dictator is non-satiated in money, he should not allocate anything to the second player. Although the theoretic prediction happens when the game is played, it is not the only behaviour that is observed. The distribution of proposals is to the left of the distribution of the proposals of the ultimatum game, but it does not collapse onto zero (Forsythe *et al.*, 1994).

The first three columns of Table 7.2 compare the results of three different experiments, which demonstrate the general level of altruism among student participants. As mentioned above, the original dictator game was played in Forsythe *et al.* (1994) which resulted in an average allocation of 23 per cent of the ten dollar pie and two modes at giving 30 per cent and giving nothing (column 1 in this table). Compare these numbers to the comparable numbers in the next two columns. In Hoffman *et al.* (1994), the experimenters increased the social distance between participants by making the experiment double blind: not only were the subjects unable to see what each other did, the experimenter also could not assign a specific response to an individual. The result is as would be predicted by a theory of behaviour in which social networks and social distance matter: allocations to the second party fell significantly, to only 9 per cent of the ten dollar pie.

Instead of increasing the social distance between players, Eckel and Grossman (1996a) effectively reduce it by changing the characteristics of the recipient. Rather than an anonymous student in the second player's role, the experimenters allowed dictators to make anonymous contributions to the Red Cross. Under this treatment, the average allocation increased to 30 per cent of the pie and new modes arose at 20 per cent of the pie and at half of the pie.

Table 7.2   A comparison of dictator game results

Study	Forsythe *et al.* (1994)	Hoffman *et al.* (1994)	Eckel & Grossman (1996a)	Carpenter *et al.* (2001)
Treatment	single blind	double blind	recipient	subject pool
Mean allocation	23%	9%	30%	50%
Modes	0%, 30%	0%	0%, 20%, 50%	50%

One interpretation is that dictators in this treatment looked at the experiment as an opportunity to invest in social capital (that is, to do the right thing socially). By contrast, increasing social distance allows participants to rationalize not giving in terms of an anonymous recipient who may not deserve one's charity.

Finally, we can consider the results of Carpenter *et al.* (2001). Compared to the single blind student game of Forsythe *et al.* (1994), workers in Kansas display significantly more generosity and altruism. Returning to the question of why this might be important for social capital investigators, these results demonstrate the relationship between the density of social networks, the average social distance between members of some specific population, and the level of generosity. Specifically, where the density of social networks is proxied by the number and importance of interactions people have with each other on a daily basis, and social distance is measured by the relative anonymity of daily interactions, we find that workers who interact very frequently in intimate settings to produce jointly their livelihood demonstrate more altruism (towards each other) than do students who interact in larger, more anonymous populations and with little at stake. This phenomenon suggests that one can play the dictator game with various populations to gather empirical measures of altruism and generosity for each population. In turn, these data can be used either to control for differences in an empirical analysis or to enter as explanatory variables alongside more traditional survey responses.

Voluntary Contribution Mechanism Game

The last experiment we will consider can be adapted to understand and measure the propensity to cooperate in social dilemmas (that is, when individual and group incentives differ). The 'voluntary contribution mechanism game', VCM, developed in Isaac *et al.* (1984), simulates the provision of a public good. For each individual there is a dominant strategy to not contribute any of one's endowment. This leads, in theory, to an inefficient equilibrium in which all players completely free-ride. However, a dilemma arises because, if all the players contributed fully, they would collectively reach the Pareto-efficient outcome. This game is interesting because it provides an incentive-compatible measure of cooperation among a participant population. The data are incentive-compatible because each player can maximize his monetary rewards by following the dominant strategy. This fact implies that deviations from the equilibrium (controlling for errors by stationary replication of the stage game) measure the propensity to cooperate (that is, there is a monetary cost to not defecting).

Table 7.3 provides a summary of the data from three different VCM experiments. The three experiments, Croson (1996b), Isaac and Walker (1988), and

Table 7.3 A comparison of VCM results (average contribution level)

Study treatment period	Croson (1996b)		Isaac & Walker (1988)		Carpenter (1999)*	
	Partners (%)	Strangers (%)	Communication (%)	No comm. (%)	Punishment (%)	No pun. (%)
1	56	41	100	54	55	49
2	53	40	88	44	57	54
3	46	36	96	35	68	50
4	50	32	92	28	67	49
5	50	28	100	15	69	41
6	48	33	93	23	65	37
7	39	27	100	17	68	36
8	30	20	100	16	67	41
9	36	21	100	8	75	45
10	19	10	100	13	71	38

Carpenter (1999), were chosen because they demonstrate three different methods that have been used to increase contributions to the public good.[11] As we
will see, each manipulation of the standard game has implications for the study
of social capital. The columns labelled 'Partners' and 'No comm.' represent
two examples of the standard decay of contributions seen in VCM experiments. As one can see, contributions usually start, in period one of a ten-period
game, at between 40 and 60 per cent of the endowment and then decay to
between 10 and 20 per cent by the last period.

A number of explanations for this decay have been put forward and tested
in subsequent experiments. We discuss two of the theories briefly and direct
the reader to Ledyard (1995) and Andreoni (1988) for more detailed discussion of this topic. One theory explains the decay of contributions by learning.
Initially, it is posited that participants have not learned the incentives of the
game and when they do, near the end, they learn to free ride. Among other
papers, Andreoni (1988) falsifies this theory in a clever experiment wherein
participants play ten rounds and then groups are reshuffled and they immediately play another three rounds. Contributions leap from low levels to much
higher levels at the beginning of the restart, which contradicts the learning
hypothesis. The alternative theory has to do with reciprocity. As discussed in
Fehr and Schmidt (1999) and Bowles *et al.* (2000), reciprocity requires that
contributors retaliate against free-riders and the only way to do this in the standard VCM game is by withholding one's contributions.

Consider first the study by Croson (1996b). In this experiment participants
are matched as 'partners' and remain in the same group for the entire ten
periods or are matched as 'strangers' and are randomly reshuffled into new
groups at the beginning of each period. The difference in the matching rule is
interesting because it either fosters or dampens the possibility for shared norms
to arise in repeated interactions. As one can see, the manipulation has a significant effect and cooperation is more sustainable when interactions are repeated.

Next, the experiment by Isaac and Walker (1988), adds the possibility for
communication between the participants of a group. Although communication
is restricted so that whatever is said can only be interpreted as 'cheap talk' and
therefore does not influence the standard prediction of complete free-riding,
there is nevertheless a strong effect of communication. As one can see, in most
periods the level of cooperation is above 90 per cent and often reaches the 100
per cent maximum. This study confirms what would be suspected from a
social capital point of view: communication is key to sustainable cooperation.
That is, communication allows the expression of shared norms and focuses the
attention of the group on the appropriate norm – do not free-ride.

The last VCM experiment with implications for the study of social capital
is the game designed by Fehr and Gaechter (1999) and expanded on in
Carpenter (1999). Here the standard game is changed so that group members

can monitor and punish free-riders at some personal cost. In the first stage, players choose contribution levels and, in the added, second stage, players see each other's contributions and have the ability to sanction each other. In effect, the new game adds a second-order public good to the first game. That is, because free-riders respond to punishment by increasing contributions in the future, the second-order public good is punishment. However, notice also that participants have to pay to punish someone else, which means no one should punish because it is costly to do so. Additionally, because the experiment uses the strangers' treatment (defined above) any benefits from getting a free-rider to contribute more in the next period will not accrue to the punisher because they will have been reshuffled into a different group.

Despite the theoretical prediction, considerable amounts of punishment are observed, which cause the level of cooperation to increase and be maintained. This result is seen by comparing the last two columns of Table 7.3. Note that this experiment is particularly interesting from the social capital point of view because the experimenter gathers data on both the propensity to cooperate and the propensity to punish free-riders.

STUDIES THAT COMBINE SURVEYS AND EXPERIMENTS

To date, few studies have used both the standard survey method and the field experimental method for gathering data on the evolution of social capital within specific populations. In this section we will briefly review the work of three research groups which have used both techniques and arrived at interesting results.

The core of the first group consists of Edward Glaeser and David Laibson, who have produced two examinations of the microfoundations of social capital (Glaeser *et al*. 1999; Glaeser *et al*., 2000). In the initial study, discussed above, the researchers used both methods to quantify trust and discovered a difference between trusting behaviour reported in a survey and the behaviour demonstrated in trust experiments. In addition, when combining their data into a meta analysis of trust, the investigators found the following results: (1) while behaviour in their experiments does not correlate with self-reported measures of trust, the data from the two experiments do correlate; (2) demographic data from their survey do seem to correlate with the behaviour in their experiments. Together, these facts argue for the use of both techniques to further understand how social capital is developed and maintained. As the authors concluded,

> Finally, we believe that this paper shows the value of using experiments and surveys together. Experiments can measure personal attributes much more convincingly

than surveys. By connecting the two forms of evidence, we can determine the socioeconomic correlates of hard-to-measure personal attributes, and test the validity of survey measures of these attributes. (Glaeser *et al.* 1999, pp. 33–4)

In Burks *et al.* (2000), the researchers examine trust and trustworthiness. As mentioned earlier, they are also unable to predict trusting behaviour by survey responses. However, differently from Glaeser *et al.* (1999), this study also employs the Machiavellian Personality Profile first developed in Christie and Geis (1970). The 'mach scale' is a series of assertions derived from Machiavelli's *The Prince* with which respondents can either agree or disagree. The scale was constructed to identify instrumental behaviour a component of which is the willingness to violate social norms for one's own benefit and, consequently, the prior hypothesis of the researchers was that instrumental behaviour would correlate (negatively) with trust and, in particular, trustworthiness. If so, then social capital could be measured in a less direct, but much cheaper, manner using the mach scale because people who exhibited Machiavellian tendencies would be less trusting and trustworthy.

As it turns out, there is a relationship between observed trusting behaviour and the mach scale, but it is not as strong as originally hypothesized. After controlling for demographic characteristics of the participants, the mach scale significantly predicts the amount someone sends as a first mover in the trust game. More specifically, as people become 'higher machs' (that is, more instrumental), they send less to their counterpart and therefore appear to trust less. This relationship does not hold, however, for trustworthiness. Here higher machs are no more or less trustworthy after controlling for personal characteristics and the amount sent. Hence these results are an example of how to calibrate or modify the study of trust. Instead of asking direct questions about trusting behaviour, which do not seem to measure trust very well, one might use the mach scale as a proxy for trusting behaviour.

To conclude our analysis of studies which employ both data-gathering techniques we consider the work of Juan-Camilo Cardenas, which is probably the most integrated example of social capital research because he not only utilizes an extensive survey and runs experiments, but he does so in the field with specific populations of participants. Cardenas has done an extensive study of cooperation in rural Columbia (Cardenas *et al.* 2000; Cardenas, 1999; also see Chapter 8 of this volume). In both papers, Cardenas examines the propensity of peasants to cooperate in a game similar to the VCM, called 'the common-pool resource game'.[12] In this game participants cooperate by refraining from overextracting a commonly held resource (such as a fishery or forest). In addition, he compares behaviour in the game with demographic characteristics of the individual participants (for example, sex, age and wealth) to find intuitive and interesting results.

Cardenas *et al.* (2000) examine the level of cooperation in villages where the participants actually face social dilemmas in their daily lives. In one region, participants gather resources from a local mangrove, which is held collectively. In another region, participants make handcrafts from fibres collected in a neighbouring, collectively held, forest. The authors show that peasants are able to restrict endogenously the consumption of a commonly held resource and the effect becomes much stronger when communication is allowed. In contrast, when the experimenter simulates a governmental solution to overextraction (that is, probabilistic monitoring by the experimenter who takes on the role of the government), the level of extraction increases significantly after an initial decline. Here Cardenas provides strong evidence of the implications of policy on endogenously maintained social capital. When government monitoring is introduced, the institution crowds out participants' inherent propensity to cooperate and the result is even more dramatic when compared to the near Pareto-optimal levels of extraction present when participants can regulate themselves using cheap talk.

In the second paper, Cardenas (1999), the author compares cooperative behaviour with survey demographics. He finds that actual wealth and occupation explain cooperation in addition to a constructed measure of social distance. More specifically, the results suggest that the participants who are more willing to cooperate have less real wealth, and are employed in occupations which revolve around commons dilemmas. Lastly, he also shows that, as the average social distance increases, participants cooperate less. These results are interesting and important because they contradict commonly held beliefs that influence policy. In particular, these results falsify the claim that the poor are more likely to destroy a commons (perhaps because of lower discount factors – another hypothesis that could be tested experimentally).

CONCLUSION

Recent results from experimental economics indicate that research on social capital should be the domain of both survey and field experimental methods because the two complement each other. Surveys are perhaps the best method for collecting demographic data, but behavioural questions on surveys should be calibrated by experiments and experiments should be the primary source of information when incentives are important. Further, it is important to stress the external benefits of conducting both surveys and experiments. Once enough data has been collected on the relationship between true (that is, experimental) behaviour and self-reports of behaviour, it will be possible to write new surveys that are much less costly to conduct than filed experiments and provide data that can be linked to and calibrated against real behaviour.

We have identified four experiments that are (relatively) easily adaptable for use in the field: the trust game which measures trust, the ultimatum game which measures the strength of norms of reciprocity, the dictator game which measures altruism and the voluntary contribution game which measures the propensity to cooperate. In fact, a number of these experiments have already been used in the field. Cooperation has been studied by Cardenas *et al.* (2000), trust has been studied by Barr (1999), and norms of fairness, reciprocity and generosity have been examined in Henrich (2000) and Carpenter *et al.* (2001). However, only a few studies have used both survey and experimental methods, suggesting that our understanding of social capital will continue to deepen as investigators increasingly measure behaviour, behaviourally.

NOTES

*   The author thanks Juan Camilo Cardenas and Corinna Noelke for inspiring discussions of this topic, and the National Science and MacArthur Foundations for financial assistance.
1.   This survey, conducted in the USA is available at *www.planetproject.com*.
2.   This problem has also plagued the contingent valuation approach to valuing environmental quality and resources (Harrison and Rutstrom, forthcoming).
3.   Another reason survey measures may not predict behaviour is that respondents frame or generalize the questions asked differently than the researchers who collect the data. This is a framing issue that also can be addressed experimentally. Credit belongs to Tom Kelly for pointing this out.
4.   One reason for the lack of external validity is that, while students are a nice cross-section of the general population (that is, the cheapest and most accessible cross-section), they may or may not have experience in the kind of social dilemma situations in which social capital is thought to be relevant. For example, students may consider free-riding on other group members when it comes time to write a collective term paper, but this is a much different decision than whether or not to defect in dilemma situations such as the provision of clean water in an urban slum or to restrain from overharvesting a common source of fish or some other regenerating, but fragile, resource.
5.   The trust game is also used in Barr (1999), Cox (1999) and Croson and Buchan (1999).
6.   The question of stakes often arises. While some experimentalists treat the stakes issue as a 'solved' problem, citing the numerous ultimatum bargaining studies that have been run for as much as three months' wages which show very robust results (Cameron, 1998). The question is still open for other games such as the dictator game (see Carpenter *et al.*, 2001).
7.   Figure 7.1 is generated by pooling the data from Berg *et al.* (1995) and Burks *et al.* (2000), which use mostly identical procedures.
8.   The ultimatum game is perhaps the most studied bargaining experiment. Interesting variations of the standard game are Blount (1995), Croson (1996a), Eckel and Grossman (1996b) and Prasnikar and Roth (1992). Also consider Camerer and Thaler (1995), Roth (1995) and Davis and Holt (1993) for reviews.
9.   Table 7.1 should be used for rough comparisons only because of protocol and stakes differences. One should also note that the Roth *et al.* (1991) data are from the first round of a ten-round game.
10. For another field experimental study making a similar point about the dislocating effects of resettlement, the reader should see Barr (1999) who uses the trust game.
11. Again, note that Table 7.3 is only useful for rough comparisons because specifics of the experiments often differ. Additionally, note that the data listed under the Croson (1996b) columns have been estimated from a graph in the original paper.
12. This game is studied extensively in Ostrom *et al.* (1992) and Ostrom *et al.* (1994).

REFERENCES

Andreoni, James (1988), 'Why free ride? Strategies and learning in public good experiments', *Journal of Public Economics*, **37**, 291–304.

Barr, Abigail (1999), 'The effects of social disruption on bargaining and investment behavior: an experimental study from Zimbabwe', mimeo.

Ben-Ner, Avner and Louis Putterman (1999), 'Reciprocity in a two part dictator game', mimeo.

Berg, Joyce, John Dickaut and Kevin McCabe (1995), 'Trust, reciprocity and social history', *Games and Economic Behavior*, **10**, 122–42.

Bertrand, Marianne and Sendhil Mullainathan (2001), 'Do people mean what they say? Implications for subjective survey data', *American Economic Review Papers and Proceedings*, **91**, 67–72.

Blount, Sally (1995), 'When social outcomes aren't fair: the effect of causal attribution on preferences', *Organizational Behavior & Human Decision Processes*, **62**, 131–44.

Bornstein, G., E. Winter and H. Goren (1996), 'Experimental study of repeated team-games', *European Journal of Political Economy*, **12**, 629–39.

Bowles, Samuel, Jeffrey Carpenter and Herbert Gintis (2000), 'Mutual monitoring in teams: the effects of residual claimancy and reciprocity', mimeo.

Brewer, M. (1979), 'In-group bias in the minimal intergroup situation: a cognitive–motivational analysis', *Psychological Bulletin*, **86**, 307–24.

Burks, Steven, Jeffrey Carpenter and Eric Verhoogen (2000), 'Playing both roles in the trust game: the golden rule and machiavellian behavior', mimeo.

Camerer, Colin and Richard Thaler (1995), 'Anomalies: ultimatums, dictators and manners', *Journal of Economic Perspectives*, **9**, 209–19.

Cameron, Lisa A. (1999), 'Raising the stakes on the ultimatum game: experimental evidence from Indonesia', *Economic Enquiry*, **37** (1), January, 47–59.

Cardenas, Juan-Camilo (1999), 'Real wealth and experimental cooperation: evidence from field experiments', mimeo.

Cardenas, Juan-Camilo, J. Stranlund and C. Willis (2000), 'Effectiveness of communication and regulation in local commons: some evidence from experiments in the field', *World Development*, **28**, 1719–33.

Carpenter, Jeffrey (1999), 'Mutual monitoring in teams: theory and experiments', mimeo.

Carpenter, Jeffrey, Stephen Burks, Eric Verhoogen and Gary Carpenter (2001), 'High stakes bargaining with non-students', mimeo.

Christie, R. and F. Geis (eds) (1970), *Studies in Machiavellianism*, New York: Academic Press.

Cox, James (1999), 'Trust, reciprocity and other-regarding preferences of individuals and groups', mimeo.

Croson, Rachel (1996a), 'Information in ultimatum experiments: an experimental study', *Journal of Economic Behavior and Organization*, **30**, 197–213.

Croson, Rachel (1996b), 'Partners and strangers revisited', *Economics Letters*, **53**, 25–32.

Croson, Rachel and Nancy Buchan (1999), 'Gender and culture: international experimental evidence from trust games', *American Economic Review* (papers and proceedings), **89**, 386–91.

Davis, Douglas and Charles Holt (1993), *Experimental Economics*, Princeton: Princeton University Press.

Eckel, C. and P. Grossman (1996a), 'Altruism in anonymous dictator games', *Games and Economic Behavior*, **16**, 181–91.

Eckel, C. and P. Grossman (1996b), 'Chivalry and solidarity in ultimatum games', mimeo .

Fehr, Ernst and Simon Gaechter (1999), 'Cooperation and punishment in public goods experiments', *American Economic Review*, **90**, 980–94.

Fehr, Ernst and Klaus Schmidt (1999), 'A theory of fairness, competition and cooperation', *Quarterly Journal of Economics*, **114** (3), 817–68.

Fehr, Ernst, Simon Gaechter and Georg Kirchsteiger (1997), 'Reciprocity as a contract enforcement device', *Econometrica*, **65**, 833–60.

Fershtman, C. and U. Gneezy (1998), 'Trust and discrimination in a segmented society', mimeo.

Forsythe, R., J. Horowitz, N. Savin and M. Sefton (1994), 'Fairness in simple bargaining experiments', *Games and Economic Behavior*, **6**, 347–69.

Fukuyama, Francis (1995), *Trust: the Social Virtues and the Creation of Prosperity*, New York: The Free Press.

Glaeser, Edward, David Laibson and Bruce Sacerdote (2000), 'The economic approach to social capital', NBER Working Paper 7728 .

Glaeser, E., D. Laibson, J. Scheinkman and C. Soutter (1999), 'What is social capital? The determinants of trust and trustworthiness', NBER Working Paper 7216.

Gueth, Werner, Rolf Schmittberger and Bernd Schwarz (1982), 'An experimental analysis of ultimatum bargaining', *Journal of Economic Behavior and Organization*, **3**, 367–88.

Harrison, Glenn and Elisabet Rutstrom (forthcoming), 'Experimental evidence of hypothetical bias in value elicitation methods', in C.R. Plott and V.L. Smith (eds), *Handbook of Experimental Economic Results*, New York: Elsevier Press.

Henrich, Joe (2000), 'Does culture matter in economic behavior? Ultimatum game bargaining among the Machiguenga Indians of the Peruvian Amazon', *American Economic Review*, **90**.

Hoffman, E., K. McCabe, J. Shachat and V. Smith (1994), 'Preferences, property rights and anonymity in bargaining games', *Games and Economic Behavior*, **7**, 346–80.

Isaac, Mark and James Walker (1988), 'Communication and free-riding behavior: the voluntary contribution mechanism', *Economic Inquiry*, **26**, 585–608.

Isaac, Mark, James Walker and S. Thomas (1984), 'Divergent evidence on free-riding: an experimental examination of possible explanations', *Public Choice*, **43**, 113–49.

Isham, Jonathan and Satu Kähkönen (2002), 'How do participation and social capital affect community-based water projects? Evidence from central Java, Indonesia', in Christiaan Grootaert and Thierry Van Bastelaer (eds), *Social Capital and Development*, Cambridge: Cambridge University Press.

Isham, Jonathan and Satu Kähkönen (forthcoming), 'Institutional determinants of the impact of community-based water projects: evidence from Sri Lanka and India', *Economic Development and Cultural Change*.

Kollock, P. (1996), 'Transforming social dilemmas: group identity and cooperation', in P. Danielson (ed.), *Modelling Rational Moral Agents*, Oxford: Oxford University Press.

Ledyard, John (1995), 'Public goods: a survey of experimental research', in John Kagel and Alvin Roth (eds), *The Handbook of Experimental Economics*, Princeton: Princeton University Press, pp. 111–94.

Molinas, J.R. (1998), 'The impact of inequality, gender and social capital on local-level cooperation', *World Development*, **26** (3), 413–31.

Ockenfels, Axel and Joachim Weimann (1999), 'Types and patterns: an experimental East–West-German comparison of cooperation and solidarity', *Journal of Public Economics*, **71**, 275–87.

Ostrom, Elinor, Roy Gardner and James Walker (1994), *Rules, Games and Common-Pool Resources*, Ann Arbor: University of Michigan Press.

Ostrom, Elinor, James Walker and Roy Gardner (1992), 'Covenants with and without a sword: self-governance is possible', *American Political Science Review*, **86**, 404–17.

Prasnikar, V. and A. Roth (1992), 'Considerations of fairness and strategy: experimental data from sequential games', *Quarterly Journal of Economics*, 865–88.

Putnam, Robert (1995), 'Bowling alone: America's declining social capital', *Journal of Democracy*, **6**, 65–87.

Roth, Alvin (1995), 'Bargaining experiments', in John Kagel and Alvin Roth (eds), *The Handbook of Experimental Economics*, Princeton: Princeton University Press, pp. 253–348.

Roth, Alvin, Vesna Prasnikar, Masahiro Okuno-Fujiwara and Shmuel Zamir (1991), 'Bargaining and market behavior in Jerusalem, Ljubljana, Pittsburgh and Tokyo: an experimental study', *American Economic Review*, **81**, 1068–95.

8. Rethinking local commons dilemmas: lessons from experimental economics in the field

Juan-Camilo Cardenas[1]

This chapter considers two fundamental questions related to the role of social capital in the management of common-pool resources (CPRs) like local fisheries or forest reserves. Why do some local groups around the world succeed in collectively managing CPRs while other local groups drive such resources close to exhaustion? Why do some individuals who extract resources from CPRs behave like *homo economicus* – that is, act only to maximize their own welfare without regard for others' welfare – while others do not? While many theoretical and empirical studies have addressed these questions (Ostrom, 1990; Putnam, 1993; Bowles, 1999), much of the discussion of CPR management still does not refer to new theoretical, empirical and experimental contributions that have emerged since Garret Hardin's prediction about the 'tragedy of the commons' (Hardin, 1968) and Mancur Olson's characterization of 'the logic of collective action' (Olson, 1965). This chapter emphasizes those contributions.

The chapter begins by highlighting recent advances in the analysis of CPRs. The chapter then presents a set of results from field experiments conducted in actual CPR settings in rural Colombia. The results of these experiments provide empirical evidence of some of the new developments in the literature, thereby shedding additional light on the limits of the conventional view about CPR dilemmas and human behaviour. The chapter concludes by highlighting the prospects for a methodological approach that includes economic experiments in the field and in the classroom, and in which the participants (villagers or students) become an active part of the analysis.

MAKING THE COMMONS LESS TRAGIC AND MORE COMPLEX

Garret Hardin (1968) famously argued that access to a commons would 'bring ruin to all'. Mancur Olson (1965) explained that, without selective incentives, coordinated action to provide a collective good would not occur. Yet the fate of all commons is not tragic, and collective goods do get produced through coordinated action. As detailed in this section, outcomes that diverge from the predicted tragedy depend on the nature of access to a commons and the characteristics of the local institutional setting.

First, the so-called 'tragedy' is more likely to occur in the conditions of open access, when potential users cannot be prevented from exploiting a divisible natural resource (Bromley and Cernea, 1989).[2] By contrast, when potential users can be prevented from exploiting a CPR, the tragedy is less likely when local institutions conform to a set of design principles. These include clearly defined boundaries, congruence between appropriation rules and local conditions, collective choice arrangements that can be modified, monitoring and sanctions, and collective-resolution mechanisms (Ostrom, 1990). For example, the fishers of Alanya, Turkey, have developed an arrangement for rotating among a set of fishing locations so that no overcapitalization occurs and the fishery, their common property resource, is managed sustainably (Berkes, 1989).

Under what related conditions is the governance of a local commons improved? First, norms of reciprocity partially determine the behaviour of group members who face a collective action dilemma. Second, communication among group members prior to the individual decision is critical: 'exchanging mutual commitment, increasing trust, creating and re-enforcing norms, and developing a group identity appear to be the most important processes that make communication efficacious' (Ostrom, 1998). Third, monitoring alone does not help reduce the aggregate level of extraction from the common pool; credible sanctions involving the actual enforcement of rules are required (Ostrom *et al.*, 1994; Moir, 1997). Fourth, in contrast to the prediction in Olson (1965), asset inequality can diminish the provision of the public good. For example, the net effect of the behaviour of the privileged group depends on several factors: rather than cooperate or free-ride, rich members may simply leave a group that is attempting to provide a public good (Dayton-Johnson and Bardhan, forthcoming). Furthermore, different types of inequalities – in assets, in exit and fallback options, and in enforcement powers – will affect the preservation of a local commons (Bowles and Gintis, 1997; Bardhan *et al.*, 1998)[3]

To illustrate, consider a group of farmers in a village who are trying to improve soil quality with soil erosion control practices, as in the case of the Groupement Naam in Burkina Faso (Smale and Ruttan, 1997).[4] One farm's isolated investment in an erosion control barrier is not enough; a critical number of farmers must undertake the investment. When the individual investment cost is low enough or the expected benefits from cooperation are large enough for even the smallest farmer, individual cooperation is likely:

building erosion control barriers will be efficient for both the individual and the collective. In such a case, larger landowners will have an extra incentive to conserve because of their larger stake in the commons. However, smaller land-holders have less of an incentive since their stake is small (Baland and Platteau, 1997a).

Overall, these results point to a richer view of CPR problems. In particular, they suggest that self-governing institutions based on reciprocal fairness among community members may emerge, thereby inducing solutions to local commons problems that require neither external intervention nor the reallocation and individualization of property rights.

Testing New Theories with Experiments

Many economic experiments have shown that, in perfectly competitive systems, individuals behave as the *homo economicus* model predicts, and markets can effectively solve allocation and distribution problems. The set of experiments summarized in this section shows that, in public good and CPR settings, individuals do not always behave as *homo economicus*: the tragedy of the commons can often be avoided.

As Carpenter discusses in Chapter 7 of the present volume, experimental economists began in the 1990s to study individual and group behaviour in the presence of different externalities. Experimental studies on voluntary public goods provision and CPRs expanded the evidence on the complexity of individual behaviour when facing a group-based dilemma. Ledyard (1995) surveyed much of the experimental work on public goods and described a set of weak and strong factors that help to explain the conditions under which behaviour does not yield the Nash suboptimal equilibrium.[5] Ostrom *et al.* (1994) used experimental techniques to establish a new area of research on institutional factors that induce cooperative behaviours in groups facing CPR dilemmas.[6]

The lessons from this area of research are that the game-theoretical prediction is not always consistent with actual behaviour in the lab or the field and that decentralized (self-governing) mechanisms and institutions do not always guarantee a socially efficient use of the commons. Many equilibria can result from the interactions of institutional factors and incentives that affect each individual's decision to extract or conserve a resource. Moreover, the experimental evidence from the public goods and the CPR literatures shows a wide variation within and across groups that cannot be explained by variables controlled in the laboratory. One plausible explanation is that many types of 'rational' agents are found in groups. For example, Ostrom (1999) uses an evolutionary model with two types, rational egoists and conditional cooperators, in a collective action setting. When members of these two types interact, the resulting equilibrium depends on the fraction of each type in the population. Generally, evolutionary arguments that explain multiple equilibria (Gintis, 2000; Bowles, 2002) provide a rich set of modelling techniques for the study of CPR dilemmas.

BRINGING THE EXPERIMENTAL LAB TO THE FIELD

For the study detailed in the rest of this chapter, an experimental CPR dilemma was brought to the field. The experiment, undertaken in the summer of 1998 in three Colombian villages, included 200 actual users of local CPRs. As summarized in this section, the experimental results complement new theories and evidence on local commons dilemmas.[7]

The First Stage: Resource Extraction without Communication

In the experiment, each participant in a group of eight participants was asked to make repeated economic decisions. The participants were compensated, in kind and cash, in proportion to their decisions. (They were also compensated for the time that they spent participating in the experiment and attending a follow-up community workshop. The participants' average earnings were equivalent to earnings from two days of minimum-wage work.)

The first stage of the experiment had eight rounds. During each round, each participant had to choose the number of months (from 0 to 8) that she would allocate to extract resources from a jointly used forest. To guide this choice, each participant received a pay-off table (Table 8.1) with the possible outcomes (in Colombian pesos) for each player in each round: critically, the outcomes depend on her decision (the columns in Table 8.1) and the decisions by other participants (the rows in Table 8.1). With this information at hand, each participant was given time to choose her 'months in the forest'. A monitor then added the months chosen by all eight participants and publicly announced this total. Each player was then asked to calculate her earnings in that round by finding the cell at the intersection of her choice and this total. In the first stage, participants were not allowed to cooperate at any time during this process.

The pay-off matrix illustrates the group's CPR dilemma: each participant's earnings are increasing in her individual allocation but decreasing in the group's total allocation. If each participant chose only one month in the forest, the social optimum solution would be achieved: group earnings would be maximized at 645 pesos per participant.[8] If each player in the group chose six months, all eight players would find themselves in the Nash suboptimal equilibrium, with earnings at 155 pesos per participant.

Table 8.1   Individual pay-offs and Nash responses in a field experiment

Their months in the forest	My months in the forest									
		0	1	2	3	4	5	6	7	8
0		619	670	719	767	813	856	896	933	967
1		619	669	717	764	809	851	890	926	959
2		617	667	714	760	804	845	883	918	950
3		615	664	711	756	798	838	875	909	940
4		613	660	706	750	792	831	867	900	929
5		609	656	701	744	784	822	857	889	917
6		605	651	695	737	776	813	847	877	905
7		600	645	688	729	767	803	836	865	891
8		595	638	680	720	757	792	824	852	877
9		588	631	672	711	747	780	811	838	862
10		581	623	663	700	735	768	797	823	846
11		573	614	653	689	723	755	783	808	830
12		565	605	642	678	711	741	768	792	813
13		556	594	631	665	697	726	752	775	795
14		546	583	619	652	683	711	736	758	776
15		536	572	606	638	668	695	719	739	757
16		525	560	593	624	653	678	701	721	737
17		513	547	579	609	636	661	683	701	717
18		501	534	565	594	620	643	664	681	696
19		488	520	550	578	603	625	645	661	674
20		475	506	535	561	585	606	625	640	653
21		461	491	519	544	567	587	605	619	630
22		447	476	502	527	548	567	584	597	608
23		433	460	485	509	529	547	563	575	585
24		418	444	468	490	510	527	541	553	561

25	402	428	451	472	490	506	520	530	538	25
26	387	411	433	453	470	485	498	507	514	26
27	371	394	415	434	450	464	476	484	490	27
28	355	377	396	414	430	443	453	461	466	28
29	338	359	378	395	409	421	431	438	442	29
30	322	341	359	375	389	400	409	415	418	30
31	305	324	341	355	368	378	386	392	394	31
32	288	306	322	336	347	357	364	368	371	32
33	272	288	303	316	327	335	341	345	347	33
34	255	270	284	296	306	314	319	323	324	34
35	238	253	266	277	286	293	297	300	300	35
36	221	235	247	257	265	272	276	278	278	36
37	205	218	229	238	245	251	254	256	255	37
38	189	200	211	219	226	231	233	234	233	38
39	173	184	193	201	206	211	213	213	212	39
40	157	167	175	182	188	191	193	193	191	40
41	142	151	159	165	169	172	174	173	171	41
42	127	135	142	148	152	154	155	154	152	42
43	113	120	126	131	134	136	137	136	133	43
44	99	106	111	115	118	119	119	118	115	44
45	86	92	961	100	102	103	103	101	99	45
46	73	78	82	86	87	88	88	86	83	46
47	61	66	69	72	73	74	73	71	68	47
48	51	54	57	59	60	61	60	58	55	48
49	40	44	46	48	49	48	47	45	43	49
50	31	34	36	37	38	37	36	34	32	50
51	23	25	27	28	28	28	27	25	23	51
52	16	18	19	20	20	19	18	17	15	52
53	10	12	12	13	13	12	11	10	8	53
54	6	7	7	7	7	7	6	5	4	54
55	2	3	3	3	3	3	2	2	1	55

Their months in the forest

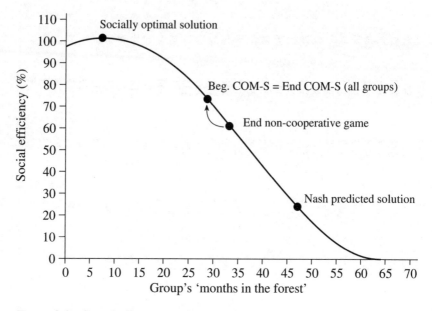

Figure 8.1   Social efficiency with no coordinating institution

   This pay-off structure creates a curve of social efficiency, shown in Figure 8.1, where group efficiency is shown as a function of group effort.[9] At the socially optimal solution (each player allocating one month) social efficiency is 100 per cent; at the Nash solution (each player allocating six months) social efficiency is only at 24 per cent (155×8 pesos$/645 \times 8$ pesos $= 0.24$).

   How did the experimental results from the first stage – with no coordinating institution – compare to these two possibilities? As shown by the point 'End non-cooperative game' in Figure 8.1, participants in the 15 groups that faced these incentives did not regularly choose the game-theoretic Nash result. In the last three rounds of the first stage, the groups chose an average of 34 months in the forest, for a group efficiency of almost 60 per cent. Under a setting of private, non-coordinated choices, the symmetric Nash prediction does not accurately predict the individual behaviour.

The Second Stage: Resource Extraction with Communication or External Regulation

In the second stage of the game, players faced one of two alternative new rules over ten additional rounds: the chance to cooperate or external regulation. Ten village groups faced the first alternative, in which they were able to converse for five minutes per round – before allocation decisions were made. (Threats or promises of earnings transfers were not permitted during conversations.)

What behaviour was observed in this new setting? Confirming a widespread, consistent pattern from other experimental evidence, face-to-face communication induced more cooperative behaviour. The results reject the 'cheap talk' argument, that when agents make promises with no enforceable consequences, promises are not fulfilled.[10] On average, as summarized by the point 'Beg-COM-S' in Figure 8.1, these ten groups improved social efficiency by about 10 per cent (from 60 per cent to 70 per cent).

However, behaviour across groups varied widely. Although each group faced the same incentives and rules in similar environments, some groups almost achieved the socially optimal solution, while others achieved almost no improvement from the non-cooperative first round. This wide variation, consistent with other evidence (Ostrom *et al.* 1994), can be partially explained by the evolution of specific conditions in each group. For instance, the development of norms of reciprocity based on choices made in previous rounds is likely to determine choices in subsequent rounds. Moreover, emotions such as guilt, respect and spite are likely to have affected each individual's choice – in ways that are unique to the personalities and repeated conversations in each group

Emotions are hard to observe, but one can ask: do participants' demographic, economic and social characteristics explain some of the observed variance in behaviour? Empirical analysis of the group decisions, summarized in Figure 8.2, shows that group composition partially determined the effectiveness of the intra-group communication. For these ten groups, the standard deviation of the wealth of group participants was measured (based on individual ownership of land, livestock and equipment.)[11] The three least homogeneous groups barely improved their efficiency through communication: they achieved efficiency gains of only 3 per cent (compared to the first stage). By contrast, the three most homogeneous groups achieved gains of almost 30 per cent by the final round (for an overall efficiency level of almost 90 per cent).[12]

Furthermore, holding other factors constant, players within all groups chose fewer months in the forest if the difference between their wealth and the average of the wealth of the other seven players was smaller.[13] In addition, players whose real-life income was more dependent on the use of a commons (and less dependent on private assets like land) behaved more cooperatively (again holding other factors constant). Finally, there was no statistically significant relationship between behaviour and demographic variables like age, education or gender, at individual or group levels. Overall, outcomes were improved through group communication and self-government, particularly when a smaller social distance separated players. Group composition and an

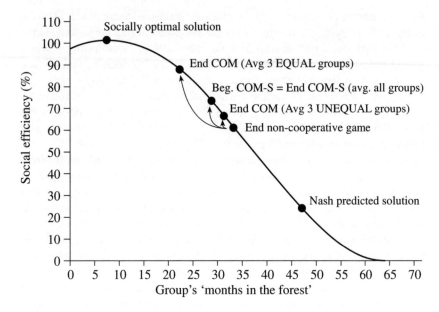

Figure 8.2   Social efficiency with intra-group communication

individual's personal experience in similar CPR dilemmas significantly affect choices about resource extraction.

Next, five village groups faced the second alternative, in which an external regulator with enforcement capabilities (but with imperfect information and monitoring capacity) could affect individual earnings. In this case, participants were told at the end of the first stage that an external regulator (who wanted the group to achieve the socially optimal solution) would try to enforce a rule that players choose only one month. Each participant faced a 1/16 (random) probability of being inspected by the regulator at the end of each round: if she were not in compliance with the 'one month' rule, she would pay a penalty of 100 pesos (approximately 15 per cent of each individual's earnings, had the entire group complied) for each month in excess of the rule. Given the expected penalty, the game-theoretical prediction is that this rule would raise social efficiency from 24 per cent (the Nash equilibrium result) to 42 per cent.

These benchmarks and the experimental results from this set of groups are summarized in Figure 8.3. At the end of the first stage, these groups achieved about 60 per cent of social efficiency, a group extraction effort of 35 months. After the new rule was established for the second stage, the immediate reaction of most players in the first round was to comply with the rule (point Beg. REG-S in Figure 8.3) by reducing their months in the forest: now the groups achieved about 80 per cent of social efficiency. But in the next round, several

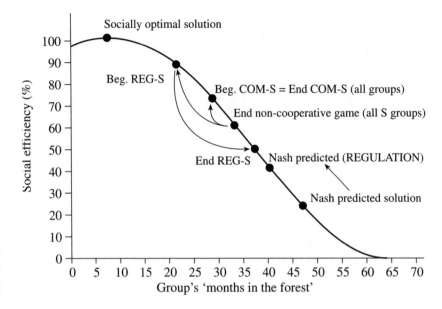

Figure 8.3 Social efficiency with outside regulation

players increased their months in the forest, and this behaviour continued over the next few rounds. Negative reciprocity began to affect individual behaviour: increased extraction rapidly drove down efficiency levels. In fact, even by the third round, the groups were back to the same efficiency levels achieved in the first stage *without the regulator*. In the subsequent rounds, efficiency continued to decrease (to the point End REG-S for the last three rounds of stage 2). Compared to either the first stage under a non-cooperative game or the alternative second stage with the group communication, the groups under the external regulation ended up even closer to the Nash suboptimal equilibrium.[14] One plausible explanation for this behaviour (further detailed in Cardenas *et al.*, 2000) is that the explicit monetary incentives drove the partici-pants away from group-oriented behaviour and towards more individualistic actions (Frey, 1997; Frey and Jegen, 1999).

An Alternative CPR Game with Asymmetric Marginal Returns

In the case of many CPRs – for example, local forest reserves with a hetero-geneous dependent population that includes indigenous extractors and commercial loggers – the marginal return from not contributing to a CPR may be asymmetric. That is, the opportunity cost of their effort (what they could gain by expending time and resources in the next best private alternative) is vastly different across group members. Indigenous extractors, for example, may depend more on a local forest reserve because the marginal return on their private alternative is so much lower.

Olson (1965) first explored the theoretical effect of intra-group inequality in public good settings. He argued that, if a member of a 'privileged group' benefits individually from providing a public good, she might provide it despite the anticipated free-riding of other group members. That is, if the marginal returns from contributing to the collective action are higher for some, these members of the privileged group are more likely to cooperate.[15]

This aspect of the CPR problem was also explored in this set of experiments. In each of five new groups, each participant was (randomly) assigned one of two pay-off tables. Two participants received 'high pay-off' tables (H) that included a relatively high marginal return on months *not* allocated to the forest; the remaining six participants received 'low pay-off' tables (L) with a relatively low marginal return. All participants were informed of this asymmetry and knew which received the H and L tables, respectively. Otherwise, tables H and L have a similar incentive structure to Table 8.1: each participant's earnings are increasing in her individual allocation but decreasing in the group's total allocation. With these asymmetric incentives, the Nash theoretical equilibrium is that players with L tables allocate all eight months in the forest, and players with H tables allocate no months.

These asymmetric groups (HL) went through the same two stages as the symmetric baseline groups (S): in the first stage, no communication; in the second stage, five minutes of group discussion at the start of each round.

Once again, as summarized in Figure 8.4, the experimental results failed to confirm the Nash theoretical behaviour. (Note that the socially optimal and Nash benchmarks are the same for the HL and S groups because the average group marginal return on the private alternative was the same and the marginal returns from forest extraction were equal for all group members.) First, compare the results at the end of the first stage for the two groups: the HL groups achieved an efficiency level of 72 per cent; the S groups achieved 60 per cent. This is consistent with Olson's proposition: heterogeneity seems to increase collective action. However, these outcomes evidently were not related to the 'privileged group' argument: by the end of the first stage, it was the six players with the L tables that exhibited more cooperative behaviour. At the levels of high extraction predicted by the Nash equilibrium, earnings were quite low, so any reduction in individual extraction would bring improvements to the group *and* to each individual.

The introduction of communication in the second stage reinforced this cooperative behaviour. Group discussions among all eight participants focused on reducing individual months in the forest, but only the L players showed statistically significant changes towards more cooperative behaviour. The H

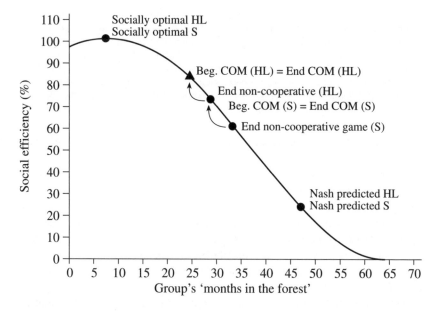

Figure 8.4   Social efficiency with asymmetric marginal returns

players remained with the same individual levels chosen before communication. This combination of factors induced a group increase in earnings, and therefore in social efficiency, as shown in Figure 8.4.[16]

To summarize, the experimental evidence detailed in this section accords with recent theoretical models, fieldwork and other experimental work on CPRs. These field-based experiments demonstrate that many institutional factors determine whether groups can approach the socially optimal solution. In particular, an institutional setting that permits communication among homogenous agents, without the intervention of a regulator, can promote relatively effective 'governing of the commons'.

CONCLUSION: LESSONS FOR STUDYING AND TEACHING COMMONS DILEMMAS

These field-based experiments among actual CPR users in three Colombian villages took to heart the reflections of Sanz de Santamaria (1992), who highlights in his own economic research the legacy of Paulo Freire on rethinking the social scientist–subject relationship and the student–teacher relationship:

Collective participation by academics *and* the investigated communities [is crucially important] in the processes of production and use of economic knowledge that will affect the living conditions of these communities. Attaining this participation requires tremendous efforts in the construction of communication channels between science (economists) and society (the investigated communities). These communication channels can be constructed only if economists are willing to stop ignoring (abstracting from) in their concrete research practices the cultural complexity of how the communities they investigate perceive their own realities.

This section discusses how field-based experiments can enhance these two relationships.

After these experiments were completed and the data were partially analysed, each set of participants was invited to join a one-day community workshop that was designed to promote a two-way information flow. The information provided by the researchers about the behaviour of the subjects – the main trends and differences across groups and the effects of the different experimental treatments – was ethically motivated: to assure the participants of the well-motivated reasons for the experiments, the monetary incentives and the different rules.

The information provided by the subjects to the researchers was scientifically motivated. Given the overall variation of outcomes, the researchers sought plausible explanations for behaviour within and across groups. For this, the community workshops proved invaluable. Participants gave a variety of credible explanations (that led to the exploration of some of the hypotheses detailed in the previous section): for example, the 'social distance' hypothesis about why some groups were more effective in increasing group earnings through face-to-face communication. Further, these conversations demonstrated that preconceived hypotheses, for example that lack of education or variation in age might create methodological problems and affect the results, were incorrect.

Overall, when can field-based experiments like these yield richer results than laboratory experiments? First, in many field-based experiments, participants are familiar with the theoretical question under study (unlike, say, many college students). Therefore, their behaviour and reactions to institutional changes might be closer to reality. Accordingly, their experiences in similar settings can inform a subsequent participatory analysis of the problem. Second, a wider variation in participant characteristics, including demographic, economic and cultural variables that affect values and preferences brought into the lab, can better explain certain behaviours that seem unrelated to the experimental institutions. The lack of variation in college student pools can restrict such analysis. Third, within a field-based group, the relative familiarity among participants better enables the trust and recognition that affect decision making in social dilemmas. Institutions devised for governing CPRs build on a history of previous interactions among group members as well as a relatively high probability of reciprocal exchanges in the future.

One could argue that these factors bring more 'noise' to the experiment than is found in a more controlled laboratory setting. This is undoubtedly true. The proposition here is that such noise can be used as data. 'Real-world' (non-laboratory) complications influence real behaviour. Since participants would find it difficult not to bring their own tastes, preferences and experiences to an experiment, they should be accounted for explicitly. They can help explain the variation in behaviour that the experimental institutions and environment cannot, thereby enhancing research quality.

Similar reflections about allowing participants to be part of the analysis hold for the student–teacher relationship. The 'principles' textbook for experimental economics (Bergstrom and Miller, 1996) begins its preface thus: 'Taking a course in experimental economics is a little like going to a dinner at a cannibal's house. Sometimes you will be the diner, sometimes you will be part of the dinner, sometimes both.' In fact, active involvement in an experiment can significantly change the process of learning. Frank (1997) sought to determine whether participation in a simple classroom experiment, among students studying the tragedy of the commons, affected academic performance. On a multiple-choice test, those participating in the experiment and those present during the experiment outperformed those who were not exposed to it at all. In addition, experiments create opportunities for creative teacher–student interactions in the exploration of complex areas of economics where puzzles remain to be solved.

In summary, what are the methodological lessons of field-based experimental research for educators and policy makers concerned with CPR dilemmas? By bringing the lab experiment to the field, one can learn from and with actual commons users. It is they who face daily the decision to extract more or less fish, more or less firewood – and the decision to comply with, redefine or create rules of self-governance for improving social outcomes. And bringing experimental tools to the classroom can prove effective in creating a deeper (experiential) understanding of why a group may – or may not – manage sustainably a common-pool resource.

In both cases, the use of the term 'participant' rather than 'subject' captures this 'hands-on' approach. People as 'subjects' are mere sources of data as they respond to a survey or make choices in an experiment. People as 'participants' get involved in the experimental process and contribute from their own perspectives. Scholars and practitioners in other social sciences have for some time explored the value of participatory research, rapid rural appraisal and the like (Perez, 1988; Fals-Borda and Rahman, 1991). Economists, who have participated less in this exploration, could benefit greatly from considering such approaches, as illustrated by the examples and arguments given in this chapter.

NOTES

1. I would like to thank, above all, the people in Nuquí, Encino, Circasia and Filandia (Colombia) who opened their doors during 1998 and 1999 and allowed me to learn from their experience and knowledge about solving commons dilemmas from the bottom up. I must also thank the field practitioners and fellows from the Instituto de Investigación de Recursos Biológicos Alexander von Humboldt (Colombia), The World Wide Fund (WWF-Programa Colombia), and Fundación Natura (Colombia) who helped pre-test and conduct the experiments. Very special thanks to Luis Guillermo Baptiste and Sarah Hernandez at Humboldt, Carmen Candelo at WWF-Colombia, and Juan Gaviria, Nancy Vargas and Danilo Salas who worked at Natura at the time. Financial support for the field work was provided by the MacArthur Foundation, the Instituto Humboldt, the WWF Colombia programme and Fundación Natura. Thanks to Sam Bowles, Jeff Carpenter, Elinor Ostrom, John Stranlund, James Walker and Cleve Willis for advice at different stages of the research. And finally, thanks to the excellent job by the editors of this volume.
2. With strategic behaviour of individuals, the Nash game-theoretical equilibrium does not predict the open access point where average product is equal to average cost of extraction – the outcome that corresponds to the spirit of Hardin's prediction; only when the number of users approaches large numbers would the Nash solution coincide with the open access point (Cornes and Sandler, 1983).
3. The rural inequality and poverty questions are then related. In a methodologically interesting paper, Reardon and Vosti (1995) argue that there are several types or components of asset poverty in rural contexts, and each of them may have a different relation with possible environmental outcomes. Rural poverty could be in terms of natural resources assets, human resources poverty, or on-farm or off-farm assets.
4. Other types of local commons that involve a typical collective action dilemma at the village level are watershed management, wind erosion control, water erosion control, fishery management, forestry management, and weed and pest control management as discussed by Baland and Platteau (1977a).
5. The difference in the structure of incentives between a pure public good and a common-pool resource problem precludes a simple extrapolation between experimental results with these types of goods. Public goods and CPRs are excludable, but only CPRs are rival: one unit of a resource extracted from a CPR is no longer available to other potential users in the group, while one unit of the pure public good produced and consumed is still available for the benefit of others.
6. In addition, recent economic experiments that address the roles of transaction costs and incomplete information have generated results that challenge the core elements of the neoclassical paradigm (Kagel and Roth, 1995).
7. Further details of the experimental results that follow can be consulted in several sources (Cardenas, 2000a, 2000b; Cardenas *et al.*, 2000).
8. To see this, note that, if a participant defected from an allocation of one month to two months, she would gain an additional 37 units (from 645 to 688), but the remaining seven would each lose seven units, for a net loss to society of 12 units.
9. Group efficiency is calculated as the actual group's earnings divided by the potential group's earnings had they played the socially optimum strategy.
10. Non-cooperative game theory predicts that 'verbal promises to keep agreements lack credibility when individuals know they will face future choices where sticking with an agreement would be costly' (Ostrom *et al.*, 1994).
11. Other measures of heterogeneity like the Gini of wealth, Herfindahl, and the log of the variance of wealth all yield similar results.
12. These results are discussed in more detail in Cardenas (2000a). In a related study, Alesina and La Ferrara (1999), using a General Social Survey (1974–94) sample from US citizens, showed that participation in social activities as contributions to their neighbourhoods decreased for more unequal and more racially or ethnically heterogeneous groups.
13. See Cardenas (2000b) for a more detailed analysis of this result.

14. Note that the data points in the graph are inside the social efficiency curve: under the regulation regime, penalties result in social losses for the entire group, so that actual group earnings decrease.
15. Sandler (1992) develops the Olsonian propositions in detail and shows that, depending on the production function for the public good, that claim may or may not hold.
16. Chan *et al.* (1996) have shown similar results from a pure public goods experiment. Caution must be exercised in comparing these results because the CPR and public goods incentives are different in nature. Nevertheless, it is interesting to note that Chan *et al.* found that, when they introduced asymmetric income distributions within groups, aggregate contributions increased because of comparatively higher contributions by those endowed with higher income levels.

BIBLIOGRAPHY

Alesina, Alberto and Eliana La Ferrara (1999), 'Participation in heterogeneous communities', NBER Working Paper no. 7155, National Bureau of Economic Research, Washington, DC.

Andreoni, James (1995), 'Cooperation in public-goods experiments: kindness or confusion?', *American Economic Review*, **85** (September) (4), 891–904.

Axelrod, Robert (1984), *The Evolution of Cooperation*, New York: Basic Books HarperCollins.

Baland, Jean-Marie and Jean-Philippe Platteau (1996), *Halting Degradation of Natural Resources: Is There a Role for Rural Communities?*, Oxford and New York: Oxford University Press.

Baland, Jean-Marie and Jean-Philippe Platteau (1997a), 'Coordination problems in local-level resource management', *Journal of Development Economics*, **53**, 197–210.

Baland, Jean-Marie and Jean-Philippe Platteau (1997b), 'Wealth inequality and efficiency in the commons: the unregulated case', *Oxford Economic Papers*, **49**.

Bardhan, P., Samuel Bowles and Herbert Gintis (1998), 'Wealth inequality, wealth constraints and economic performance', in *Handbook on Income Distribution*, Amsterdam: North Holland.

Bergstrom, Theodore C. and John H. Miller (1996), *Experiments with Economic Principles*, New York: McGraw-Hill.

Berkes, Fikret (ed.) (1989), *Common Property Resources: Ecology and Community-Based Sustainable Development*, London: Belhaven Press.

Bowles, Samuel (1999), ' "Social Capital" and Community Governance', *Focus* **20** (Fall), 6–10.

Bowles, Samuel (2002), *Economic Institutions and Behavior: An Evolutionary Approach to Microeconomics*, Princeton, NJ: Princeton University Press.

Bowles, Samuel and Herbert Gintis (1997), 'The evolution of pro-social norms in communities', mimeo, Department of Economics, University of Massachusetts Amherst.

Bromley, D. and M. Cernea (1989), 'The management of the common property natural resources: some conceptual and operational fallacies', World Bank Discussion Paper no. 57, The World Bank, Washington, DC.

Cardenas, Juan-Camilo (2000a), 'Rural institutions, poverty and cooperation: learning from experiments and conjoint analysis in the field', PhD dissertation, Department of Resource Economics, University of Massachusetts Amherst.

Cardenas, Juan-Camilo (2000b), 'Real wealth and experimental cooperation: evidence from field experiments', Research Medals Competition, Second Global Development Network Conference GDN2000 Tokyo, 11–13 December. (http://www.gdnet.org/awards-shrtlist.htm).

Cardenas, Juan-Camilo, John K. Stranlund and Cleve E. Willis (2000), 'Local environmental control and institutional crowding out', *World Development* **10** (October) (28), 1719–33.

Chan, K., S. Mestelman, R. Moir and R.A. Muller (1996), 'The voluntary provision of public goods under varying income distributions', *Canadian Journal of Economics*, **29** (1), 54–69.

Cornes, Richard and Todd Sandler (1983), 'On Commons and Tragedies', *American Economic Review*, **4** (September) 73.

Dasgupta, Partha, Peter Hammond and Eric Maskin (1980), 'On imperfect information and optimal pollution control', *Review of Economic Studies*, **47**, 857–60.

Dayton-Johnson, Jeff and Pranab Bardhan (forthcoming), 'Inequality and conservation on the local commons: a theoretical exercise', *Economic Journal*.

Fals-Borda, Orlando and Muhammad Anisur Rahman (eds) (1991), *Action and Knowledge: Breaking the Monopoly with Participatory Action Research*, London: Intermediate Technology Publications, Apex Press.

Fehr, Ernst and Jean-Robert Tyran (1996), 'Institutions and reciprocal fairness', *Nordic Journal of Political Economy* (January), 1–18.

Field, Barry (1985), 'The Optimal Commons', *American Journal of Agriculture Economics* (May), 364–7.

Field, Barry C. (1989), 'The evolution of property rights', *Kyklos*, **3** (42), 319–45.

Frank, Bjorn (1997), 'The impact of classroom experiments on the learning of economics: an empirical investigation', *Economic Enquiry*, **XXXV** (October), 763–9.

Frey, Bruno (1997), *Not Just for the Money: an Economic Theory of Personal Motivation*, Cheltenham, UK and Lyme, US: Edward Elgar.

Frey, Bruno and Reto Jegen (1999), 'Crowding theory: a survey of empirical evidence', mimeo, University of Zurich.

Gintis, Herbert (2000), *Game Theory Evolving*, Princeton, NJ: Princeton University Press.

Hardin, Garret (1968), 'The tragedy of the commons', *Science*, **162**, 1245–8.

Kagel, John H. and Alvin E. Roth (1995), *The Handbook of Experimental Economics*, Princeton, NJ: Princeton University Press.

Ledyard, John O. (1995), 'Public goods: a survey of experimental research', in John H. Kagel and Alvin E. Roth (eds), *The Handbook of Experimental Economics*, Princeton, NJ: Princeton University Press.

Lewis, Tracy (1996), 'Protecting the environment when costs and benefits are privately known', *Rand Journal of Economics*, **27** (4), 819–47.

Loewenstein, George (1999), 'Experimental economies from the vantage point of behavioural economics', *The Economic Journal*, **109** (February), F25-F34.

Moir, Robert (1997), 'Costly monitoring and sanctioning in a common-pool resource environment', Department of Economics, University of Brunswick, Canada.

Olson, Mancur (1965), *The Logic of Collective Action: Public Goods and the Theory of Groups*, Cambridge, MA: Harvard University Press.

Ostrom, Elinor (1990), *Governing the Commons: The Evolution of Institutions for Collective Action*, Cambridge, UK and New York: Cambridge University Press.

Ostrom, Elinor (1998) 'A behavioral approach to the rational choice theory of collective action', *American Political Science Review*, **92** (March) (1), 1–22.

Ostrom, Elinor (1999), 'Context and collective action: four interactive building blocks for a family of explanatory theories', Working Paper W99–17, Workshop in Political Theory and Policy Analysis, Indiana University, Bloomington, IN.

Ostrom, Elinor, Roy Gardner and James Walker (1994), *Rules, Games and Common-Pool Resources*, Ann Arbor: University of Michigan Press.

Perez, Edelmira (1988), 'Enfoques Metodólogicos sobre la Investigación Participativa', *Cuadernos de Agroindustria y Economia Rural*, no. 20 Primer Semestre de 1988, Universidad Javeriana, Bogotá.

Putnam, R. (1993), *Making Democracy Work: Civic Traditions in Modern Italy*, Princeton, NJ: Princeton University Press.

Reardon, Thomas and Vosti, Stephen A. (1995) 'Links between rural poverty and the environment in developing countries: asset categories and investment poverty', *World Development*, **9** (September) (23), 1495–1506.

Sampson, S.W. Raudenbush and F. Earls (1997), 'Neighborhoods and violent crime: a multilevel study of collective efficacy', *Science*, **277** (August).

Sandler, Todd (1992), *Collective Action: Theory and Applications*, Ann Arbor: University of Michigan Press.

Sanz de Santamaria, Alejandro (1992), 'Economic science and political democracy', in Paul Ekins and Manfred Max-Neef (eds), *Real-life Economics: Understanding Wealth Creation*, London: Routledge.

Segerson, Kathy (1988), 'Uncertainty and incentives for nonpoint pollution control', *Journal of Environmental Economics and Management*, **15**, 87–98.

Smale, M. and V. Ruttan (1997), 'Social capital and technical change: the Groupement Naam of Burkina Faso', in C. Clague (ed.), *Institutions and Economic Development: Growth and Governance in Less-Developed and Post-Socialist Countries*, Baltimore, MD: Johns Hopkins University Press.

Spulber, Daniel (1988), 'Optimal environmental regulation under asymmetric information', *Journal of Public Economics*, **35**, 163–81.

Wade, Robert (1988), *Village Republics: Economic Conditions for Collective Action in South India*, Cambridge, UK and New York: Cambridge University Press.

Weitzman, Martin (1974), 'Free access vs private ownership as alternative systems for managing common property', *Journal of Economic Theory*, **8** (June) (2), 225–34.

PART III

Investing in Social Capital in the Field

9. Can investments in social capital improve local development and environmental outcomes? A cost–benefit framework to assess the policy options

Jonathan Isham

INTRODUCTION

This chapter asks the question: 'So what?' What, really, are the policy implications of empirical and case study evidence – including the evidence presented in Part II – that forms of social capital affect well-being in a range of different settings?[1] After all, one of the most striking empirical conclusions on the relationship between social capital and economic outcomes can be found in the ground-breaking work of Putnam (1993): that the forms of reciprocity and trust which are key determinants of the relative economic success of northern Italy in the late 1900s were established in the early 1200s. It is hard to imagine a more depressing conclusion for policy practitioners: mix a pinch of trust with a dash of social cohesion, then let simmer for six or seven centuries! Such path-dependence seems to leave little room for the efforts of eager policy makers.

In this chapter, the challenges of the concept of social capital are addressed from the perspective of a development practitioner. Specifically, the material in this chapter focuses on investments in development projects whose objective is the improvement of well-being among a subset of target beneficiaries.[2] In particular, the focus is on projects whose primary objective is the improved delivery of local services and whose implementation will (to some degree) depend on decentralized service provision from the staff of government ministries who are working in the field, the staff of local NGOs and the intended beneficiaries. This would include developmental projects, for example, whose objective is cleaner drinking water, better health facilities or more effective primary schools.

This chapter argues that, in three related ways, recent empirical and case study results do matter for development practitioners, even as they imply that such practitioners should not always be advocating 'investments' in forms of social capital. First, potential investments in social capital should be considered only alongside potential investments in physical and human capital during the planning of most development projects. Second, even where investments in social capital may not be called for, the potential effect of social capital on a proposed development project should be assessed in the first phase of planning of most development projects. Third, development practitioners may, in selected cases, be faced with a dilemma that undertaking *no activity at all* in low social capital communities is the correct policy prescription, unless equity considerations dictate that certain projects be aimed at the poorest communities.

The chapter is organized as follows. The first section presents a policy-oriented perspective on what social capital is and how it may affect local development and environmental outcomes. The second section argues that the potential influence of social capital critically depends on the nature of economic goods that development projects are designed to deliver. The third section shows how one can evaluate the expected stream of benefits and costs associated with various forms of social capital. The fourth section presents such an evaluation in the case of the provision of clean water. The fifth section summarizes the chapter's arguments.

SOCIAL CAPITAL AND DEVELOPMENT OUTCOMES

For the development practitioner, the usefulness of the concept of social capital begins with the observation that recurring and patterned social interactions within a well-defined boundary form a local 'social structure',[3] and that the characteristics of this social structure will affect many economic decisions of agents within that boundary. Specifically, the local social structure may affect economic decisions and outcomes through four main mechanisms: information sharing, the impact on transaction costs, the reduction of collective action dilemmas and mitigation of risk.[4]

First, social structures can affect information sharing among agents. When agents interact frequently in local networks and in the observance of local norms (for example, at an annual community festival), they are more likely to observe each other's behaviour (one-way information sharing) and to exchange information about their daily lives (two-way information sharing). By contrast, when local networks and norms exclude different groups of agents (for example, lower castes), they can diminish the frequency of one-way and two-way information sharing.[5]

Second, social interactions can affect the level of transaction costs associated with many market exchanges. When agents frequently and regularly interact in social settings, they establish patterns of expected behaviour and build bonds of trust. Combined with the possibility of social sanctions, this lowers the likelihood of opportunistic behaviour by agents that are in the same social structure. By contrast, the lack of cooperative norms within social structures can lead to higher transaction costs and more inefficient markets.[6]

Third, without selective constraints, agents in many settings will not have an incentive to participate in mutually beneficial collective action (Olson, 1965) such as the construction of a community-based water system or maintaining a feeder road. Frequent and regular interactions in social settings lead to the development of institutions that can serve as such constraints, thereby lowering the incentives of individual agents to free-ride.

Fourth, established networks and norms can help those who are suddenly in need, thereby mitigating risk. Household-to-household transfers and informal credit institutions can ensure consumption smoothing for most members of poor communities, particularly those who do not face contemporaneous exogenous shocks. For example, in Chapter 5 of this volume, Grootaert, Oh and Swamy detail how the incidence of consumption crises in Burkina Faso is substantially lower in communities in which community lending institutions are active.

As illustrated by these four mechanisms, networks and norms often serve as constraints on economic decisions among the poor. Accordingly, a social structure can be regarded as an institution, a 'set of constraints that governs the behavioral relations among individuals or groups' (Nabli and Nugent, 1989). Importantly, this definition encompasses both formal institutions such as the rule of law and informal institutions such as 'cultural rules and codes of conduct which . . . can constrain the relationships between different individuals and/or groups' (ibid.). Following this definition, networks and norms are informal institutions: they affect the optimizing behaviour of economic agents and can increase (or decrease) overall levels of well-being within a community. As detailed in Chapter 1 of this volume, networks and norms – as forms of social capital – can thus be introduced as fixed inputs into a model of household production.

This institutional perspective, which as argued below can help development practitioners to assess how specific characteristics of social structures may affect the stream of costs and benefits of development projects, also conforms to the definition of social capital by Schiff (1992): 'Social capital is the set of elements of the social structure that affect relations among people and are inputs or arguments of the production and/or utility function.' This 'functional' definition is consistent with the influential formulation of Coleman (1990): 'Social capital is defined by its function. It is not a single entity, but a variety of different entities having two characteristics in common. They all consist of some aspect of a social structure, and they facilitate certain actions of individuals who are within the structure.'

SOCIAL CAPITAL AND THE NATURE OF ECONOMIC GOODS

This section argues that the expected relationship between elements of the social structure and the proposed deliverable – through information sharing, the impact on transaction costs, the reduction of collective action dilemmas and risk mitigation – critically depends on the nature of economic goods that development projects are designed to deliver. Following a standard public economics framework, Table 9.1 begins by delimiting the nature of economic goods that development projects may be designed to deliver.[7]

Private Goods

Where projects are promoting the delivery of private goods, collective action dilemmas are less likely to affect directly their delivery because of their non-exclusive and non-rival nature. By contrast, forms of social capital may affect the delivery of private goods through the other three mechanisms: information sharing, transaction costs and risk mitigation. Take the example of a project that is trying to promote the adoption of an improved fertilizer among agricultural households. First, the adoption of such a private good may be more likely when networks and norms promote information diffusion: much economic and non-economic research suggests that local networks and norms are critical determinants of the way that information is diffused among such households (Rogers, 1995).[8] Second, the initial distribution of supplies of improved fertilizer may be detrimentally affected by opportunistic behaviour by local leaders if norms and networks do not hold them accountable. Third, adoption is more likely if agricultural households have access to local institutions that can mitigate the risk associated with trying a new technology.

Toll Goods and Collective Goods

Where projects are promoting the delivery of toll goods (for example, many kinds of irrigation systems[9]) or community goods (for example, a feeder road), the potential influence of social capital through information sharing and risk mitigation is relatively low: in general, the use of such a good by a community member is not characterized by large information spillovers or dependent on the presence of institutions that mitigate risk.[10] However, the potential influence through transaction costs is high. In most settings in the developing world, sustained management of decentralized toll goods and collective goods depends on the performance of local leaders and (in the case of most development projects) the performance of staff of government ministries or local NGOs. Where norms of mutual trust between these stakeholders and project beneficiaries are low, opportunistic behaviour – in the form of financial

Table 9.1 The characteristics of economic goods and the likelihood of influence of social capital

Type of good	Characteristics of economic good		Example of good	Potential influence of social capital mechanism				
				Information sharing	Transaction costs	Collective action	Risk mitigation	
Private good	rival	exclusive	improved fertilizer	high	high	low	high	
Toll good	non-rival	exclusive	irrigation system	low	high	high	low	
Common property resource	rival	non-exclusive	community forest	low	high	very high	low	
Collective good	non-rival	non-exclusive	feeder road	low	high	high	low	

Note: See text for descriptions of the mechanisms and their relationship to the characteristics of economic goods.

corruption or shirking – will be more prevalent. In addition, because of their non-rival nature, collective action dilemmas may also affect the delivery of these goods, particularly in the early stages of service design. Consider projects that finance the delivery of 'demand-driven' community-based water systems (Garn, 1998) or local feeder roads (Heggie, 1995), where the mobilization of some community resources for construction of the required infrastructure is a necessary but not sufficient condition for receiving project assistance. In such cases, unless a small number of households have an encompassing interest to contribute most of the community inputs (Olson, 1965), community norms of generalized reciprocity are necessary if individual households are to commit their time and resources to construction (as opposed to trying to free-ride on the expected commitments of others).[11]

Common Property Resources

Where projects are promoting the enhancement of selected common property resources (for example, a community forest), the potential influence of social capital through transaction costs is also high. As in the case of toll goods and collective goods, sustained management of common property resources often depends on the performance of local leaders and (in the case of most projects) of project staff. Because of the non-exclusive and rival nature of these goods, the potential influence of social capital through collective action is even higher. As in the case of toll goods and collective goods, the presence of active networks and norms of reciprocity will provide a critical incentive for individual households to commit their time and resources to *initiate* such an activity. But in the case of common property resources, networks and norms can also improve the *management* of common property resources in diverse settings (Ostrom, 1990). In the case of community forests, for example, community norms of reciprocity will affect the likelihood that households will harvest only their allocated share of trees.

To summarize, the information in Table 9.1 suggests that social capital is likely to have a high influence on outcomes in projects designed to promote the adoption of private production goods with large information spillovers, provide toll or collective goods that depend on design and construction by community members and implementation by local agents and improve the management of common property resources.

SOCIAL CAPITAL FROM A COST–BENEFIT PERSPECTIVE

This section illustrates how, in the case of each type of economic good discussed above, a cost–benefit framework can help to guide project investment decisions.

To begin the development of this argument, equation 9.1 presents a functional relationship between the deliverable of a development project in year t (Q_t) – for example, the quantity of clean water available per household per week in a specific community – and vectors of available productive inputs in that year ($\mathbf{K_t}$, $\mathbf{L_t}$, $\mathbf{H_t}$ and $\mathbf{S_t}$):[12]

$$E_{t' < t} \, Q_t = A_t{}^* F(\mathbf{K_t}, \mathbf{L_t}, \mathbf{H_t}, \mathbf{S_t}) \tag{9.1}$$

where $\mathbf{K_t}$ is physical capital, $\mathbf{L_t}$ is labour, $\mathbf{H_t}$ is human capital, $\mathbf{S_t}$ is social capital, A_t is a (factor neutral) productivity shifter, and $E_{t' < t}$ denotes that this is the expected[13] productive relationship of a development project in a previous year t'.

This equation illustrates how development practitioners, by adopting a cost–benefit framework, can consider networks and norms alongside more standard productive inputs. Four alternative possibilities for the way forms of social capital may affect the expected production of a specific deliverable Q_t are considered below.

First, if the expected direct productivity of at least one form of social capital (S_{it}) is positive:

$$E_{t' < t} \, (\partial F_t / \partial S_{it}) > 0, \tag{9.2}$$

then there may exist some justification for investments in that form of social capital. For example (as further discussed below), if experience in a region suggests that the presence of active civic associations is associated with the improved delivery of clean drinking water, this is a necessary but not sufficient condition for a possible investment in these civic associations.

Second, if the expected direct productivity of all j forms of local social capital is nil:

$$E_{t' < t} \, (\partial F_t / \partial S_{it}) = 0, \qquad i = 1 \ldots j, \tag{9.3}$$

there still may exist some justification for investments in some element of the social structure as a form of social capital, as long as one of the following conditions holds:

$$E_{t' < t} \, (\partial \mathbf{K_t} / \partial S_{it}) > 0; \; E_{t' < t} \, (\partial \mathbf{L_t} / \partial S_{it}) > 0;$$
$$\text{or } E_{t' < t} \, (\partial \mathbf{H_t} / \partial S_{it}) > 0, \qquad i = 1 \ldots j. \tag{9.4}$$

In other words, if some element of the social structure has a productive role in the creation of physical capital, labour or human capital, which in turn affects the desired output (so that $E_{t' < t} \, (\partial F_t / \partial K_{it})^*(\partial \mathbf{K_t} / \partial S_{it}) > 0$), there still may exist some justification for investments in that form of social capital. For example, if participation among women in local women's groups is positively associated with higher levels of knowledge among women, including productive knowledge about maintaining clean water taps and drinking vessels, a possible investment in such local women's groups may be justified.

Finally, there is also a real possibility that, in some cases, some forms of social capital can have a negative effect on the expected output, either directly or indirectly:

$$E_{t' < t} (\partial F_t / \partial S_{it}) < 0, \tag{9.5}$$

$$E_{t' < t} (\partial \mathbf{K}_t / \partial S_{it}) < 0; \ E_{t' < t} (\partial \mathbf{L}_t / \partial S_{it}) < 0;$$
$$\text{or } E_{t' < t} (\partial \mathbf{H}_t / \partial S_{it}) < 0, \qquad i = 1 \ldots j. \tag{9.6}$$

For example, in regions where social norms prohibit the education of girls, this element of the social structure will (indirectly) lower outcomes that depend on the productive role of local human capital. In such cases, while investments in this form of social capital are ruled out by definition, the presence of this form of social capital may (as further discussed below) call into question the implementation of the proposed development project.

With this perspective at hand – that networks and norms can be viewed as potential inputs into the production of the deliverable of a development project – one can begin to evaluate the expected stream of benefits and costs associated with various forms of social capital.

Let the expected net benefits (at time $t' < t_0$) of a potential project which may be undertaken from time t_0 to t_n be $\{B(t_0), B(t_1) \ldots . B(t_n)\}$, so that the expected net present value of the project at time t_0 is:

$$E_{t' < t_0} NPV_{t_0} = \Sigma[B(t_i)/(1 + r)^i] \qquad i = 1 \ldots n \tag{9.7}$$

(where the summation is indexed over i from 0 to n).

In addition, let the expected benefits of the potential project be increasing and concave in production of the deliverable in each year, so that

$$E_{t' < t_0} \partial B(t)/\partial Q_t > 0, \ \partial^2 B(t)/\partial Q_t^2 < 0. \tag{9.8}$$

In other words, the benefits of the project, for example improved health due to cleaner and more reliable drinking water, will be positively related to the quantities of the deliverable, and the marginal benefits of increasing amounts of the deliverable are decreasing.

By combining material in equations (9.1)–(9.8), one can formally note that

$$E_{t' < t_0} \partial NPV_{t_0} / \partial S_{it} > 0, \tag{9.9a}$$

when (9.2) holds or when (9.3) and (9.4) hold; and that

$$E_{t' < t_0} \partial NPV_{t_0} / \partial S_{it} < 0, \tag{9.9b}$$

when (9.5) or (9.6) hold. In other words, social capital will have a positive (negative) effect on the expected present value of a development project only when at least one element of the local social structure has a positive (negative) effect on the production of the deliverable at some time in the future.[14]

Why are (9.9a) and (9.9b) useful as one is thinking about assessing the policy options associated with a potential development project? These equations formalize the potential relationship between elements of the local structure, other potential productive inputs and project benefits. Addressing the implications of these equations suggests that development and environment practitioners need to take the potential effects of social capital into account, even as they imply that such practitioners should not always be advocating investments in social capital.[15]

First, using this kind of cost–benefit framework shows that potential investments in social capital should be considered only alongside potential investments in physical and human capital during the planning of most development projects. While (9.9a) summarizes the possibility that social capital will be expected to have a positive effect on the present value of some development projects, the relative magnitude of this positive effect – at the margin – should be compared to the corresponding (expected) effects of physical capital, labour and human capital.

This is particularly true because, in some cases, the production of social capital may demonstrate increasing returns to scale.[16] When productive forms of social capital are absent, large investments may be required for them to reach a threshold where their marginal affects are relatively large. This might be true, for example, when a community lacks the most basic norms of generalized reciprocity that are required for the management of a community-based water project. By contrast, when productive forms of social capital are prevalent, small investments in forms of social capital may have a high pay-off. This will be true when a community has a well-established community tradition of building and maintaining local schools: in such a case, a moderate amount of financial or educational support for local organizations may have a high pay-off.[17]

This leads to the conclusion that only in a limited number of cases will investments in social capital, for example through training of local organizations, be called for. These cases are when the project is designed to promote the adoption of private production goods with large information spillovers, to provide toll or collective goods that depend on design and construction by community members and implementation by local agents, or to improve the management of common property resources; when the discounted stream of expected benefits of incremental social capital is significantly greater than the corresponding discounted stream of expected costs; and when the uncertainty about potential damages to the local social structure through such investments is minimal. This latter case is particularly important because, in many villages, outside intervention has the potential to harm local social structures significantly (Ostrom, 1990; Narayan and Pritchett, 1999).

Second, since social capital may be a substitute for a complement to other inputs which affect project performance (equation (9.9a), when (9.3) and (9.4) hold), the potential effect of social capital on a proposed development project should be assessed in the first phase of planning of most development projects
– even when potential investments in forms of social capital are unlikely. Take again the example of girls' education: investing in new schools and materials to increase girls' enrolment is likely to be less productive in the case of restrictive social norms. Knowledge about the presence and strength of such norms is important, even when investments in women's groups are not likely to be productive.

Development practitioners can learn about the characteristics of such forms of social capital through social assessments, 'systematic investigations of the social processes and factors that affect development impact and results' (World Bank, 1994). Since the early 1990s, they have been used in a wide range of development initiatives to identify key local stakeholders, to ensure that social differences are taken into account in the design of development projects, and to ensure that social differences do not limit service delivery (McPhail and Jacobs, 1995a). The fixed costs of social assessments will in many cases be relatively small: the average cost of social assessments in 42 reviewed development projects was less than $100 000 (McPhail and Jacobs, 1995b).

Accordingly, using social assessment in the design of many development projects is likely to be a cost-effective way to enable outside stakeholders, including government officials, representatives of NGOs and staff of donor agencies, to identify communities within a target region that have relatively high (and low) levels of local social capital. Specifically, social assessments may also help to identify how other characteristics of communities impede the flow of information among different sets of households, affect transaction costs, reduce collective action dilemmas or mitigate risk. For example, in communities with high levels of inequality and norms that discourage social contacts between the rich and the poor, these norms would hinder the flow of public information about agricultural practices from the rich to the poor.

Overall, this information can provide information on which communities will, *ceteris paribus*, have higher expected returns to a specific development project.

Thus, by using social assessments and by considering the costs and benefits of potential investments in social capital, development and environmental practitioners may be faced with a dilemma that undertaking *no activity at all* in low social capital communities is the correct policy prescription, unless equity considerations dictate that certain projects should be aimed at the poorest communities, including those with very low levels of social capital. Using the cost–benefit framework presented above, this would be in the case of (9.9b) and when (9.5) or (9.6) hold, and when the economic rate of return of a proposed project in a specific region[18] is below some standard criterion.

Less formally, this would be true when the costs of investing in any form of capital in a certain region do not generate enough benefits, precisely because levels of social capital in that region are low. For example, this framework suggests that, if guided only by a rate of return criterion, investments in community water systems should not be undertaken in communities in which the characteristics of local social capital dramatically reduce the likelihood of project success.

If equity considerations dictate that certain projects be aimed at the poorest communities, the allocation of investment resources for such projects may need to be adjusted according to this cost–benefit perspective. Consider, for example, investments in agricultural extension. If national policy dictates that investments in extension should be aimed at the poorest villages, possible adjustments that take the characteristics of local social structures into account include investments in the strengthening of local organizations (for example, through direct training in new agricultural techniques) and in more direct follow-up with individual farmers to counteract likely patchwork patterns of adoption in areas where the social structure impedes the flow of information.[19]

SOCIAL CAPITAL AND THE PROVISION OF CLEAN WATER

The following case studies from communities in Sri Lanka and Indonesia illustrate how differences in social capital can affect the provision of clean water – and how investment decisions can be guided by this difference.[20]

Sri Lanka

In Gallella, a community-based water service (supported by a World Bank-financed project) provided connections to 214 households that had previously consumed water from unprotected wells, springs or streams. As service design began, community members, collaborating with government and NGO representatives, agreed that household connections be provided and that the connection cost would depend on household distance from the main pipeline. Households contributed about 43 per cent of total construction costs (well above the required 20 per cent) in the form of unskilled labour. As the project began, the water committee in Gallella, which had many pre-existing community groups and civic activities, coordinated community participation, monitored household construction contributions and hired caretakers to handle routine maintenance. The committee established clear procedures for tariff collection to cover operations and maintenance (O&M) expenses: caretakers collect monthly fees and retain written records of payments. Ninety per cent of households pay the required fee, and households get together monthly to clean the water tank. Overall, water services in Gallella have had substantial impacts: 21 per cent of households report that the incidence of diarrhoea has decreased, and the time saving for women has been dramatic – an average daily reduction of an hour.

In Passaramulla, another village supported by a World Bank-financed water project, only one pipe-borne gravity system was in operation three years after service implementation. Seven other systems were in place but inoperable; many others were incomplete. As service design began, a local NGO was hired to mobilize the community and to help to launch a water committee. The local government failed to monitor the efforts of this NGO, which were half-hearted: staff members conducted social mobilization programmes poorly and remained detached from the community. They managed to establish a water committee but did not ensure that committee members had adequate information and training. The committee did not organize monitoring and quality control of construction, which resulted in defective construction work. The subsequent performance of the water committee has been poor. Committee members meet rarely, and financial records have been kept haphazardly. Further, operations have not been transparent: while most households do not receive any water, the committee chairman has a working household connection.

Indonesia

Closeness and familiarity characterize the social relationships among households in Wonorojo. For example, both men and women say that neighbours tend to help one another in various tasks (such as building houses) and usually participate actively in various community groups and associations, including those established by the government. This social cohesion has affected the performance of the community-based water service that was supported by a World Bank-financed project. Once a week, households get together to clean the water tanks. They also clean the drains collectively (at the same time as they are maintaining community roads). Of households interviewed, 64 per cent reported that they contributed to the O&M of the service, and all 25 households that were surveyed said that the service functioned every day without any major problems. Overall, 82 per cent of households report that their health has improved since the implementation of this service.

In Tlogo, a local NGO helped households to design and construct a gravity-fed piped water service with public standposts. For the most part, community leaders rather than households participated in service design: only 32 per cent of households reported that they participated in the selection of the type of service, and 76 per cent of households reported that leaders made the final decision about the service technology. Initially, the service functioned well. In 1997, however, several community officials illegally tapped the pipeline to build private connections. These illegal connections diverted water to private households, severely hampering the functioning of the service and reducing the flow of water to public standposts. In the absence of a formal water committee or a group to manage water services, households have been unable to act collectively and take up the issue with community leaders. One reason for this inability to act collectively is that households in Tlogo are not accustomed to working together or interacting socially: they have been involved in very few community activities, such as maintaining roads, and relatively few households report that they regularly spend time with their neighbours or even invite them over for special occasions. Instead of attempting to organize themselves, households report that they are hoping for outside intervention to rectify the situation. In the meantime, only 12 per cent of households report that they are very satisfied with the service.

These case studies imply that the allocation of investment resources for community-based water services should be adjusted to take into account the characteristics of local networks and norms. The chance of successfully introducing water services is significantly enhanced in communities with more productive forms of social capital. In communities with active community groups and norms of generalized reciprocity, households are used to working together and social ties deter free-riding. This suggests that designers of community-based water projects need to pay attention to the prevailing levels of social capital, as one of the factors that will influence service performance, in communities to be served by the project. In particular, the allocation of investment resources for water services may need to be adjusted to take into account the low levels of social capital.

CONCLUSION

This chapter has used a cost–benefit framework to argue that, in three related ways, recent empirical and case study results concerning the effects of social capital on well-being really do matter for development and environment practitioners. First, potential investments in social capital should be considered alongside potential investments in physical and human capital during the planning of most development projects. Using a cost–benefit framework leads to the conclusion that only in a limited number of cases will investments in forms of social capital be called for. Second, even where investments in social capital may not be called for, the potential effect of social capital on a proposed development project should be assessed in the first phase of planning of most projects, since social capital may be a substitute for or a complement to other inputs which affect project performance. The fixed costs of this kind of formal 'social assessment' will in many cases be relatively small. Third, by using social assessments and by considering the costs and benefits of potential investments in social capital, development practitioners may, in selected cases, be faced with a dilemma that undertaking *no activity at all* in low social capital communities is the correct policy prescription, unless equity considerations dictate that certain projects should be aimed at the poorest communities – including those that have very low levels of social capital.

NOTES

1. Other recent microempirical evidence that, at least for some types of economic goods, social capital has a relatively large effect on developmental and environmental outcomes is found in Narayan and Pritchett (1999), Grootaert (1999), Isham and Kähkönen (2002a; forthcoming) and Maluccio *et al.* (2000).
2. Following the perspective on capabilities and well-being of Amartya Sen, which is related to the analysis of well-being of Partha Dasgupta. In Chapter 1 of the present volume, Isham, Kelly and Ramaswamy explore the connection between this perspective and the concept of social capital.
3. A social structure can be defined as 'recurrent and patterned interactions between agents that are maintained through sanctions' (Swedberg, 1994).
4. In Chapter 2 of this volume, Woolcock gives an overview of the way local social structures are associated with information diffusion, transactions costs, collective action and risk mitigation. Additional discussions can be found in Esman and Uphoff (1984), Nugent (1993), Dasgupta (2000) and Collier (2002).
5. For example, Barr (2000) finds empirical evidence that information diffused via social networks helps to explain productivity difference among Ghanaian enterprises.
6. For example, Brautigam (1997) finds empirical and case study evidence that culturally based networks have reduced information uncertainties and principal–agent problems in eastern Nigeria's manufacturing zone; and Gambetta (1988) documents how norms reinforced by the Mafia in southern Italy lead to higher transaction costs and poorer quality of goods and services.
7. See World Bank (1994) for a more detailed presentation on how development initiatives

(particularly infrastructure projects) can be helpfully classified according to their rival and exclusive characteristics.

8. Isham (forthcoming) finds that, among agricultural households in the plateau zone of Tanzania, tribally based and participatory local organizations act as a form of social capital in the decision about adopting improved fertilizer.

9. Not all irrigation systems are toll goods: where the water source is limited or congestion effects are large, irrigation systems have a higher degree of rivalry, so that a household-by-household pricing system is more appropriate than a toll-based pricing system.

10. Information diffused from project staff to project beneficiaries may play a role, of course, in the performance of a toll good. But, except as it is affected by principal–agent problems (as discussed later in the chapter), such information diffusion is not likely to be affected by the local social structure.

11. In many such cases, as shown by Olson (1965) and others, no activity will be undertaken.

12. A similar production function framework that incorporates social capital is presented in Dasgupta (1998) and Grootaert (1999), among others.

13. Expected by, say, a team of development practitioners who are beginning to design a project in year t.

14. It is, of course, possible that some elements of the local social structure have a positive effect on the production of the deliverable while others have a negative effect.

15. Note that the advocacy here of this kind of cost–benefit approach is consistent with the fact that exact cost–benefit calculations are being de-emphasized at the World Bank and in other development institutions. As advocated here, an understanding of the potential relative effect of social capital on the stream of costs and benefits is consistent with the policy-based arguments of Devarajan *et al.* (1997) that there should be a 'shift in emphasis away from a concern with precise rate of return calculations to a broader examination of the rationale for public provision'.

16. Following equation (9.2), this would be true when $E_{t<t}(\partial^2 F/\partial S_{it}^2) > 0$.

17. In Chapter 6 of this volume, Molinas notes the likelihood of increasing returns in the production of some forms of social capital in the case of rural households in Paraguay.

18. The discount rate r that sets the net present value of the deliverables in that region equal to zero.

19. As, for example, in areas of the central plateau region in Tanzania, with ethnically diverse and non-participatory local organizations (Isham, forthcoming).

20. These case studies, and others that discuss the role of social capital in the effectiveness of community-based water projects in Sri Lank, India and Indonesia, can be found in Isham and Kähkönen (2002a; forthcoming).

REFERENCES

Barr, Abigail M. (2000), 'Social capital and technical information flows in the Ghanaian manufacturing sector', *Oxford Economic Papers*, **52** (3), 539–59.

Brautigam, Deborah (1997), 'Substituting for the state: institutions and industrial development in eastern Nigeria', *World Development*, **25** (7), 1–19.

Coleman, James S. (1990), *Foundations of Social Theory*, Cambridge, MA: The Belknap Press of Harvard University Press.

Collier, Paul (2002), 'Social capital and poverty', in Christiaan Grootaert and Thierry Van Bastelaer (eds), *Social Capital and Development*, Cambridge: Cambridge University Press.

Dasgupta, Partha (2000), 'Economic progress and the idea of social capital', in Partha Dasgupta and Ismail Serageldin (eds), *Social Capital – A Multifaceted Perspective*, Washington, DC: World Bank.

Devarajan, Shantayanan, Lyn Squire and Sethaput Suthiwart-Narueput (1997),

'Beyond rate of return: reorienting project appraisal', *World Bank Research Observer*, **12** (1), 25–46.

Esman, Milton and Norman Uphoff (1984), *Local Organizations: Intermediaries in Rural Development*, Ithaca, NY: Cornell University Press.

Gambetta, Diego (1988), 'Mafia: the price of distrust', in Diego Gambetta (ed.), *Trust: Making and Breaking of Cooperative Relationships*, Oxford: Basil Blackwell.

Garn, Harvey A. (1998), 'Managing water as an economic good', in *Proceedings of the Community Water Supply and Sanitation Conference*, Washington, DC: The World Bank.

Grootaert, Christiaan (1999), 'Social capital, household welfare and poverty in Indonesia', Local Level Institutions Working Paper no. 6, The World Bank, Washington, DC.

Heggie, Ian. G. (1995), 'Management and financing of roads: an agenda for reform', World Bank Technical Paper no. 27, Africa Technical Series, The World Bank, Washington, DC.

Isham, Jonathan (forthcoming), 'The effect of social capital on fertilizer adoption: evidence from rural Tanzania', *The Journal of African Economies*.

Isham, Jonathan and Satu Kähkönen (forthcoming), 'Institutional determinants of the impact of community-based water projects: evidence from Sri Lanka and India', *Economic Development and Cultural Change*.

Isham, Jonathan and Satu Kähkönen (2002a), 'How do participation and social capital affect community-based water projects? Evidence from central Java, Indonesia', in Christiaan Grootaert and Thierry Van Bastelaer (eds), *Social Capital and Development*, Cambridge: Cambridge University Press.

McPhail, Kathryn and Sue Jacobs (1995a), 'Social assessment', *Environment Department Dissemination Notes*, Washington, DC: The World Bank.

McPhail, Kathryn and Sue Jacobs (1995b), 'Social assessment structured learning: preliminary findings', *Environment Department Dissemination Notes*, Washington, DC: The World Bank.

Maluccio, John, Lawrence Haddad and Julian May (2000), 'Social capital and household welfare in South Africa: 1993–1998', *Journal of Development Studies*, **36** (6).

Nabli, Mustapha K. and Jeffrey B. Nugent (1989), *The New Institutional Economics and Economic Development*, New York: North-Holland.

Narayan, Deepa and Lant Pritchett (1999), 'Cents and sociability: income and social capital in rural Tanzania', *Economic Development and Cultural Change*, **47** (4), 871–97.

Nugent, Jeffrey B. (1993), 'Between state, market and households: a neoinstitutional analysis of local organizations and institutions', *World Development*, **21** (4), 623–32.

Olson, Mancur (1965), *The Logic of Collective Action*, Cambridge, MA: Harvard University Press.

Ostrom, Elinor (1990), *Governing the Commons: The Evolution of Institutions for Collective Action*, Cambridge: Cambridge University Press.

Putnam, Robert D. (1993), *Making Democracy Work*, Princeton, NJ: Princeton University Press.

Rogers, Everett M. (1995), *Diffusion of Innovations*, New York: The Free Press.

Schiff, Maurice (1992), 'Social capital, labor mobility and welfare: the impact of uniting states', *Rationality and Society*, **4** (2), 157–75.

Swedberg, Richard (1994), 'Markets as social structures', in Neil Smelser and Richard

Swedberg (eds), *The Handbook of Economic Sociology*, Princeton, NJ: Princeton University Press, pp. 255–82.

World Bank (1994), *World Development Report 1994: Investing in Infrastructure*, New York: Oxford University Press.

10. Social capital and environmental management: culture, perceptions and action among slum dwellers in Bangkok

Amrita Daniere, Lois M. Takahashi and Anchana NaRanong[1]

Research on the general role of social capital in economic development has blossomed in the last decade, but few studies have examined the connection between social capital and environmental management. Improving environmental management is especially important for low-income groups, which are disproportionately affected by the environmental impacts of rapid development (Cairncross et al., 1990). Central government agencies in developing countries often lack the capacity to manage or regulate environmental problems. However, government agencies may be able to create an enabling setting that allows local residents, communities, and organizations to devise and implement community-based environmental management mechanisms. In urban slums, indirect governmental action can effectively encourage local mobilization that improves public services such as electricity, safe drinking water, public toilets, and drains (Douglass 1992, 1995, 1998; Douglass and Zoghlin, 1994; Douglass et al., 1994; Majumdar, 1995).

In rapidly developing metropolitan areas, low-income groups differ significantly by geographic locale, tenure security, their relationships to other low-income settlements, and other sociodemographic and environmental variables. This chapter analyses how the capacity of low-income groups for collective environmental action is affected by these variables, focusing on the role of social capital. In particular, using data from household interviews in five slum communities in Bangkok, Thailand, the chapter explores the connections between environmental problems, health behaviours and beliefs, and forms of social capital. The chapter also presents evidence that the differences in environmental management among these communities critically depend on social integration and linkages with external authorities. Accordingly, we argue that incorporating an understanding of local social capital into urban planning and design can improve local environmental conditions of urban slums.

This chapter is organized into four sections. The first details the socioeconomic and institutional contexts for environmental change in Bangkok. The second introduces the characteristics of the five communities in this study. The third section details the results of the survey, focusing on environmental problems, health behaviours and beliefs, and forms of local social capital within the different communities. The final section explores the implications of this research for environmental policy and planning, focusing on the potential role of investing in social capital to improve collective environmental action.

SLUM CONDITIONS AND SERVICE PROVISION IN BANGKOK[2]

The population of the Bangkok Metropolitan Region (hereafter 'Bangkok'), Thailand's capital city, grew rapidly in the 1980s: from 5.7 million in 1980 to 10.8 million in 1990 (National Statistical Office, 1993). The city has also expanded physically, particularly in the central core and the periurban areas. Approximately 630 square kilometres of rural land were urbanized within Bangkok between 1974 and 1988 (Dowall, 1992). Consequently, many Bangkok residents live in slums or squatter communities that are extremely crowded and unsanitary. Crane and Daniere (1996) present evidence that access to services in Bangkok has continued to deteriorate in the face of increased economic growth and settlement density. According to Setchell (1992), 1400 physically separate slums in the metropolitan area were home to about 300 000 households (approximately 1.7 million persons) in 1992.[3]

Per capita annual income in 2000 in Thailand was approximately US$1500 (World Bank, 2001). Among households in the slums of Bangkok, per capita annual income is only about US$655.[4] The relatively low income level of households in these slums, as well as expensive and rising land prices, is associated with inadequate and crowded housing conditions.

As with households in most cities of the developing world, slum dwellers and squatters in Bangkok are vulnerable because they lack tenure security. According to Thailand's National Statistical Office, between 30 and 60 per cent of dwellers in medium and large slums were squatters in 1995/6: these households admitted to dwelling rent-free on land to which they have no title. Without tenure security, households are less likely to invest in housing. Additionally, lack of tenure security can hamper access to basic public services that are typically provided to urban residents by the public sector.

Overlapping and inefficient bureaucracies characterize public administration in Thailand; politicians and bureaucrats face little public pressure to improve their performance. In the case of Bangkok's water supply and treatment, two agencies have primary management responsibility. The Metropolitan Waterworks Authority (MWA) is supposed to deliver piped water to all residents and businesses within the jurisdiction of the Bangkok Metropolitan Authority (BMA), which is the geographically defined administrative unit responsible for the core area (but not for the surrounding provinces) of the metropolitan region. The Provincial Waterworks Authority (PWA) is supposed to supply water to all the other regions of Thailand, including those provinces within the Bangkok metropolitan region but outside the BMA. The Public Works Department (PWD) is responsible for the development, operation and maintenance of sewerage and drainage systems of the entire country.[5] Other agencies within the labyrinth of the Thai bureaucracy also influence the design and implementation of water supply and sanitation services. Authorities in these agencies generally hold overlapping responsibilities and, unfortunately, are under the jurisdiction of disparate ministries within the central government.

The current mix of agencies does not effectively provide water and sanitation services in Bangkok (Daniere, 1996). The Thai government has never authorized a specific agency to take direct responsibility for sewage and waste management at the provincial and local levels. However, in 1994, the BMA took the initiative and identified several priority areas within Bangkok that were to receive sewage connections to treatment plants within ten years. These areas were apparently selected because of higher than average population density and pollution levels. As is typical of many urban infrastructure initiatives, it is likely that this was a top-down planning decision. It is, for example, unlikely that low-income residents requested these services, especially not those with informal land tenure arrangements who are often refused public services as a result of their 'illegality'. It is not surprising that many residents of Bangkok are resisting the imposition of charges for water and sewage services, particularly in low-income slum areas.

As the MWA tries to provide access to piped water in an ever-expanding Bangkok, the water quality in the Chao Phraya River has rapidly deteriorated.[6] Large quantities of industrial and household waste in Bangkok are released without treatment into open sewers, canals and leaky septic tanks. In 1990, the river water had dissolved oxygen concentration of 0.5 to 1.0 milligrams per litre, well below the 2.0 milligrams per litre standard recommended for household consumption and industrial utilization purposes (Asian Development Bank, 1990). Under the management of the BMA, the Si Phraya wastewater treatment plant began operating in 1994; the plant, the first in the entire region, can treat only about 6 per cent of the city's daily wastewater. The BMA proposed to start charging Bangkok residents for wastewater treatment services in 1995, but the public objected and the proposal has been shelved while the country continues to deal with economic problems caused by the 'Asian Flu' of 1997 and 1998. Most observers realize, however, that these services will require user charges and that the Thai government must begin to educate and work with its constituents to design and implement a sustainable system (Srisawaskraisorn and Bamroong-ua, 1994).

By contrast, the institutional structure for solid waste collection and treatment in Bangkok is relatively straightforward. The BMA provides residents of wealthier households with door-to-door collection.[7] Residents in poor squatter communities typically organize their own collections, since door-to-door collection is not affordable – or even physically possible, because of the small impassable lanes and byways that serve as the means of egress to most slum communities. Slum communities often request that the BMA place a large dumpster at the entrance of their settlement; the BMA then regularly collects garbage from these skips, usually once or twice a week. However, unlike other cities in Asia such as Calcutta or Ho Chi Minh City, the BMA devotes few resources to controlling the spread of vermin and pests within the city, the source of significant health problems. Furthermore, neither the BMA nor the central government provides resources or incentives for communities to clean up their own communal areas and pathways. Overall, this system of waste disposal has worked well in some squatter communities and poorly in others.[8]

IDENTIFICATION OF COMMUNITIES

To assess how social networks and community governance structures affect local environmental management practices, a survey was implemented among representative low-income residents in five communities in Bangkok.[9] Table 10.1 summarizes the age of each community as well as population and household size. Each community, as discussed below, has distinct characteristics that have influenced its capacity for social capital formation and environmental management.

- Community 1, Klong Toey, on a swath of land surrounding the Port of Thailand, comprises a geographically distinct section of the Klong Toey slum, one of Southeast Asia's best known. Many neighbourhood-based NGOs are active in Klong Toey: the Duang Prateep Foundation (founded by a Magsaysay Award recipient living in the community) tries to improve the physical conditions of community residents.[10] It runs a day care centre, operates a microcredit project, is associated with an infrastructure/community development initiative and has negotiated on behalf of residents for land exchanges.

Table 10.1   Demographic and socioeconomic characteristics of five slum communities in Bangkok

	Klong Toey	Ruam Samakkhi	Samut Prakan	'Railroad slum'	Pathum Thani
Community characteristics					
Total population	2 800	160	185	538	600
Location	urban	urban	suburb	urban	suburb
Survey respondent characteristics					
Age	42.7	40.6	42.8	41.2	41.8
Born in community	32%	3%	38%	9%	29%
Lived in community	92%	72%	88%	79%	72%
Household characteristics					
Number of adults	3.1	3.4	3.7	3.2	3.1
Number of children	1.8	1.0	1.8	1.6	1.5
Monthly household expenses (baht)					
Food	4 971	4 790	5 124	4 523	3 844
Rent	225	640	873	169	99
Electricity	510	372	647	578	594
Education	327	197	460	407	283
Entertainment	430	324	625	458	327
Legal and illegal lotteries	509	917	1 404	556	326
Loan and interest	1 816	1 378	2 200	1 168	987
Other expenses	2 775	3 272	2 715	2 605	2 024
Total expenses	11 561	11 890	14 048	10 464	8 482

Note: The exchange rate during data collection was 40 baht/US$.

- Community 2, Ruam Samakkhi, developed during the late 1990s along a small very contaminated *klong* (canal) in inner Bangkok. The most prominent features of the community's geography are the housing structures, which rest on concrete stilts that are six feet above the surface of the canal. The brackish water below the housing structures releases odours into and around these dwellings.
- Community 3, a suburban slum in Samut Prakan province, adjoins central Bangkok. Land in this urbanizing community is owned by a nearby Buddhist temple and private landlords, among others; wealthy households have even begun to build large homes in the midst of crowded slum lanes. Although this is the wealthiest of the five communities, solid waste lies beneath many houses and on undeveloped tracts of land, and aggressive rats abound.
- Community 4, the 'Railroad Slum', is adjacent to a major railroad line that intersects downtown Bangkok. The housing stock here, mostly composed of wood, is particularly poor. Standing water and garbage are common beneath many houses. The value of real estate is quite high in this community's central Bangkok location, which means that the likelihood of eviction is greater than in the other four locations. The conditions here are among the worst in the city of Bangkok, but there do appear to be several community organizations engaged in improvement activities as well as trying to negotiate with the State Railroad Authority of Thailand for land ownership.
- Community 5, a suburban slum in Pathum Thani province, is a quasi-rural environment along the banks of a large *klong* that teems with plants and animals. Residents of this slum are very poor and earn significantly less than households in the other four locations. They are dispersed within two distinct areas, differentiated by age and land ownership. The first area, on land that is owned by the Irrigation Department, is about 20 years old. The second area, on land that was recently transferred from a member of the royal family to an insurance company, is about 30 years old. Both communities are actively threatened with eviction. However, the Department of the Interior has intervened, and slum members on the plot owned by the insurance company now have the opportunity to purchase property through their savings groups. Many are trying to assemble the required down payment. Unfortunately, there is not enough space in this plot to accommodate all households even if all of the members of both communities were interested in moving there. Households living on land owned by the Irrigation Department have been given the option of moving to other sites owned by the housing authority. The community has resisted this option because the land is far away and residents would have to

purchase the land and try to find jobs in the new area. In response, a local group has formed to resist attempts to move the community from along the edges of the canal.

SURVEY METHODS AND RESULTS

The household surveys that were implemented in these five neighbourhoods were designed to assess environmental problems, health behaviours and beliefs, and forms of social capital. The survey consisted of three major sections. Section I concerned environmental attitudes and practices, including questions about the time spent in water- and sanitation-related activities, the type of facilities used, monthly expenditures and household satisfaction with existing services (including perceptions of cleanliness, convenience and reliability). Section II concerned health behaviour, including the frequency of illness and visits to medical facilities, as well as household knowledge about the relationship between environment and health. Section III concerned different forms of social capital, including participation in community organizations, the number and type of people upon whom the household relies for daily assistance, and social connections of household members that affect employment and the provision of shelter, energy and water.[11]

Community Characteristics

As detailed in Table 10.1, the five communities differ in demographic and socioeconomic characteristics. Some of these differences are likely to affect stocks of community-wide social capital. For example, only 3 and 9 per cent of respondents in Ruam Samakkhi and the Railroad Slum, respectively, are native born, compared to about a third of the respondents in the other three communities. While most survey respondents have lived in their current community for at least five years, a higher proportion of respondents in Klong Toey and Samut Prakan has lived in their communities at least that long. Since the length of time that people have lived in their communities is likely related to the quantity and quality of their social networks, one might expect, *ceteris paribus*, households in Klong Toey, Samut Prakan and Pathum Thani to have access to more social capital than households in Ruam Samakkhi and the Railroad Slum.

The five communities have similar average household sizes: three to four adults and about one-and-a-half children per household (except in Ruam Samakkhi, with about one child per household). Since children are often a source of community interaction and networking (for example, through community projects in education and health [*Editors' note*: see the discussion by Grootaert *et al.*, in this volume, Chapter 5]), one might expect that households in this community would have less access to social capital, *ceteris paribus*, than households in the other communities.

The five communities have important differences in average household expenditures (which are used as a proxy for household income). Households in the three urban slums have monthly expenditures of about 1000 to 12 000 baht (about $25 to $300 at July 2000 exchange rates.) Average household expenditures in the suburban slums differ significantly from each other and from those of the urban slums: monthly expenditures in Samut Prakan and Pathum Thani are about 14 000 and 8500 baht, respectively: households in Samut Prakan spend almost 70 per cent more per month on basic needs than households in Pathum Thani.[12] The possible effects of these differences on social capital formation are ambiguous. With more income, households may be able to allocate more time to networking and community mobilization, thereby increasing social capital formation. But they may also become less reliant on fellow community members for mutual assistance.

Environmental Problems and Personal Behaviour

Tables 10.2 and 10.3 summarize environmental and health characteristics of the surveyed households. As detailed in Table 10.2, communities share environmental concerns but differ about their relative importance. Land rights, for example, are a principal problem for about two-thirds of all residents of Ruam Samakkhi, the Railroad Slum and Pathum Thani (all of whom face eviction on a permanant basis), but they are not a principal problem for most residents of Klong Toey and Samut Prakan. More than two-thirds of residents of Klong Toey are very concerned about both rats and mosquitoes; four of every five residents in Ruam Samakkhi, along the *klong* in inner Bangkok, are very concerned about mosquitoes.

Almost all of the households in the first four communities have metered, piped water and private toilets (as do households in most slum communities in Bangkok). In Pathum Thani, where only one in five households have piped water, many residents retrieve household water from the *klong* and from a mobile water tank that the BMA regularly drives into the community.[13] As detailed in Table 10.3, although most residents in the five communities do not boil their drinking water before use (regardless of the source),[14] at least half of the residents of the first four communities always (or sometimes) filter their water; 80 per cent of the residents of Ruam Samakkhi do.

In Pathum Thani, by contrast, less than 5 per cent filter their drinking water, despite their dependence on the *klong*, an extremely unclean source. As noted above, this is the poorest of the five communities, so residents may not have the resources to boil or otherwise treat their drinking water on a regular basis.

Table 10.2   Environmental problems in five communities in Bangkok

Community concerns	Klong Toey	Ruam Samakkhi	Samut Prakan (per cent)	'Railroad slum'	Pathum Thani
Land rights					
Not a problem	43	3	50	18	24
A notable problem	28	30	34	17	16
A principal problem	3	67	14	63	59
Mosquitoes					
Not a problem	12	0	6	12	16
A notable problem	30	20	44	44	42
A principal problem	69	80	50	43	42
Rats					
Not a problem	12	10	14	18	28
A notable problem	18	43	38	46	39
A principal problem	70	47	48	37	34
Children's health					
Children's health is good or okay	9	5	62	44	74
Children sometimes get ill	32	6	28	34	14
Children's health is poor	10	19	10	22	10

The daily costs of both types of water treatment are about 50 cents to $1, depending on family size.

The residents of Samut Prakan, the wealthiest community, are the most likely to have sought some kind of formal medical assistance. Given that members of this community are the wealthiest respondents, it is likely that they can afford to go to the doctor or health clinic when they are ill. Respondents in the lower-income Pathum Thani visit a doctor only when absolutely necessary.[15] The combination of unsanitary conditions and less frequent doctor's visits leads to relatively poor health of the children in the Railroad Slum and Pathum Thani. Among households with children in the Railroad Slum and Pathum Thani, almost 56 and 45 per cent, respectively, are sometimes or always sick. This compares to 30 per cent or less in the other three communities.

What is the perceived connection between household health and water quality? Food preparation techniques in Thailand are extremely clean compared to those in many other Asian countries, primarily for cultural reasons: careful food preparation and water treatment practices are passed from one generation to the next. Nevertheless, only two-thirds of all respondents in four communities (excluding Ruam Samakkhi) believe that there is a

Table 10.3   Health behaviours and beliefs in five communities in Bangkok

	Klong Toey	Ruam Samakkhi	Samut Prakan (per cent)	'Railroad slum'	Pathum Thani
Treatment of water					
Frequency of boiling					
Never	68	83	76	73	89
Sometimes	14	3	16	13	5
Always	18	13	8	13	5
Frequency of filtering					
Never	53	20	48	51	95
Sometimes	6	3	2	3	2
Always	42	77	50	46	2
Health behaviours and beliefs					
Number of doctor visits in previous year					
More than 3 times	26	33	22	18	19
2 or 3 times	23	10	30	20	25
Once	18	10	14	13	10
None	34	43	21	48	4
Don't know	1	3	2	1	2
How is the general health of the children in your household?					
Good/OK	66	75	72	44	54
Get ill sometimes	26	6	18	34	24
Poor/always sick	8	19	10	22	20
Believe that health and the quality of water are related?					
Yes	83	37	70	73	65
No	17	47	30	20	33
Don't know	1	17	0	4	2

connection between their health and the quality of their water; in Ruam Samakkhi (along a very polluted *klong*), only 37 per cent believe this. This is quite disturbing, since, in many cases, visibly contaminated water flows adjacent to (or below) respondents' homes. At first glance, it is also perplexing, since so many households report that they filter their drinking water. It is likely that these cultural food and water practices are passed on without a full understanding about why they matter: poorly educated household members in these communities have not yet been formally or informally taught about the relationship between microorganisms and health. In addition, since enteric or gastrointestinal illness is a daily occurrence in the lives of most Thai people, the contribution of water to chronic poor health may not be well appreciated.

Community Governance and Social Networks

As noted above, Section III of the survey instrument was designed to begin to measure social integration and linkages within the five communities. Assessments of intra-community support systems, social ties and general trust were derived from the social integration questions. For example, households were asked about household and other community participation in community groups and projects and in environmental improvements (such as disposing of solid wastes in a community collection, as discussed above).

Assessments of inter-community networks were derived from the linkage questions. For example, households were asked about their reliance upon and trust in government officials and NGOs, community efforts to obtain help from outside groups for expertise and resources, and community willingness to appeal for additional government resources for community betterment. The survey instrument also included linkage-related questions about seeking and paying for appropriate technical inputs. A willingness and capacity among community group members to work with government officials and NGOs would suggest that the community has exhibited a commitment to develop extra-community networks.

Responses related to social integration are detailed in Table 10.4. They indicate that community 5 (Pathum Thani) – the poor suburban community along the *klong* in Pathum Thani in which residents are widely dispersed and face the threat of eviction – has significantly lower social integration than the other four communities. First, the share of community members that participate in community groups differs across the five communities: 20 per cent of households participate in the Railroad Slum, compared to only 3 per cent in Pathum Thani. Second, in the first four communities, households are relatively active in community projects: at least 60 per cent of households in each of these communities report that the community had a project in the previous year and that they participated in the project.

Table 10.4 Social integration in five communities in Bangkok

	Klong Toey	Ruam Samakkhi	Samut Prakan	'Railroad slum'	Pathum Thani
			(per cent)		
Community groups					
Belong to a community group (%)	18	13	8	20	3
Community projects					
Community had project in previous year (%)	60	77	80	74	21
Household participated in project in previous year (%)	58	80	56	63	25
Community assistance					
Potential sources of non-familial help within the community					
Neighbours (%)	42	37	34	43	28
Community money lenders (%)	36	7	10	8	21
Community groups (%)	1	57	10	3	0
Community leaders (%)	1	3	2	1	1
Solid waste					
Use municipal collection (%)	56	40	88	99	40
Use community collection (%)	36	60	12	1	5
Do not use collection service (%)	8	0	0	0	55
Waste collection					
Average municipal waste collection cost (baht/month)	240	267	0	600	73
Average community waste collection cost (baht/month)	2 583	0	1 340	0	85
Average BMA bin collection cost (baht)	1 120	667	20	1 278	185

In Pathum Thani, by contrast, only about one in four households reported being aware of a community project and participating in one. Third, in the first four communities, at least one in three households report that they could borrow money from neighbours if they were very short of food.[16] In Pathum Thani, by contrast, 28 per cent reported that they could, and community money lenders (as opposed to groups or leaders) are the only other significant source of funds in this community.[17] Overall, these responses suggest that Pathum Thani has relatively little social integration.

How do the previous results on social integration compare to the willingness (and ability) of community members to raise significant resources and contribute to environmental improvement (Table 10.4)? Households in the first four communities have access to waste collection bins that are serviced (more or less regularly) by the BMA. As detailed in Table 10.4, all (or almost all) respondents in these communities claim to dispose of their waste in bins, and are willing to pay for their waste disposal service. Residents of Klong Toey pay between 11 and 25 baht per month for waste collection, while residents of the other communities pay between six and 13 baht per month.

By contrast, in Pathum Thani, only 45 per cent of households dispose of their waste in bins.[18] Like the other results detailed in Table 10.4, such low involvement in waste collection also suggests that Pathum Thani has relatively low social integration. Unlike so many communities in Bangkok, it has not been able to organize community-centred methods of disposing of solid waste, which contribute less to environmental pollution than methods of individual disposal.

Responses related to linkages are detailed in Table 10.5. They reinforce the findings on social integration in these five communities. In particular, Pathum Thani also lacks linkages with potentially useful outside sources.

One way to assess community linkages is to characterize local efforts to gain assistance from outside networks. The survey tabulated in Table 10.5 asked residents if outside organizations or the government had responded to requests about improving local environmental problems. Many respondents reported that the government, in response to community outreach, has responded positively. For example, as detailed in the first part of Table 10.5, most households in the first four communities felt that the government (the BMA, in this case) had helped to resolve garbage collection problems. This is particularly true in Ruam Samakkhi and Samut Prakan (97 per cent and 82 per cent, respectively). In the case of Ruam Samakkhi, the BMA and the Department of Public Works have been very helpful: when the *klong* was lined with cement, the BMA offered to pay part of the cost for a bridge over it, greatly increasing the safety of residents.

By contrast, in Pathum Thani, only 38 per cent of respondents stated that the government had helped. Community leadership here claims that the

Table 10.5   Linkages in five communities in Bangkok (percentage of responses)

	Klong Toey	Ruam Samakkhi	Samut Prakan	'Railroad slum'	Pathun Thani
Relationship with government					
Has the government helped the community to solve 'the garbage problem'?					
Yes	63	97	82	63	38
No	38	0	18	31	59
Trust in the government and NGOs					
Government officials that can be trusted					
None	39	3	6	16	20
Some	26	33	36	47	29
Most or all	3	3	26	19	8
Don't know	25	60	26	18	37
NGOs that can be trusted					
None	22	7	8	9	12
Some	20	33	38	39	12
Most or all	18	3	16	23	2
Don't know	33	57	34	27	65

government has been very slow to help residents improve living conditions or to provide security of tenure.

As detailed in the second part of Table 10.5, the communities reported differing levels of trust in government officials and NGOs. A relatively large share of respondents in Ruam Samakkhi (60 per cent) and Pathum Thani (37 per cent) did not know whether or not they could trust government officials; a small share (3 per cent and 8 per cent, respectively) said that most or all government officials could be trusted. This pattern is replicated, in these two communities, with respect to NGOs: a large share of respondents (57 per cent and 65 per cent, respectively) did not know whether or not they could trust NGOs; a small share (3 per cent and 2 per cent, respectively) said that most or all NGOs could be trusted. In Klong Toey, respondents were more knowledgeable about governments and NGOs, but the level of complete mistrust in government officials (39 per cent) and NGOs (22 per cent) was relatively high. Overall, according to these questions about trust, Klong Toey, Ruam Samakkhi and Pathum Thani appear to have fewer reliable linkages with public and NGO officials who might offer development assistance.[19]

These results must be interpreted with caution. Many critics of surveys that attempt to measure 'trust' argue that responses to these types of questions do not correlate with real trusting behaviour towards anonymous strangers, even friends or acquaintances (for example, Glaeser, 2001). In an effort to get better measures of trust in these communities, the present authors will be returning to Bangkok to conduct a series of experimental economic games based on methods illustrated by Carpenter (Chapter 7, this volume) and Cardenas (Chapter 8, this volume). Comparing responses to the survey with actual behaviours in experiments will help us to judge how much confidence we should place in responses to questions about trust and may provide new insights about trust in slum contexts.

ANALYSIS OF RESULTS AND PLANNING IMPLICATIONS

Building on the results reported in the previous section, the following conclusions emerge about social capital, community governance and environmental management in the slums of Bangkok. First, communities that appear to share many of the demographic and socioeconomic characteristics – such as Ruam Samakkhi and the Railroad Slum – may contain very different endowments and forms of social capital, and thus have very different capacities to engage in welfare-increasing collective action. For example, residents of Ruam Samakkhi have managed to improve solid waste disposal using the linkages they have developed with key officials in the Bangkok government. Residents of the Railroad Slum, by contrast, have not achieved the same success: despite their high levels of social integration, they have not been able to resolve water and sanitation problems, partly because they lack the necessary government linkages. As noted above, respondents in the Railroad Slum were more likely than respondents in other communities to say they would help or assist those community members in need; at the same time, they felt that they received relatively little assistance from the government.[20]

Second, economic and geographic isolation – the case for Pathum Thani – is associated with low levels of social integration and linkages. According to this research, social capital in poor, isolated slums is likely to be low. In communities in which the majority of households are very poor, it seems difficult to develop productive social networks. Undoubtedly, this relationship is two-way: the relative poverty of Pathum Thani is partly caused by a lack of social capital among its residents.[21] In very poor communities, investing in social capital will most likely be costlier, *ceteris paribus*, than in relatively well-off communities.

Third, even in communities where one would expect to find very high levels of social capital, assessing the role of social capital in improving well-being is challenging. Community 1 (Klong Toey), for example, is located within the well networked and vibrant Klong Toey slum. Yet the survey evidence does not suggest that it has more social integration or linkages than smaller and less known Bangkok slums. Social capital needs to be analysed from a variety of perspectives if we are to understand its local sources and effects.

This research has the following planning implications. First, the forms of social capital within a community should be assessed prior to project implementation since they can critically affect the probability of success of a project.[22] Second, policies that are designed to create or reinforce social capital need to tread carefully: complex social relations that exist in even the least socially integrated groups can be detrimentally affected by planning initiatives. This may be particularly true in very poor communities: households that are struggling to meet basic needs are less likely to respond to incentives that are designed to create social capital. For example, poor households may not have the time to serve on a new water user's association. Therefore, without significant financial resources, policies designed to increase social capital may do little to improve well-being.

Finally, what are the implications of this research for understanding environmental management and community governance more generally? As international donors and government agencies continue to advocate community-based programmes, they must recognize that social capital is a vast and uneven terrain across communities. Undoubtedly, some forms of social capital are available to residents in all communities. Yet only specific forms of social capital can effectively leverage and mobilize environmental improvements. For example, communities with a history of designing and maintaining other collective goods, such as a local health clinic, will be more likely to be successful in managing community-based waste collection. In addition, these forms of social capital are likely to be related to resource availability: a basic level of material resources is necessary before households can contribute to communal activities.[23] In poor communities without permanent land status, access to reliable public services and stable sources of income, mobilization of social capital for collective action is likely to be very difficult, if not impossible. Therefore, as international donors and government agencies try to promote collective action to improve well-being, they must concurrently address basic issues of poverty and public health in order to cope effectively with environmental degradation. If basic survival needs are ignored, communities will participate unevenly in environmental management and improvement, since their resources are unevenly distributed. If basic survival needs are taken into account, community-based environmental improvements can be distributed more equitably across diverse communities.

NOTES

1. The authors would like to acknowledge the substantial contributions of Viroj NaRanong at the Thailand Research Institute for Development, and Molly Davidson-Welling, a graduate student in the Department of Geography at the University of Toronto. In addition we thank the graduate students at Thailand's National Institute for Development Administration for

their untiring efforts to help us conduct our household-level research. We are indebted to both the University of California Pacific Rim Research Program and the Social Science and Humanities Research Council of Canada for funding this research and to the Middlebury College Department of Geography that provided one of the authors with the time and space to write this chapter.

2. Much of this section is based on a similar description from Daniere and Takahashi (1999a).
3. Setchell's (1992, Appendix A) estimate of 968 slum households relied on the official definition of a slum as proposed by the Bangkok Metropolitan Administration; that is, 'a group of deteriorated and disorderly housing with improper environment harmful to the health and security of residents. A congested community is defined by the criteria of housing density, i.e., 15 houses per one rai of land'.
4. This estimate is based on the survey data described below.
5. For a more detailed account of the organizational relationships among agencies involved in water and sanitation provision, see Daniere and Takahashi (1997).
6. The Chao Phraya River is one of Southeast Asia's primary rivers and flows through the centre of Bangkok into the Gulf of Thailand.
7. Most of the discussion regarding solid waste disposal services relies on Mekvichai and Kritiporn (1990).
8. A related issue is the unsanitary disposal of collected waste in Bangkok. A majority of this waste is placed in unlined dumps, which increases health risks through groundwater contamination and the prevalence of vermin. Yet these dumps do offer economic opportunities for scavengers who live nearby. Ironically, limiting the use of these unlined dumps would improve the health of most residents but limit the economic opportunities of some of the city's poorest residents.
9. This survey was implemented in July 2000. For the initial sampling frame, low-income neighbourhoods in different geographic areas with differing access to services were identified from national housing data and through consultation with local researchers (Daniere and Takahashi, 1999b). Permission to conduct household interviews was sought through community leaders: communities were selected only if leaders and the randomly selected households agreed to participate.
10. The Ramon Magsaysay Award seeks to acknowledge individuals and organizations in Asia whose contributions exemplify the ideals and service for which President Ramon Magsaysay of the Philippines is remembered. Many refer to this prize as the Asian equivalent of the Nobel Peace Prize although, of course, it is not accompanied by a financial award of the same magnitude.
11. Following the United Nations *Statistical Handbook* (1987), households were defined as any group of people who live together and pool their resources to manage their day-to-day existence. The initial version of the household questionnaire, which was developed in English and then translated into Thai, was pre-tested in 25 households. The primary enumerators for the survey were generally graduate students recruited from a local university who were given intensive training in survey administration. About 15 per cent of all households were surveyed in each community. In each household, the individual most responsible for water, sanitation and solid waste management was asked to respond. In many cases, the respondent was female, as domestic divisions of labour generally place women in charge of these tasks (Daniere and Takahashi, 1997). The respondent was thanked for participating in the survey with a small health kit which was purchased from the Ministry of Health.
12. The average household expenditure per month is calculated by summing various daily, weekly and monthly expenditures, in Thai baht, as estimated by the respondent. We then convert average monthly expenditures in baht to US dollars by dividing by the exchange rate of 40 baht per US dollar, which was the average official exchange rate during the month of July 2000 (the period in which these data were collected).
13. Thirty-five per cent of the surveyed households in Pathum Thani reported that they used the *klong* as a water source and 34 per cent reported that they used the BMA tank.
14. Residents of Klong Toey are most likely always (18 per cent) or sometimes (14 per cent) to boil their water; residents of Pathum Thani are least likely always (5 per cent) or sometimes (5 per cent) to do so.

15. Although public clinics/hospitals in Thailand are technically free to the poor, their quality is notoriously low; most low-income dwellers cannot afford the time for hospital visits or medicines associated with private doctors. A check-up at a private hospital can cost the equivalent of between US$5 and US$20 dollars per visit, depending on the reputation of the facility.
16. The survey asked each respondent: 'If your household was very short of money and food, could you ask people in this community beyond your relatives for help?' If the respondent responded 'yes', the survey then asked about the potential sources of funds in the community: neighbours, money lenders, groups and leaders.
17. In Klong Toey and the Railroad Slum, community money lenders are also the only other significant alternative source of funds. However, in these communities, neighbours are a much greater source of potential assistance than in Pathum Thani.
18. In addition, residents of both Klong Toey and Pathum Thani claim to dump waste in open areas as well as burn it on a regular basis.
19. By contrast, in Samut Prakan and the Railroad Slum, 62 per cent and 66 per cent of respondents, respectively, state that at least some public officials can be trusted; the comparable figures for NGOs are 54 per cent and 62 per cent.
20. In the next round of research in these communities, the authors share these survey results with respondents and ask them to detail why the government has not responded to requests for improving infrastructure and environmental conditions.
21. For a discussion of the feedback effects between poverty and social capital in rural communities, see Molinas (Chapter 6, this volume).
22. For additional advocacy of social assessments in the planning of environmental projects, see Isham (Chapter 9, this volume).
23. This is especially true in Thailand, where sociocultural norms emphasize individualism and patron–client relationships (Daniere and Takahashi, 1997).

BIBLIOGRAPHY

Asian Development Bank (1990), 'Asian Development Outlook 1990 Manila', The Philippines.

Cairncross, Sandy, Jorge E. Hardoy and David Satterthwaite (eds) (1990), *The Poor Die Young: Housing and Health in Third World Cities*, London: Earthscan Publications.

Coleman, James (1988), 'Social capital in the creation of human capital', *American Journal of Sociology*, **94** (Supp.), S95–S120.

Coleman, James (1990), *Foundations of Social Theory*, Cambridge, MA: The Belknap Press of Harvard University Press, pp. 300–325.

Cooke, Philip and Kevin Morgan (1993), 'The network paradigm: new departures in corporate and regional development', *Environment and Planning D: Society and Space*, **11** (5), 543–64.

Crane, Randall and Amrita Daniere (1996), 'Measuring access to basic services in global cities: descriptive and behavioral approaches', *Journal of the American Planning Association*, **62**, 203–21.

Daniere, Amrita (1996), 'Growth, inequality and poverty in Southeast Asia: the case of Thailand', *Third World Planning Review*, **18**, 373–95.

Daniere, Amrita and Lois Takahashi (1997) 'Environmental policy in Thailand: values, attitudes and behaviors among the Slum Dwellers of Bangkok', *Environment and Planning C*, **1**, 305–27.

Daniere, Amrita and Lois Takahashi (1999a), 'Environmental behavior in Bangkok, Thailand: a portrait of current practices, attitudes and values', *Economic Development and Cultural Change*, **47** (3), 525–58.

Daniere, Amrita and Lois Takahasi (1999b), 'Poverty and access: differences and commonalities across slum communities in Bangkok', *Habitat International*, **23** (2), 271–88.

Davern, Michael (1997), 'Social networks and economic sociology: a proposed agenda for a more complete social science', *The American Journal of Economics and Sociology*, **56** (3), 287–302.

Douglass, Mike (1992), 'The political economy of urban poverty and environmental management in Asia: access, empowerment and community based alternatives', *Environment and Urbanization*, **4** (2), 9–32.

Douglass, Mike (1995), *Urban Environmental Management at the Grass Roots: Towards a Theory of Community Activation*, Honolulu: East–West Working Papers.

Douglass, Mike (1998), 'World city formation on the Asia Pacific Rim: poverty, "everyday" forms of civil society and environmental management', in Mike Douglass and John Friedmann (eds), *Cities for Citizens*, Chichester: John Wiley & Sons, pp. 107–38.

Douglass, Mike and Malia Zoghlin (1994), 'Sustaining cities at the grassroots: livelihood, environment and social networks in Suan Phlu, Bangkok', *Third World Planning Review*, **16** (2), 171–99.

Douglass, Mike with Orathai Ard-Am and Ik Ki Kim (forthcoming), 'Urban poverty and the environment – social capital and state–community synergy in Seoul and Bangkok', in Peter Evans (ed.), *Livable Cities? Urban Struggles for Livelihood and Sustainability*, Berkeley: University of California Press.

Douglass, Mike, Yok-Shiu F. Lee and Lowry Kem (1994), 'Introduction to the special issues on community-based urban environmental management in Asia', *Asian Journal of Environmental Management*, **2** (1), vii–xiv.

Dowall, David E. (1992), 'A second look at the Bangkok land and housing market', *Urban Studies*, **29** (1), 25–37.

Drakakis-Smith, David and Chris Dixon (1997), 'Sustainable urbanization in Vietnam', *Geoforum*, **28** (1), 21–38.

Edwards, Bob and Michael Foley (1997), 'Social capital and the political economy of our discontent', *American Behavioral Scientist*, **40** (5), 669–78.

Evans, Peter (1997), 'State–Society Synergy: Government and Social Capital in Development', International and Area Studies, University of California at Berkeley.

Erickson, Bonnie (1998), 'Social capital and its profits, local and global', paper presented at the Sunbelt XVIII and 5th European International Conference on Social Networks, Sitges, Spain, 27–31 May.

Gertler, Mark (1997), 'The invention of regional culture', in Roger Lee and Jane Wills (eds), *Geographies of Economies*, London: Edward Arnold, pp. 47–58.

Gertler, Mark (2000), 'Social capital', in R. Johnston, Derek Gregory, G. Pratt, David Smith and M. Watts (eds), *The Dictionary of Human Geography*, 4th edn, Cambridge, MA: Blackwell Publishers.

Gibbs, David and Andrew Jonas (2000), 'Governance and regulation in local environmental policy: the utility of a regime approach', *Geoforum*, **31**, 299–313.

Glaeser, Edward (2001), 'The formation of social capital', *ISUMA*, **2** (1), 34–40.

Granovetter, Mark (1973), 'The strength of weak ties', *American Journal of Sociology*, **78** (6), 1360–80.

Granovetter, Mark (1985), 'Economic action and social structure: the problem of embeddedness', *American Journal of Sociology*, **91** (2), 481–510.

Granovetter, Mark (1995), *Getting a Job: A Study of Contacts and Careers*, Cambridge, MA: Harvard University Press.

Grieco, Margaret (1995), 'Time pressures and low-income families: the implications for "social" transport policy in Europe', *Community Development Journal*, **30** (4), 347–63.

Jessop, Bob (1998), 'The rise of governance and the risks of failure: the case of economic development', *International Social Science Journal*, **50** (1), 29–45.

Kim, Won Bae, Mike Douglass, Sang-Chuel Choe and Kong Chong Ho (1997), *Culture and the City in East Asia*, Oxford: Oxford University Press.

Kreinin, Mordechai and Michael Plummer (1992), 'Effects of economic integration in industrial countries on ASEAN and the Asian NIEs', *World Development*, **20**, 1345–66.

Lee, Yok-Shui F. (1998), 'Intermediary institutions, community organizations and urban environmental management: the case of three Bangkok slums', *World Development*, **26**, 993–1011.

Lin, Nan (1998), 'Social networks and status attainment', *Annual Review of Sociology*, **25**.

Majumdar, T.K. (1995), 'Social networks, people's organization and popular participation – process, mechanisms and forms in the squatter settlements', *Norsk Geograisk Tidsskrift*, **49** (9), 161–76.

McGee, Terence G. (1995), 'The urban future of Vietnam', *Third World Planning Review*, **17** (3), 253–77.

Meagher, Kate (1995), 'Crisis, informalization and the urban informal sector in Sub-Saharan Africa', *Development and Change*, **26**, 259–84.

Mekvichai, Banasopit and Phanu Kritiporn (1990), 'Urban environmental issues', *Background Report No. 7-1*, National Urban Development Framework (NUDF) Project, Bangkok: Thailand Development Research Institute (TDRI).

Minkoff, Debra (1997), 'Producing social capital: national social movements and civil society', *American Behavioral Scientist*, **40** (5), 606–19.

Mitchell, Kathryne (1995), 'Flexible circulation in the Pacific Rim: capitalism in cultural context', *Economic Geography*, **71** (4), 365–83.

Morgan, Kevin (1997), 'The learning region: institutions, innovation and regional renewal', *Regional Studies*, **31**, 491–503.

National Statistical Office (1993), 'Statistical Yearbook: Thailand 1993', Office of the Prime Minister, Bangkok, Thailand.

Parenteau, René (1997), 'Habitat et environnement au Vietnam: Hanoi et Ho Chi Minh-Ville', Paris: Editions Karthala.

Portes, Alejandro and Patricia Landolt (1996), 'The downside of social capital', *The American Prospect*, **26** (May–June), 18–21.

Putnam, Robert (1993), *Making Democracy Work*, Princeton, NJ: Princeton University Press.

Rowley, Dunham (2000),'Building social capital for school governance in southern Ethiopia', Beso-Community School Activity Program, USAID-Funded Program in Southern Ethiopia, World Learning, Inc.

Satterthwaite, David (1995), 'Viewpoint – the underestimation of urban poverty and of its health consequences', *Third World Planning Review*, **17** (4), iii–x.

Setchell, Charles (1992), 'Final report of the Greater Bangkok Slum Housing Market Study, Volume 1', Bangkok, Thailand: Regional Housing and Urban Development Office, United States Agency for International Development.

Simmel, Georg (1971 [1908]), 'Group expansion and the development of individuality', in D. Levine (ed.), *Georg Simmel: On Individuality and Social Forms*, Chicago: University of Chicago Press.

Statistical Yearbook (1987), New York: United Nations Statistical Office.

Srisawakraisorn, Saengroaj and O. Bamroong-ua (1994), 'Bankokians to pay for waste water', *The Bangkok Post*, 49, number 364, 30 December.

Storper, M. (1997), *The Regional World*, New York: Guilford.

Takahashi, Lois M. and Rigoberto Rodriguez (1999), 'The social construction of access: social networks and daily routines among persons living with HIV/AIDS', working paper, Department of Urban and Regional Planning, University of California-Irvine.

Whittington, Dale, Donald T. Lauria, Kyeonge Choe, Jeffrey A. Hughes and Venkateswardlu Swarna (1993), 'Household sanitation in Kumasi, Ghana: a description of current practices, attitudes and perceptions', *World Development*, **21** (5), 733–48.

Woolcock, Michael (1998), 'Social capital and economic development: toward a theoretical synthesis and policy framework', *Theory and Society*, **27**, 151–208.

11. Building networks of social capital for grassroots development among indigenous communities in Bolivia and Mexico

Kevin Healy

The *Central Regional de Cooperativas Agropecuaria y Industrial Regional del Alto Beni, El Ceibo* and the *Unión de Museos comunitarios de Oaxaca* are community-based federations that have crafted innovative and long-lasting programmes for tackling complex social, economic and cultural problems for the micro-regions in which they work. They have achieved social empowerment by exercising greater control over their local economic, social and cultural environments and brought tangible and valued benefits to their communities. This chapter explores the history of these two organizations, illustrating how social capital can be utilized by rural indigenous organizations in strategies of grassroots development.

This chapter begins with brief histories of the two organizations, highlighting their main achievements and strategies for change, and then examines in each case the nature of their social capital and the strategies deployed to utilize it for grassroots development. There follows a theoretical discussion about investment in indigenous cultural resources, contrasting the way in which these two organizations have utilized social capital in order to draw some lessons about the viability of such investments in other parts of the developing world.

EL CEIBO'S GRASSROOTS DEVELOPMENT FEATURES

El Ceibo is a Bolivian peasant federation of 37 community-based service cooperatives located in the country's northern region of Alto Beni. Since its founding in 1979, the federation has become one of the country's most widely respected small farmer organizations. The widespread participation by the group's members has expanded their industry, improved environmental stewardship of the tropical forest environment and promoted social equity in the distribution of social and economic benefits to rural communities.

El Ceibo provides interrelated agricultural services to its 900 small farmer members from the Aymara, Quechua and Moseten ethnic groups and generates 'spillover benefits' to non-member peasant households as well. Most of its efforts focus on the production and marketing of cocoa beans grown by its members on small farms in the tropical forest. By transporting, marketing and adding additional value to a large share of the micro-region's cocoa beans, El Ceibo has been able to regulate the prices for its most important cash crop, enabling peasant farmers to defend themselves from powerful price gouging commercial middlemen and urban industrialists and to compete more effectively for higher, more stable prices.

To bolster the productive capacity of its members, the federation provides diverse skill training and farmer services in agroprocessing, agricultural extension and research. The services are provided by a self-managed organizational structure staffed by 84 members and leaders. Over half its members have been internationally certified as bona fide organic producers of cocoa beans as a result of their use of improved agroecological practices in the Amazonian rainforest.

El Ceibo's agroindustry currently markets 23 different cocoa bean and chocolate products with average annual revenues of over $1 million during the past four years. This includes revenues from an innovative marketing strategy to introduce several organic chocolate products to fair trade and health food markets in western Europe and the United States over the past decade.

El Ceibo's accomplishments are more remarkable in view of the logistical demands placed on its routine operations and labour forces, which are drawn from peasant communities with weak public schooling. Its offices, infrastructure and service programmes function in two vastly different environments: La Paz, the world's highest capital city, and the remote tropical Amazonian rainforest, a ten-hour drive away over the rugged eastern slopes of the Andes. The operations of the farm-to-market system between these two physical environments requires active coordinated teamwork of small workgroups, performing diverse work tasks in a long synchronized chain of interconnected actions.

This teamwork unfolds as follows. Rural activities are coordinated from Sapecho, a small town in the Alto Beni jungle. From this site, which includes processing facilities, warehouses and a training centre, El Ceibo members schedule pick-ups of cocoa harvests from local farmers, and then weigh, grade and store the beans through their own work brigades. Business managers purchase cocoa from local cooperatives, and peasant extension agents bicycle out to farm sites for demonstrations and training courses. Other workers rake cocoa beans for drying in the sun or load bags of dried beans into bags for shipment by truck to La Paz.

When the beans arrive in La Paz, they are taken to a federation warehouse for storage and marketing. At this site, the labour force at El Ceibo's modern chocolate factory transforms the beans into chocolate products, and then packs, stores and ships these products to local, national and international markets. The entire urban labour force – including project planners, accountants, sales agents, radio communicators, industrial machine operators, drivers and industrial workers – are youths recruited from the cooperatives of the alto Beni.

A HISTORICAL OVERVIEW OF SOCIAL NORMS IN THE ALTO BENI REGION

In 1953, agrarian reform in Bolivia, including the liquidation of the hacienda system, freed peasant families from social bondage to the landlord. Many families resettled in colonization zones such as the Alto Beni to create new homesteads, roads, farms, schoolhouses, communities and farmer associations. Numerous colonists organized rural *sindicatos*, which had served them well in their highland home communities as the basic organization for managing a range of local tasks. They also organized rural cooperatives to undertake grassroots development tasks needed to improve their incipient and fragile farm economies.

The first agricultural service cooperatives in the Alto Beni emerged within the context of resettlement programmes established by the Bolivian government and international donors. The objective of these programmes was to integrate the remote eastern lowland regions with the rest of the nation, increase the production of tropical agricultural products and improve living standards of impoverished farm families. Specifically, the cooperatives were shaped by intensive cooperative training and technical assistance programmes organized by the national government and NGOs during the 1970s.

Notably, both the *sindicatos* and the cooperatives mobilized available social capital (democratic assemblies, rule by consensus, rotating leadership, an egalitarian ethos and so forth) that the Aymaras and other groups had brought with them from the Andean highlands.

In the 1970s, one of the first activities of the cooperatives was to rent private trucks for transporting cocoa beans to market. Their objective was to attain economies of scale and a better position for negotiating prices of cocoa beans with industrialists in La Paz. In 1979, 12 of these coops organized the El Ceibo federation. Once again, they were focused on attaining greater economies of scale in transport and marketing operations in order to break the monopolistic grip of the commercial truck-owning middlemen over this micro-region. This new organizational framework opened up opportunities to tackle many other deficiencies in producing and marketing cocoa faced by the members.

Soon, El Ceibo mounted other service programmes requested by their membership. They instituted a broad array of training programmes to improve membership skills; these included elementary bookkeeping, the management of sustainable farming practices, agroprocessing services to ferment and dry beans in centralized locations and agricultural extension services. A training programme that was introduced also included sponsoring select members to study in other Latin American countries in order to upgrade the technical staffing requirements of their growing service programmes. This reduced their dependency on external NGOs and government agencies (although German volunteer programmes provided a stream of invaluable young professionals who specialized in business and agronomy).

Overall, the most important component of El Ceibo's strategy for adding value to its product was the organization of its own industry, whose 22-year history has passed through various stages of scaling up. It began in an almost symbolic fashion, as a tiny artisanal enterprise, and eventually became a small factory with modern automated processing equipment and machines that could turn out 23 chocolate products. The processing of value-added chocolate has enabled the federation to further diversify its products for the domestic and international market place.

El Ceibo's most dynamic membership growth occurred during the first half of the 1980s when the number of cooperative members tripled, reaching 37 separate member organizations. International organizations – including the Inter-American Foundation, COTESU (an agency of the Swiss government) and other European donors – underwrote programmes in training, transport and infrastructural investments during this period of consolidation and expansion.

While the gains of El Ceibo are impressive, the federation has also had to contend with a wide range of recurring problems, which threaten to undermine its service programme and leave lasting damage to the organization in their wake. Its rank-and-file constituents and member cooperatives have consistently had to muster considerable tenacity and ingenuity to overcome record-shattering hyperinflation, radical international price swings and severe crop disease problems. In addition, various management foibles have taken a toll on their organizational performance and growth (Healy, 2001).

EL CEIBO'S USE OF SOCIAL CAPITAL

El Ceibo's service programmes employ about 84 members and are effectively managed by designated leaders from the federation's two administrative councils. Both El Ceibo and its member cooperatives display the democratic features of a vibrant communal assembly: collective decision making by consensus, multiple posts for providing community service, leadership and worker rotation, and an egalitarian ethos in the distribution of responsibilities and rewards. For example, El Ceibo has built its participatory service programme by involving Quechuas as well as Mosetenes (members of the ethnic group from the lowlands) in self-management and self-help practices.

The success of these programmes critically depends on forms of social capital that El Ceibo itself, as well as its member cooperatives, have skilfully cultivated throughout their history. El Ceibo's social capital consists of social norms, democratic and egalitarian practices, which reflect well-honed institutional arrangements that have been a fundamental part of village life in the Andes for generations. These practices have proved essential in holding together an organization of 37 widely scattered cooperatives which sprawl over rugged terrain, and in enabling them to accomplish a number of impressive grassroots development gains for the Alto Beni communities.

The cultural and political roots of these highly democratic organizational practices date back two centuries to the time when political changes swept through rural highland areas of what is today the Bolivian Republic. Historians view this era of the eighteenth century as a period of transition to more democratic forms of organization in the countryside, as hereditary rule gave way to institutions such as communal assemblies and rotational practices that began to ensure greater leadership, accountability and expressions of grassroots village democracy. Sinclair Thomson, a historian specializing in this period of colonial history, has written that

> political power formerly centralized and concentrated at the apex of the political formation on a permanent basis was redistributed in a more diffuse pattern on a rotating, temporary basis. The overall political transformation had two clear consequences. First as the hereditary patriarchal elite declined, there was a reduction in ascriptive authority (deriving that is from conditions in this case associated with estate, class and gender into which individuals were born). Second there was more direct and broader political participation for community members. In addition to collective decision-making, all families with full membership were expected to exercise authority on a rotating annual basis. Rotating and temporary office holding was coordinated in accordance with the principle of egalitarian representation for the diversity of local *ayllu* units. Office holders viewed the exercise of authority as obligatory service, which would leave them materially impoverished if symbolically enriched. While community members held respect for the person and position of local authorities, the effective control from below meant that authorities had to follow and enforce the common will. (Thomson, 1996)

In another section he argues that 'the community assembly acquired greater prominence as the space for political debate, elaboration and decision-making. Community forces at large could demand more from below, or in anticipation of the forthcoming republican conditions, they could well up like subterranean springs on the highland plateau to displace them all together' (ibid.).

Ethnographic community-based rural studies in the Bolivian *altiplano* during the 1960s and 1970s also documented the continuity and vibrancy of these communal, self-governing democratic traditions in Aymara communities (Albo, 1977). Although, for various critics of the Bolivian agrarian reform, the rural *sindicato* was a western organizational form imposed for purposes of cultural assimilation on the rural native masses, other observers have pointed out that the dynamism of Andean culture soon took over and reworked these institutions along Andean lines to resemble these older community norms shaped during the eighteenth century. Subsequently, these democratic practices endured major incursions such as the great advance over their territories by the hacienda system, along with many other important political and economic forces.

When El Ceibo emerged from the peasant aspirations in the Alto Beni, it was partially guided by the principles, rules and regulations stipulated by the British Rochdale cooperative doctrine, which was brought to Bolivia by western aid agencies. Yet from its first days it also incorporated its traditional form of social capital into its organizational characteristics. These democratic and participatory norms have remained the bedrock of El Ceibo's flexible operating approach. The footprints of these Andean social norms, which can be viewed in all phases of its work, have represented a kind of comparative advantage for scaling up an agroservice programme, and therefore benefited a widely scattered constituency.

One of the most important expressions of El Ceibo's Andean social capital has been its commitment to relatively frequent assemblies and decision making by consensus within them. Since its initial years, the federation has opted to hold more frequent and longer assemblies than most cooperatives in rural Bolivia. They have brought delegates together from affiliated communities three times a year rather than the customary 'annual meeting' advocated by established cooperative promotional agencies. Each cooperative sends three delegates (including one slot for women) to the three-day assemblies. When pressing business matters cannot be adequately handled during this event, seminars take place soon thereafter to resolve them in an equally deliberative manner. The local cooperatives belonging to El Ceibo exhibit many of these same organizational practices in their own management and decision making practices, which are related both to services within the El Ceibo orbit of action and to independent local development actors. Their own strong base of social capital enables the federation to operate a system that blends centralized and decentralized forms of decision making and execution.

Another organizational feature of El Ceibo which suggests an egalitarian structure rooted in Aymara cultural traditions is that the top management of the federation has been placed in the hands of a council of elected leaders. Until 1998, they served (in one-to two-year terms) in lieu of a general manager or an outside technical specialist. This structure has allowed each member of the administrative council to assume responsibility for a specific division such as transport, industry, training, marketing and agricultural extension. This management system remained operational until 1998 when it was modified under the pressures of competition from Bolivia's globalizing economy. Subsequently, important management functions were transferred from the rotating elected leaders from the administrative council to several specialists with open-ended work contracts.

The vigilance council also shares in management responsibilities and performs annual audits of the federation. As the federation has continued to diversify its activities and reach higher levels of complexity, its leadership and management personnel have been hard-pressed to maintain an efficient form of management. Yet, on balance, the gains from using such a participatory mechanism appear to have outweighed the losses.

El Ceibo's assignment of leadership and management posts within this institutional hierarchy must also be viewed in relation to its established rotational practices. Similar to the internal democratic practices of Andean communities, the frequent rotation of leaders helps to avoid the entrenchment of a privileged, corrupt leadership, or a paid staff oftentimes of external non-members divorced from the needs and experiences of its members. Under El Ceibo's rules of rotation, leaders have been elected to one- or two-year terms, which enable the federation to tap an ever-widening pool of potential leaders throughout the Alto Beni.

El Ceibo also takes measures to minimize the disruptive aspects of these practices by disallowing more than half the administrative officers to depart from their councils in a given year and scheduling a six-month apprenticing period for new presidents prior to assuming office. Over the course of time, the terms in office for their leadership have also been extended.

El Ceibo also regularly rotates its 84 or so cooperative workers staffing the different service divisions and performing the myriad of tasks as bookkeepers, accountants, sales agents, agricultural extension agents, trainers, radio operators, drivers and planners. All this mobilization of member energy serves to propel its multi-tiered organizational structure and service programme. The local cooperatives send their members and sons and daughters of members to fill these positions as a service to the community, in very much the same way that Andean service allotments took place for different work assignments within highland communities. Although most job tenures through El Ceibo's history have been of two years' duration, there are important exceptions, such as with the agricultural extension agents who serve for four years preceded by a full year of on-the-farm training.

Another established federation practice that goes hand-in-hand with this rotation of members into these leadership and work positions is the '*jornal única'* or uniform wage earned for holding these posts. In 1986, the *jornal única* was $1.70 plus three meals a day; by the 1990s it had increased to $2.50, plus additional allotments for dependants, years of membership and per diem. This wage level is uniform for all leaders and coop workers regardless of their level of skill, experience or responsibility: it typically represents lower remuneration than that earned from cocoa and other farm plots. However, the mentioned bonuses for dependants and seniority enable some members to earn as much as 80 per cent above the '*jornal única*'. The low remuneration implies a community service ethos underlying these positions (as they involve something of a material sacrifice), yet they also provide non-monetary rewards such as increased social status, an opportunity to learn new skills and access to personal networks in the capital, including contacts with foreign aid representatives.

The policy of paying equal and then equitable wages was one of those early consensus solutions used to construct the organization on the basis of egalitarianism. It has become an important instrument for bonding the members more closely together and building further solidarity and legitimacy among the federation's stakeholders. When El Ceibo began to distribute its cocoa profits in the late 1970s, proposals to establish a graduated wage structure for workers stirred up much resistance from cooperative members. The solution turned out to be an idealistic one that emphasized that federation jobs were opportunities for service rather than material improvement.

However, in 1998, El Ceibo instituted a greater hierarchy of compensation for its leadership and workforce from its earnings as a self-financed agroindustry. Under these modified rules, which reward superior skill levels vital to the industry, adjustments to compensation are made to take seniority and dependency of up to two children into account, resulting in a difference of five to one between the highest and lowest paid worker. The general manager, for example, receives $500 monthly and the president and vice-presidents $260 and $250, respectively, while the lowest paid workers without these additional bonuses receive $104 monthly. According to El Ceibo leaders, the chief benefit to the federation from these changes is the reduction in the brain drain from some of their best-trained and most-skilled individuals to other organizations. One could also point to the increasing quality and competitiveness of their chocolate products in recent years. However, at the same time, member complaints about the pay differences are not infrequent and some members find that the organization's overall solidarity has been compromised and thus advocate a return to former levels of egalitarianism. Today El Ceibo's agroindustry is self-financing, yet its service programme in sustainable agricultural development in the Alto Beni receives grants for its activities of various kinds from the German donor agency Agro-Aleman.

Nonetheless, all of these *organizational* features illustrate how traditional

Andean social norms comprise a form of social capital that has been critical for El Ceibo and its member cooperatives. El Ceibo has been able to build on these norms to sustain a representative institution that has faced many critical problems and engendered community empowerment. The organizational system, which blends centralized and decentralized practices, requires the teamwork of small groups in order to succeed. The social capital available in Andean communities and transferred via migration to the Alto Beni has been a major factor in enabling this system to work over this rugged and sprawling physical landscape and in macroeconomic conditions that are difficult for peasant farming.

THE COMMUNITY MUSEUM MOVEMENT IN OAXACA

In the central valleys and western Sierra *Mixteca* of the state of Oaxaca in rural Mexico, another federation-building experience, illustrating tourism promotion within a depressed agricultural setting, demonstrates how social capital can be mobilized from rural communities to foster a new grassroots development strategy. This second case involves the utilization of traditional organizational structures and strategies for combining this form of social capital with forms of financial capital in order to improve well-being for its members.

The Oaxaca region has one of the largest indigenous populations among Mexican states, with 14 native languages. The region has a rich endowment of archaeological sites, the most spectacular of which attracts half a million visitors annually. For historical reasons, the single state of Oaxaca contains half the country's municipalities, which provides it with a dense political landscape of decentralized political units with indigenous majorities and leadership (Stephens, 1991). Events such as the Chiapas uprising have enabled Oaxaca's indigenous municipalities to gain greater autonomy from the grip of the monopolistic tendencies of the *Partido Revolucionario Institucional* (PRI) in forging a distinctive brand of working democracy under the indigenous practices popularly referred to as '*usos y costumbres*'.[1] At the same time, the municipalities of the Central Valleys and Sierra *Mixteca* face wrenching economic problems and consequently suffer a continual leakage of their younger male labour force to the United States.

The *museos comunitarios* (community museums) represent the creation of cultural spaces in village settings where individual and community cultural identity such as that of the *Zapotecas* and *Mixtecas* can be reconstructed and reinforced in a multifaceted educational programme. This involves a participatory process which has revitalized elements of indigenous culture such as local history, music and dance, traditional medicine, native languages and archaeology (Erickson, 1996; Barrera, 1990). As one observer wrote, 'The museum not only represents memory but it preserves and vitalizes that memory, particularly such themes as pueblo autonomy and valid ownership over pueblo cultural patrimony' (Erickson, 1996).

The participating villages work together with anthropologists, the Institute of Anthropology and History (INAH), and cultural activists drawn from their own ranks to shape these innovative cultural institutions. The *museos comunitarios* are administered and maintained by holders of the civil posts of the local municipality: they thus represent an alternative to the centralized large museums administered by specialists and high-level government officials from the INAH. In addition to becoming important repositories of local indigenous culture and enabling community members to rebuild their cultural identity, the *museos comunitarios* have espoused the objective of attaining a beneficial engagement for their villages with Mexico's tourist industry through attractions that can be managed by and benefit the indigenous communities themselves.

The *museo comunitario* movement began in Oaxaca in 1985, when community members in the town of Santa Ana del Valle in the Central Valley discovered a tomb full of pre-hispanic artifacts under the main plaza and acted to retain this cultural patrimony for community benefit. To create this first *museo comunitario* of Oaxaca, the Santa Ana del Valle authorities submitted a funding proposal to a government fund which supported conventional community development investments such as irrigation and agricultural marketing endeavours. The two applied anthropologists in charge of this small projects fund became fascinated by the unusual proposal for an alternative type of museum. They provided the necessary resources to renovate a local building and then worked together with INAH to provide the technical backstopping to mount a professionally designed museum with smartly organized exhibit halls, adequate lighting and well displayed cultural artifacts assembled by the *Zapotec* community (Erickson, 1996).

The demonstration effect of this new rural institution inspired members of other similar villages of Oaxaca who were also concerned about protecting local cultural patrimony. This set in motion processes of establishing various museums based on this model. This social process has relied greatly on the talent and commitment of the two leading anthropologists who put together a support structure (including the creation of an NGO) for getting these *museos comunitarios* planned, designed, financed and renovated within a framework that built upon participatory norms which were familiar to the local communities. This form of social capital mobilization was complemented by an intensive training and technical assistance programme which covered a number of aspects for museum management and community involvement.

A key organizing methodology from the outset has been to foster exchanges among representative community members from participating *museos comunitarios* to share information, ideas and experiences. Concepts and methodologies from the field of popular education were adapted to the emerging requirements for these new alternative cultural institutions. For example, the publications of various instructional manuals for oral history research and the organization of a *museo comunitario* and other didactic literature of the popular education genre reflect the serious professional effort behind this cultural and grassroots development process. Over the last several years, five additional *museos comunitarios* in *Zapotec* and *Mixteca* towns have emerged from this institution-building process. Each has presented its own particular set of cultural interests, resulting from its oral history research and paths of thematic exploration by community members.

As a result of the groundswell of this grassroots organizing and participation, communities with *museos comunitarios* have opted to take a more proactive stance and exercise greater collective influence over the spread of this movement. In 1991, 13 communities organized themselves into the *Unión de Museos comunitarios de Oaxaca*, a federation of six museums dedicated to working closely with the anthropologists to spearhead the consolidation and expansion of their network. During the remainder of the 1990s, this institution building resulted in six other *museos comunitarios* among *Zapotec* and *Mixteca* communities being founded and joining this growing movement of cultural promoters who are celebrating their village roots.

The *museo comunitario* movement of Oaxaca has turned heads in other parts of Mexico. Outsiders are noting that these are exciting cultural institutions with possibilities of fostering grassroots development and protecting the nation's cultural patrimony in new ways. The first national meeting of *museos comunitarios* was in 1994, with representatives from 18 Mexican states. Subsequent national meetings have taken place throughout the decade, and the number of participating museums and Mexican states have continued to grow.

The national organization holds the *Unión de Museos comunitarios de Oaxaca* as its prototypical model and continues to receive technical assistance from them. Yet, given the varying cultural conditions throughout the country, most *museos comunitarios* tend to utilize other forms of locally available social capital. The *Unión*'s own training workshops aim to prepare the participants with instruments to identify and subsequently utilize social capital within Mexico's vast civil society in adapting the museums to other localities outside Oaxaca.

The *Unión* has also opened an international front for its work in recent years by sending exhibits from Oaxaca's *museos comunitarios* to Los Angeles, where many Oaxaca migrants reside, and by providing training courses for interested and incipient museum groups in Guatemala and Venezuela. Recently, it also formed a Latin American network of community museums in eight countries to provide training and exchanges and to solidify Oacaxa's role as a central training centre rooted in ten years of experience. Indigenous peoples such as the Kuna of Panama and the Mayas of Guatemala have joined this network to begin the planning and training towards establishing their own community museums.

Another step in the evolution of the *museo comunitario* movement was the creation by the *Unión* of a cooperative enterprise for conducting activities of cultural tourism within the network opened by the proliferation of the *museos comunitarios*. The cooperative offers cultural tours in 15 villages of the Central Valleys, the *Mixteca* region and even the Pacific coast of Oaxaca. They sponsor a variety of tours, which include visits to the museums themselves, to archaeological historical and natural sites, as well as demonstrations of traditional crafts and medicines. Over the past five years, the visits to the museum communities sponsored by Oaxaca's cooperative enterprise have involved 4742 tourists (60 per cent are students from the United States) and almost $600 000 have been spent by them for the benefit of communities within the museum network. In their brochure, they state that

> as Native Americans and *mestizo* communities of Oaxaca, we have taken the initiative to create community museums to strengthen our identity and culture through the preservation of our cultural patrimony. We intend to make the testimonies of our history and current traditions widely known and valued by our own youth and the people who visit us.

They have focused particularly on bringing university programmes from the United States to engage in this people-to-people style of tourism. Although still incipient, these cultural tours demonstrate the grassroots development dimensions to this cultural recuperation and revitalization movement.

THE *UNIÓN DE OAXACA*'S DEPLOYMENT OF SOCIAL CAPITAL

The anthropologists who conceptualized this strategy to strengthen cultural identity among ethnic groups perceived the civil cargo system of the municipality as the place to anchor the *museo comunitario* in Oaxaca villages. They were aware that these elected small committees were an organic part of the village governing system of Oaxaca and therefore would give the *museos comunitarios* a legitimacy and staying power that would otherwise be difficult to transfer to a new cultural institution. The systems of local government in Oaxaca, in addition to the official governing positions of the mayor and town council, contain these unremunerated civil posts, which comprise a variety of committees for conducting vital local activities. Participation on these committees is so significant that they represent in local eyes the first step to becoming a bona fide Mexican citizen.

By performing this community service, they are beginning a process which leads up the civil cargo ladder to more important posts within this hierarchy (Barrera, 1990, p. 174). These committee representatives become elected to the posts in the town's general assembly; the assignments are generally for several years' duration. Even male members working in the United States as migrants can be called upon to return home and fulfil this assignment. Thus all males are on equal footing in this regard and are expected to assume a number of these public responsibilities for service at one time or another throughout their lives. As in the El Ceibo case in Bolivia, the posts are frequently rotated to ensure a wide distribution of these tasks and a broad level of participation within the community. For example, in the town of Santa Ana del Valle, the local line-up of these institutions includes several parents' committees, committees for potable water, for community health, for municipal transport, for festivals and for kindergarten among the wide range of activities represented (Barrera, 1990).

Historically, the civil cargo system was intertwined with a parallel hierarchy of religious offices. During the twentieth century it became secularized in many municipalities of Oaxaca (Stephens, 1991). For example, modernizing influences during recent decades have meant that community members with higher levels of education can bypass lower-ranking cargoes for a rapid advance up the hierarchical ladder of posts as a short-cut for fulfilling one's community obligations and attaining important leadership status.

The anthropologist visionaries behind the *museo comunitario* movement not only utilized this social capital of the cargo system to build and sustain each of the individual museums. They also scaled up this form of social capital through the organization of the federation in order to replace the earlier NGO that had originally been used to spread this innovative institution in Oaxaca. As such, the idea to federate grew logically from the planned efforts organized to hold frequent interchanges and discussions among the museums participating in the programme. This informal programme fostering frequent exchanges eventually led to the creation of a full-fledged federation of *museos comunitarios* constituted by the *Unión*.

The *Unión* also deploys a small cadre of cultural promoters selected from the different committees to represent the federation in launching new *museos comunitarios* (currently six are in the formative stages) as well as supporting the 12 institutions currently in being. Since the turnover in the rotating committee system is frequent, new members constantly have to be trained to assume their roles and responsibilities. The *Unión*'s policy of rotating the sites of the regular meetings of committee delegates among the different museums socializes information from diverse experiences and builds a shared understanding of the broader *museo comunitario* experience in Oaxaca. It has also become a way of socializing representatives from municipalities in the process of setting up their museum. In short, the civil cargo system becomes the glue holding together the *museo comunitario* movement, a form of social capital which has enabled the museums to adapt new ideas for social, economic and cultural change to the indigenous towns of Oaxaca within a familiar framework of action for the participants.

FINAL COMMENTS ABOUT SOCIAL CAPITAL IN BOLIVIA AND MEXICO

These two cases can be situated within the broader social science literature on social capital cited in Part I of this volume. El Ceibo represents the kind of supralocal farmers association, focused on agricultural issues, which is the main vehicle for the social process of empowerment (Uphoff, 1984). The organizational configuration for the *museo comunitario*, by contrast, shows how social capital mobilization involves the linking of indigenous institutions with state institutions (Tendler, 1997). In the *Unión* case, the two Mexican anthropologists leading this movement have received their salaries from the Mexican government since 1985. They began this process by organizing their own NGO to gain autonomy and additional financing to launch and sustain this institution building. Thus the *museo comunitario* activities have multiple institutional actors who are working in concert to link civil society and the state.

A striking common characteristic of these two cases is that the social capital being deployed, although considered by outsiders and participants to be an 'indigenous' or a 'traditional' resource, has undergone a variety of mutations over the course of its history through many cross-cutting influences of political, economic, cultural and social change. This aspect suggests that the phenomenon of cultural change should be taken into account when trying to focus on the nature of social capital in relation to grassroots development strategies. Although social capital contains elements and values often deemed unique to a given ethnic or racial group, it also reflects a cultural hybridization process which blends together traditions and influences over time from a variety of different cultural sources. The fact that the groups described in this chapter are appropriating social capital for use in new ways and in changing contexts is another illustration of this continuing process of cultural change and mixing.

It is also apparent from examining the two cases that, although social capital was indispensable for the respective development strategies, these grassroots development processes were also accompanied by other necessary elements. Both federations have given extraordinary attention to institutionalizing continuous training for their members. Training in a variety of 'modern skills' related to businesses, agriculture and alternative museums was a prerequisite for sustaining the social process, empowering these communities and achieving the significant gains reported. Yet the heavy, continuous training component of these institution-building processes, with frequent turnover among participants, gives a higher cost to this strategy of deploying social capital. Also the number of years necessary for underwriting training costs is problematic for foreign aid programmes which use much shorter time-lines for their investments in a given institution or project experience. Indeed, one of the main messages from these experiences for foreign aid agencies is to figure out ways to stretch those time-lines over longer periods for a slower allocation of economic support in keeping with the process of 'institution building' at the grassroots.

Of the two cases, El Ceibo is much more advanced in terms of its grassroots development impact. Only over the past few years has the *Unión* begun to utilize its institutional network and mobilized social capital to organize, in a systematic fashion, a cultural tourism programme to compete in Mexico's booming market. Their circuit of museums, cultural programmes and broad community interest is already providing comparative advantages for this competition. The high regard for local cultural patrimony and sense of shared responsibilities found in these towns promises, for the future, the kind of social equity and effective self-management that El Ceibo has achieved.

THE BROADER FRAMEWORK OF INDIGENOUS CULTURAL RESOURCES

By drawing on indigenous social capital, these two organizations demonstrate a strategy for change that falls within the developmental and political trends, with the potential to reverse decades of culturally assimilationist policies and recognize the indigenous contributions in development for Latin American societies during the 1990s. Within the political domain, these changes brought about by indigenous social and environmental movements are manifested by the path-breaking constitutional reforms redefining Latin American nations as multiethnic and multilingual, the opening of political spaces for indigenous representation in municipal governments and other higher-level governmental bodies, and new, more environmentally and culturally sensitive land reform legislation recognizing collective territorial rights for indigenous peoples throughout the hemisphere (Van Cott, 1994; Brysk, 2000).

These same pro-indigenous trends are evident in the two peace accords established during the 1990s to end civil conflicts in both Mexico and Guatemala. The peace accords emphasized important collective cultural rights of indigenous populations. International legislation such as the International Labour Organization's Convention 169 and Rigoberta Menchu's Nobel Peace

Prize, as well as shifts in policies and perceptions towards indigenous peoples within the multilateral development banks, are other signs of this changing institutional panorama on an international stage.

In the Andean countries, it is evident that such political changes mirror a framework for action within civil society where greater appreciation and utilization of indigenous cultural resources occur in grassroots development programmes and projects. The 'traditional' norms and networks of social organization discussed in the Bolivian and Mexican cases of this chapter then fit within a broad category of these 'indigenous cultural resources': native food, crops, pastures, trees, medicinal plants, livestock, art, languages and organizational forms that have been revitalized through the organizing efforts taking place in civil society over recent decades (Healy, 1996, 2001). Similar to the political changes mentioned above, activities directed at this kind of resource mobilization received great impetus from the indigenous and environmental movements and events such as the anti-quicentenary campaign.

These innovative efforts at recovering such resources have run counter to the melting-pot approach in which social and economic development was synonymous with a process of western cultural homogenization. Indigenous peoples were pushed by public policy as well as market forces to conform to western urban cultural norms, both in the generic sense of changing an indigenous cultural identity for a *mestizo* identity, and also in many specific ways, including changing their agricultural technologies, food, costume, religious beliefs, livestock, language, crops and choice of trees for planting and medicines for curing, in addition to various organizational forms used for community activities such as those presented in Bolivia and Mexico.

Each of these particular indigenous cultural resources has its own specific forms, and thus makes the sum of these parts greater than this whole of indigenous becoming *mestizo*. Under the pervasive ideology of western modernization and 'national integration' that gained force during the 1950s, these indigenous cultural resources were identified as features of a backward, underdeveloped economic and physical landscape that needed to be transformed and replaced by an array of superior Western institutional, technological, cultural and biological forms. Yet through civil society's organized efforts the 'obstacles' and 'irrational practices' for development became transformed into 'resources' and 'assets' to be utilized in multiple ways at the micro as well as the macro levels.

The integrationist/assimilationist development schemes of the mid-twentieth century also mirrored and gained credence from the modernization theory that became the most popular paradigm within the social sciences in the academies of the United States and Latin America for explaining underdevelopment through a form of cultural determinism. However, new insights generated by a growing body of research within the field of Andean Studies during the 1970s showed that indigenous peoples in the highlands played vital economic roles in shaping the colonial as well as early republican economies in Peru and Bolivia. Consequently, there was a strong historical basis for making claims for an important indigenous role in national development (Larson and Harris, 1995).

Both the El Ceibo and the *Federación de Unión de Museos comunitarios* form part of a larger movement pushing up from the local levels within civil society in Latin America that affirms the importance of cultural pluralism and a wide range of cultural patrimony previously underutilized in development programmes and projects. They have been able to deploy and institutionalize the utilization of these indigenous cultural resources in their local development strategies, thus overturning established canons of western-centric development planning and enhancing greater popular participation.

NOTE

1. The expression in English technically would be 'traditional practices and customs', yet, in the Oaxaca case, it signifies a local governance system for municipalities based upon the election of authorities and consensus in village assemblies along with voluntary citizen participation in committees for local development. This system became more formally incorporated into the state (Oaxaca) constitution in 1995.

BIBLIOGRAPHY

Albo, Xavier (1977), *La Paradoja Aymara: Solidaridad y Faccionalismo*, La Paz: CIPCA.
Bebbington, Anthony and German Trujillo (1993), 'Technology and rural development strategies in a small farmers organization: lesson from Bolivia for rural policy and practice', *Public Administration and Development*, **16** (879), 195–213.
Berrera, Mario (1990), *Beyond Aztlan: Ethnic Autonomy in Comparative Perspective*, South Bend, IN: University of Notre Dame Press.
Brysk, Alison (2000), *From Tribal Village to Global Village: Indian Rights and International Relations in Latin America*, Palo Alto, CA: Stanford University Press.
Camarena Mario Ocampo, Teresa Morales Lersch and Gerardo Necoechea Gracia (1994), *Reconstruyendo Nuestra Pasada Tecnicas de Historia Oral, Instituto Nacional de Antropologia e Historia*, Direccion General De Culturas Populares, Mexico, DF: Consejo Nacional para la Cultura y las Artes.
Erickson, Patricia Pierce (1996), 'So my children can stay in the Pueblo: indigenous community museums and self-determination in Oaxaca, México', *Museum Anthropology*, **20** (1).
Feldman, Tina Rossing and Susan Assaf (1999), 'Social capital: conceptual frameworks and empirical evidence, an annotated bibliography', Social Capital Initiative Working Paper 5, World Bank, Washington, DC.
Healy, Kevin (1987), 'From field to factory: vertical integration in Bolivia', *Grassroots Development*, **11** (2).

Healy, Kevin (1988), 'A recipe for sweet success: consensus and self reliance in the Alto Beni', *Grassroots Development*, **12** (1).

Healy, Kevin (1996), 'Ethnodevelopment of indigenous Bolivian communities, emerging paradigms in Tiwanaku and its hinterland', in Alan Kolata (ed.), *Archeology and Paleoecology of an Andean Civilization*, Washington, DC: Smithsonian Press, pp. 241–65.

Healy, Kevin (2001), 'Cocoa bean farmers make a chocolate covered development climb', in *Llamas, Weavings and Organic Chocolate, Multicultural Grassroots Development in the Andes and Amazon of Bolivia*, South Bend, IN: University of Notre Dame Press, pp. 123–54.

Larson, Brooke and Olivia Harris, with Enrique Tandeter (1995), *Ethnicity, Markets and Migration in the Andes: At the Crossroads of History and Anthropology*, Durham, NC: Duke University Press.

Morales, Teresa and Cuauhtemoc Camarena (1994), *Constantino Valeriano, Pasos para Crear un Museo Comunitario, Instituto Nacional de antropologia e Historia*, Direccion General de Culturas Populares, Mexico, DF: Consejo Nacional para la Cultura y las Artes.

Morales, Teresa Lersch and Cuauhtemoc Camarena, (1995) ' Fortaleciendo Lo Propio', in *Ideas para la Creación de un Museo Comunitario Instituto Nacional de Historia*, Oaxaca, Mexico: Instituto Nacional de Historia.

Stephens, Lynn (1991), *Zapotec Women*, Austin: University of Texas Press.

Tendler, Judith (1983), 'What to think about cooperatives, A Guide from Bolivia', Inter-American Foundation.

Tendler, Judith (1997), *Good Government in the Tropics*, Baltimore, MD: Johns Hopkins Press.

Thomson, Sinclair (1996), 'Colonial crisis, community and Andean self-rule: Aymara politics in the age of insurgency (Eighteenth Century La Paz)', unpublished PhD dissertation, University of Wisconsin, Madison, WI.

Uphoff, Norman (1984), *Local Organizations Intermediaries in Rural Development*, Ithaca, NY: Cornell University Press.

Van Cott, Donna (1994), 'Indigenous peoples and democracy for policymakers' in Donna Van Cott (ed.), *Indigenous Peoples and Democracy in Latin America*, New York: St Martin's Press, pp. 1–27.

Vazquez, Rojas Gonzalo (1993), 'Patrimonio Cultural y Museos Comunitarios: La Experiencia de Santa Ana del Valle, Oaxaca', unpublished Licenciatura, Escuela Nacional de Antropología e Historia, Mexico, DF.

12. Resilient communities: building the social foundations of human security

Nat Colletta and Michelle Cullen[1]

The Rwandan genocide erupted in April 1994 with widespread massacres of Tutsi by Hutu that ravaged the countryside, leaving 800 000 dead within three months. This anti-Tutsi campaign wiped out entire families, neighbourhoods and – by attacking staff at universities and hospitals – whole classes of professionals. Rwandan society collapsed: business and agricultural activities ceased, skilled people and the intelligentsia were slaughtered or fled, the infrastructure was deliberately destroyed and government operations, including legal, educational and health activities, completely dissolved (Des Forges, 1999). While Tutsi communities within Rwanda were eliminated, Hutu power groups grew stronger. Through the spread of dehumanizing hate propaganda, the Hutu elite were able to mobilize exclusionary and divisive social capital that bonded Hutu, primarily male unemployed and uneducated youth, to form such groups as the *Interahamwe* ('those who attach together' in Kinyarwanda). While some Hutu willingly participated in the massacres, others were ordered or forced to kill. Within Hutu extremism, 'bonding' took the form of exclusive social capital and powered the groups' success by providing excellent information networks and a sense of solidarity, obligation and civic duty (Prunier, 1997).

In stark contrast to this example of social capital gone awry, social capital can 'bridge' different groups by enabling cross-cutting and inclusive ties, like those that exist among indigenous Guatemalan women's groups who have united to sustain peace efforts. By establishing the Office for the Defense of Indigenous Women's Rights (Defensoria), the government solidified the first post-conflict initiative in Guatemala to incorporate indigenous participation into the management and administration of a public institution. The Defensoria has a consultative council that includes representatives from 24 different indigenous linguistic communities; a coordinating council that links members of the main indigenous women's organizations; and an interinstitutional commission that includes members from ministries, uniting the groups with government actors. The effort promotes the inclusion of one of Guatemala's most excluded groups, indigenous women, and the development of their capacity to represent their interests in working with external actors, while also bridging gaps that may exist between the groups. This kind of social capital, which forges links between excluded groups and government offices, is a good example of the optimal application and usage of social capital stocks.

This chapter asks a number of questions. What is the difference between these forms of social capital? What conditions reinforce exclusionary 'bonding' social relations and what conditions nurture inclusionary 'bridging' social relations? And how does the ebb and flow of social capital work to hold or fragment a society? These critical questions are crucial to understanding the role of social capital in promoting social cohesion and the management of conflict. Reviewing case studies conducted in four war-torn countries (Cambodia, Guatemala, Rwanda and Somalia) on social capital and its interface with violent conflict will help shed light on these questions.

VIOLENT CONFLICT AND THE TRANSFORMATION OF SOCIAL CAPITAL

There is much contention over what cognitive aspects, social dynamics and organizational structures constitute social capital, but there is little disagreement about its role in facilitating collective action, economic growth and development by complementing other forms of capital (Grootaert, 1998). As growth and development become ever more important and challenging in post-conflict environments, it is necessary to be able to assess extant social capital stocks to facilitate the recovery process. Woolcock's (1998) model of social capital facilitates analysis across various levels by presenting a comprehensive framework that incorporates four dimensions: strong ties[2] between family members and neighbours, weak ties with the outside community and between communities, formal institutions (including laws and norms) and state–community interactions. The application of this model can help to enable the directing of external interventions towards specific dimensions of social capital, either nurturing and utilizing remaining stocks or building new links that unite affected and disparate groups.

Strong ties (integration) form the primary building blocks of society, uniting nuclear and extended family members and neighbours. These relations, predominantly based on kinship, ethnicity and religion, are largely protectionist, defensive mechanisms that form a safety net for basic survival. During the Guatemalan civil war, Mayan traditions were the cultural glue that kept many communities together while seeking refuge in the mountains. Traditional Mayan institutions and spirituality served as a coping mechanism that helped the groups collectively to withstand the violence. Some of these

Mayan associations (mainly women's groups) that emerged during the war later became catalysts for the peace process.

Weak ties (linkages) are associational and connect diverse groups outside the smaller bonding communities, such as those links that exist within civic associations and networks. This dimension of social capital often bridges differences in kinship, ethnicity or religion. These cross-cutting relations are often affiliated with offensive measures, such as civic engagement and economic enterprise, which give people the strategic advantage they need to move ahead. These ties have emerged in Somalia, despite the conflict. As the warfare in Somalia has led to relative anarchy in the southern regions, community members in northern Hargeisa have reacted to the social disruption with much ingenuity while seeking to provide services and benefits no longer provided by the state. Within these endeavours, linkages between communities have arisen, geared to economic growth and development. Private entrepreneurs primarily from the diaspora have initiated business activities to reinstate services such as communications and public transport. Women's groups have opened markets in zones deemed secure that allow exchange between warring clans. The success of these new ties despite the surrounding conflict depends on varying factors, including among others the absence of (once overly powerful and authoritarian) state regulation and control, which has created the space necessary for civic activity to thrive, combined with the unleashing of market forces (through the connectivity of the worldwide Somali diaspora) to form a bridge to local actors.

The mere existence of NGOs and other civil society organizations, however, does not automatically result in the formation of bridging social capital. Non-governmental organizations in Rwanda during the early 1990s were, for the most part, apolitical, service-oriented and closely affiliated with the state, which suppressed the space necessary for civil society to truly flou-rish. Extreme poverty, inequality, clientelism and poor information networks, compounded by the social, economic and political marginalization of the rural majority, hindered the emergence of an autonomous, highly developed civil society. Thus, despite the abundance of these associative groups, the social capital present was not inclusive enough or potent enough to counterbalance the hate politics of Hutu extremists (Uvin, 1998). Social learning and social change that support bridging efforts, not just the presence of numerous types of organization, are required to make up a healthy civil society.

Social capital also occurs through more vertical, formal institutions at the macro level. This dimension of social capital (organizational integrity) encompasses state institutions and their effectiveness and ability to function, as well as the legal environment and social norms, which can also include influential and potential mechanisms of social control such as the media. The level of the state's integrity reflects whether civil society complements (enhances) or replaces state services and functions. When an authoritarian state penetrates society, there is little space for healthy civic engagement or network development. The authoritarian Barre regime in Somalia deeply penetrated communal life, particularly in the south of the country, to the point where, in order to maintain control, Barre employed divisive policies that attempted to pit clan against clan. This overly-centralized control, compounded by ineffective rule and corruption, led to the total dissolution of the government. In the north, where clans had united under the onslaught of the Barre army, despite the physical destruction, civic engagement emerged like a phoenix from the ashes, with religious institutions and women's groups stepping in to provide basic health and education services, while a de facto government concurrently established relative security.

State–community relations reflect how leaders and government institutions are engaged in and interact with the community (synergy). During civil strife in Guatemala, the government had little connection to various sections of its constituents, mainly indigenous and rural groups. In fact, the state actively implemented policies geared towards suppressing, if not eradicating, these groups. The state waged a vicious war against its people, primarily the marginalized indigenous and rural populations, who were systematically and forcefully excluded from economic, political and social opportunities. Government efforts sought to split the populace through the formation of political action committees, dividing communal allegiances and loyalties. This absolute repression afforded little space for healthy civic engagement.

The interplay of bonding and bridging social relations (horizontal social capital) with democratic and authoritarian governance (vertical social capital) manifested in state and civil society relations shapes strong or weak cross-cutting social relations and social cohesion, the bedrock for managing conflict.

SOCIAL CAPITAL, SOCIAL COHESION AND CONFLICT MANAGEMENT

To better understand the emergence of violent conflict, the relationship between social capital and the cohesiveness of a society – expressed in the construct of social cohesion, or the nexus of vertical and horizontal social capital and the balance of bonding and bridging social capital – needs to be examined. As Berkman and Kawachi (2000) note,

> Social capital forms a subset of the notion of social cohesion. Social cohesion refers to two broader intertwined features of society: (1) the absence of latent conflict whether in the form of income/wealth inequality; racial/ethnic tensions; disparities in political participation; or other forms of polarization; and (2) the presence of strong social bonds – measured by levels of trust and norms of reciprocity; the abun-

dance of associations that bridge social divisions (civic society) and the presence of institutions of conflict management, e.g., responsive democracy, an independent judiciary, and an independent media. (Berkman and Kawachi, 2000, p. 175).[3]

Social cohesion is the key intervening variable between social capital and violent conflict. The greater the degree to which vertical social capital (a capable state responsive to its citizenry) and horizontal social capital (cross-cutting, networked relations among diverse communal groups) intersect, the more likely that a society will be cohesive and thus possess the inclusive mechanisms necessary for mediating and managing conflict before it turns violent. The weaker the social cohesion, the weaker the reinforcing channels of socialization (value formation) and social control (compliance mechanisms). Weak societal cohesion increases the risk of social disorganization, fragmentation and exclusion, which may be manifested in violent conflict.

The work of Johann Galtung (1996) captures the intersection of vertical and horizontal social capital by characterizing the structure of violence in three basic social and economic phenomena: exclusion, inequality and indignity. In many developing countries, unequal patterns of development, in terms of investment as well as access to its opportunities or fruits, have been a major source of societal cleavage. The process of globalization integrates markets and values, thus facilitating growth, yet it is also a source of increasing exclusion and marginalization, widening the gap between rich and poor within and among societies and exacerbating the conditions that can give rise to violent conflict. The consequent exclusion and inequality have been compounded by the struggle for identity in a rapidly changing world; traditional values, roles and institutions are continually under assault as a result of the communications revolution and the penetration of markets and raising of expectations in even the most remote parts of the globe. The impact of market penetration has been intensified by the weakening of the state in the face of dwindling resources, endemic corruption and the rise of civil society, which can complement the state's role but can also compete with it for legitimacy. As a consequence, wars are increasingly fought over control of resources and power by social groups within states rather than by states themselves.

Conflict resulting from exclusion, inequality and indignity does not in itself necessarily lead to the eruption of widespread hostilities. The tolerance and coping capacities of the poor and marginalized are legendary and manifold. However, conflict often engenders large-scale violence if various structural conditions are present, such as authoritarian rule and a lack of political rights (as in Rwanda and Guatemala), state weakness and lack of institutional capacity to manage conflict (such as in Somalia) and socioeconomic imbalances combined with inequity of opportunity and a weak civil society (as seen in Cambodia). The risk of an outbreak of violent conflict increases when these conditions exist concurrently or are exacerbated by other problems, such as the manipulation of ethnic or other differences (in religion, culture and language), which can further fragment society and intensify the conflict (Carnegie Commission on Preventing Deadly Conflict, 1997; Collier and Hoeffler, 1999; Nathan, 1998; Reno, 1998).

Social capital can be readily perverted to undermine social cohesion and fragment society for individual and group gain, and potentially result in violent conflict. In Cambodia the *Angka*, a group of semi-literate youth led by a handful of extremist intellectuals, operated under the guise of the Cambodian government to employ inclusionary social capital within the group to strengthen its resolve and weaken those excluded from the group. The Rwanda case illustrates that the political and economic elite often use identity to mobilize and pervert extant social capital as a ready means of achieving their own ends. Meanwhile, the Guatemala study reveals that groups and individuals suffer numerous indignities at the hands of oppressive, authoritarian regimes and a greed-driven elite who pit one group, be it religious-, ethnic- or age-bounded, against another in pursuit of largesse and power. Strong bonding social capital within Somalia fortifies clan allegiances, pitting clan versus clan and impeding moves towards peace and reconciliation.

Within this complex matrix of factors underpinning violent conflict, two main features of social capital become increasingly relevant as potential kindling to fuel the fire of hostility. Vertical relations plagued by inequality and an unequal distribution of power and opportunity (and thus often accompanied by exclusion and indignity) can instigate violent conflict. Horizontal relations that lack ties between unlike groups in a multicultural society can erupt into hostilities if one group is seen as monopolizing resources and power to the disadvantage of the others. And if, within these groups, high levels of bonding social capital link only like members, differences in access to resources and power may further aggravate relations and heighten tensions between those in control and those excluded (Narayan, 1999). Thus violent conflict can be triggered by the presence of strong exclusionary bonds combined with a lack of horizontal and vertical bridging links.

FULCRUMS FOR TRANSFORMING SOCIAL CAPITAL

The broad influences on the uses and effects of social capital rest on three fulcrums, each with the potential to destroy or build communities: state policies, markets and mediating mechanisms (including civil society and the media).

In Rwanda, relations between Hutu and Tutsi deteriorated under Belgian colonial rule. By supporting the minority Tutsi through exclusionary *policies*, the Belgians entrenched socioeconomic disparities and solidified the divide between the groups along 'ethnic' (rather than class) lines. The 1926 Belgian-implemented census forced Hutu and Tutsi to choose their 'ethnic' identity. What had once been a dynamic system of classes became a static system based on 'ethnicity', which later became a (much-abused) tool for manipulation of the masses by an elite ruling group (Lemarchand, 1970; Newbury, 1988; Prunier, 1997). When the state reverted to Hutu control, government policy continued to destroy social ties between the Hutu and Tutsi by enforcing measures meant continually to marginalize the Tutsi. The rights of the Tutsi were suspended, while institutional structure and discrimination excluded them from a range of educational and employment opportunities in education, government and business. The Rwandan example illustrates all too well the ability of policies to split communities and instil divisive behaviour and actions among the populace.

The penetration of *markets* into society can foster secondary networks of social capital. Globalization, in the form of external market penetration and the spread of technology, has facilitated peace efforts in northern Somalia by enabling exchange and economic growth despite the country's adverse conditions. The Somalia diaspora, easy access to ports, telecommunications and capital (through electronic transmittal of remittances) have all facilitated this growth, which linked those groups within the northern region. Weak state penetration (especially in Hargeisa) has also enabled this development of market forces, for there is no longer the threat of overregulation.

Societies also need institutions to avoid or solve conflict. These *mediating mechanisms* mitigate and manage conflict before it can become violent. Examples of such mechanisms range from a fair, effective judicial system to an active civil society that protects the rights of the individual; the interfacing of the state with a free press enables the airing of grievances and informs the public of government actions.

Instead of acting as a mediating mechanism to distil conflict, during the genocide the media acted as a spark to ignite and inflame ethnic hatred. *Radio et Télévision Libre des Mille Collines* (RTLMC) not only used media channels to spread hate propaganda, but also went as far as broadcasting lists of Hutu in each commune who had not participated in the killings, thereby publicly pressuring them to join the genocide. By spreading hate, fear, suspicion and greed, the Hutu extremists whipped the Hutu masses into a murderous frenzy (Des Forges, 1999; Gourevitch, 1998).

A Tutsi hiding in a church could listen to the radio and hear how the killing was going. He heard the radio announcers' gentle encouragement to leave no grave half-full, and the more urgent calls for people to go here or go there because more hands were needed to complete this or that job. He heard the speeches of potentates from the Hutu Power government, as they travelled around the country, calling on the people to redouble their efforts. And he wondered how long it would be before the slow but steady massacre of refugees in the church where he was hiding caught up with him. On 29 April, 1994, RTLMC proclaimed that 5 May was 'clean-up' day for the final elimination of all Tutsi in Kigali (Gourevitch, 1998, p. 134).

Unlike the Hutu elite, Search for Common Ground and UNESCO are using the media to sow the seeds of peace. These groups jointly created Vision 2020, a series of articles in which respected writers from the Middle East present their visions, analyses, hopes, dreams and fears for the region in the year 2020. This exposes readers in each country to a variety of viewpoints that reflect a common humanity and common interest in a better future. The series is published in nine newspapers across the Middle East in five languages, reaching audiences numbering in the millions. In addition, the BBC's Arabic Service is airing a parallel series of feature interviews with the authors, synchronizing their broadcasts with the release of each article (Search for Common Ground website).

Civil society is another key mediating mechanism. The extant Cambodian civil society was deliberately destroyed by the Pol Pot regime in an attempt to erase all forms of traditional bonds, from kinship to religion and the arts, as well as modern bridges, by attacking professionals, from teachers to doctors. In its place, a perverted bonding form of social capital, the *Angka*, whose rank-and-file were a formally excluded group and whose leadership was also formally excluded, emerged to perpetrate one of the cruellest genocides in modern history.

In societies in transition from violent conflict to peace, from crisis to sustainable development, the transformation of social capital that strengthens social cohesion can play a critical role in the transition from welfare-oriented, protectionist relief to an activist development orientation. In this perspective, communities are viewed, not just as victims with needs, but also as survivors with capacities.

BUILDING RESILIENT COMMUNITIES: THE SYMBIOTIC RELATIONSHIP OF HUMANITARIAN RELIEF AND DEVELOPMENT – CREATING LINKAGES WHILE PROTECTING INTEGRATION

Humanitarian operations focus on quick response and short-term planning, while development agencies are often slow and inflexible. Both tend to focus too much on mandates rather than on the needs and capacities of those affected by war, and neither seems to rely on the knowledge and expertise of the other that may help improve operations. Two main recommendations, based on studies examining social capital, can be made to help address this gap and improve the strategies and operations of both international actors.

Relief should not strengthen bonding associations at the expense of bridging networks. Often, humanitarian actors, while supporting primary relations, can act to stifle, or at the very least they do not encourage, the development of the links and ties necessary to progress towards stable development. If not carefully implemented, relief can strengthen primary social capital but yet prevent reconciliation by strengthening exclusionary bonding ties. Relief can cater to individual rather than community needs, thus lowering levels of social cohesion, and consequently group trust, norms of reciprocity and solidarity. Relief can keep people alive, but, in worst-case scenarios, inadvertently promote polarization and more conflict.

The real challenge is in the transition from saving lives to providing sustainable livelihoods, which consciously builds social capital while providing relief and rehabilitation. It is not enough to provide food; that can inadvertently build dependence. Agencies must work to empower the victims to take back their own lives and become active producers of food again. Repatriation of refugees without social and economic reintegration is a recipe for further impoverishment. Emergency drugs and medical treatment without health services and social security may sustain life but not end suffering. The sustainability that emerges to prevent dependence stems from the emergence of bridging linkages, which unite disparate communities in efforts of social and economic growth and development.

As cross-cutting ties are being established, both humanitarian and development actors should assess existing bonding social capital bases and take care that their external efforts do not erode them. Once these local networks and associations are identified, they should be incorporated into the process of reconstruction. Even when the web of extant social capital relations is used, international actors must be wary of overloading the abilities of the local staff by giving them too many responsibilities, too much money or too much work. External interventions should also be sensitive to indigenous organizations and be careful not to wipe out the groups' own efforts and their tendencies towards self-reliance.

In the transitory phase from humanitarian relief to development, *longer-term developmental actors should be careful not to support secondary linkages at the expense of integrative relations.* More robust development sectors (telecommunications, basic services and others) promote secondary networks and economic growth. The lack of basic infrastructure (particularly roads, transport and water) is a major hurdle to sustainable development while intensifying impoverishment.

'Where a road passes, development follows right on its heels,' said an old man in Cameroon, in 1995. Roads and transport both increase physical and social connectedness and increase prices obtained for crops and products. Roads even to the next village are seen as expanding people's options and access to services. Access to clean drinking water and water for irrigation frequently emerges as a distinguishing characteristic between the poor and the rich (Narayan, 2000, pp. 217–18).

Yet, in this drive to develop, community members can begin to feel more disconnected from their own families and thus perceive their integrative relations to be diminishing. The onslaught of globalization, while encouraging open markets and the growth of bridging networks, can worsen this condition during post-conflict phases. Development efforts should also try to nurture activities that help maintain integrative links in the community, uniting nuclear and extended family members and neighbours.

ENSURING HUMAN SECURITY: CONFLICT MANAGEMENT THROUGH INTEGRATING ACTIVITIES, CONNECTING GROUPS AND EMPOWERING PEOPLE

Relief agencies must focus more on sustainable solutions, while development agencies should focus more on supporting pre-existing primary associations. Development organizations, whether involved in conflict prevention or in reconstruction efforts, should adopt policies to help strengthen and rebuild social capital at the state level, in terms of that state's capabilities, role and links to communities. These policies include establishing impartiality while maintaining a 'do-no-harm' mentality, investing in organizations of the poor and providing incentives for good governance by encouraging positive political reform to reduce inequity and to improve housing, land tenure, and political and economic participation. International actors should take care not to rush projects to meet outside expectations, for this diverts attention from the more important task of restoring good relationships, an endeavour that can only be achieved in the longer term.

Rehabilitation and reconstruction hinge on reconciliation, which successfully connects adversarial groups of a conflict. In Rwanda, for example, since the end of genocide, attempts have been made to place Hutu in government positions to balance political power. Meanwhile, space has been created for the re-emergence of civil society actors. Yet the new social fabric of Rwanda is complicated, laden with sub-groups and schisms. The Tutsi are divided both by the duration of their stay abroad and by where they sought refuge. Those returning from Uganda are perceived as being more elitist than those from Burundi, who in turn have a higher status than returnees from the Democratic Republic of Congo. Tutsi who stayed in Rwanda and survived the genocide are suspected of collaboration with the *génocidaires*, for it is doubted that any

Tutsi could have survived on his own. There are also divisions between Hutu who participated in the killings, those suspected of being involved and those who did not participate. The genocide, while reinforcing the split between Hutu and Tutsi, also created new social cleavages within ethnic groups. To compound matters, the political topography is laden with volatile 'ethnic-rooted' landmines such as the contentious issue of the resettlement of large numbers of returning Hutu and Tutsi. Cross-cutting social capital should be nurtured to link, not just Hutu and Tutsi, but also those within the sub-groups (Gourevitch, 1998; Prunier, 1997). Overcoming the new schisms and reconciling old differences may take generations. But hope prevails as cross-cutting associations of widows (single female-headed households) bridge ethnic lines to form new social capital, working together to support one another and build a pluralistic, tolerant Rwanda.

Decentralization and participation can empower people to take over development and command of hope for their future. To dismantle the legacy of centralized decision making and begin to forge these bridging links, the government initiated an inclusive community-level approach to development founded on the concepts of participation and decentralization. This approach is designed to involve Rwandans closely in the management of their own affairs and to give local administrative structures the primary responsibility for development activities, thus not only empowering the groups, but encouraging them to work together to build their connected futures.

For instance, the East Timor Community Empowerment and Local Governance programme is an excellent example empowering the people while strengthening governance and consequently building social capital. The East Timor project relies on NGOs and donors to help facilitate community members electing their own village development committees, building community capacity to manage their own resources and decision-making processes in an efficient and transparent manner. The beneficiaries themselves remain in the driver's seat, empowered to make and learn from their own mistakes, share credit for their successes and hold one another responsible and accountable for their communities' development.

Anticipative forward thinking is crucial to success for development in post-conflict countries. Measures of civic engagement, along with human security and government efficacy, transparency and stability, are key social capital indicators for comprehensive reconstruction. Peace building involves not only economic reconstruction, or the rebuilding of physical infrastructure and economic stabilization, but also fundamental revitalization of positive social capital and the strengthening of social cohesion. The answers to conflict prevention lie not only in demilitarization and in jump-starting the economy, although these are important. They lie also in good governance – the rule of law, justice and human rights – and in strengthening social capital at every level. The crucial challenge is how to build societal capacity to manage diversity and prevent social capital from being transformed into an instrument of exclusion and violent conflict. This integral part of rehabilitation, reconstruction and reconciliation can only be accumulated over years of support and nourishment, and thus requires long-term, flexible approaches that allow adaptation to interim change.

In the end, the voices of the poor and war-affected cry out for a new kind of security, a human security free of oppression and fear, absence of hunger and with manifold opportunities, that empowers them to take decisions that affect their own lives. Resilient communities rely on all forms of social capital: bonding, primary ties to protect and survive in times of crisis, bridging links to act and develop in times of hope, efficient and functional state and norms and synergistic government–community relations that allow civic engagement to thrive. Development needs to nurture and build on such social capital in order to create and maintain the mechanisms and institutions necessary for preventing violent conflict and managing diversity.

NOTES

1. This chapter draws heavily on the authors' book, *Violent Conflict and the Transformation of Social Capital: Lessons from Cambodia, Rwanda, Guatemala and Somalia*. Special thanks are given to Bruce Ross-Larson and Molly Lohman for their editorial assistance.
2. The concepts of strong and weak ties can be traced back to Granovetter (1973, pp. 1360–80).
3. Berkman and Kawachi (2000, pp. 174–90).

REFERENCES

Berkman, Lisa F. and Ichiro Kawachi (eds) (2000), *Social Epidemiology*, New York and Oxford: Oxford University Press.

Carnegie Commission on Preventing Deadly Conflict (1997), *Preventing Deadly Conflict: Executive Summary of the Final Report*, New York: Carnegie Corporation of New York.

Colletta, Nat J. and Michelle L. Cullen (2000), *Violent Conflict and the Transformation of Social Capital: Lessons from Cambodia, Rwanda, Guatemala and Somalia*, Washington, DC: World Bank.

Collier, Paul and Anke Hoeffler (1999), 'Justice seeking and loot seeking in Civil War', World Bank, Washington, DC (available at <http://www.worldbank.org/research/conflict/papers/justice.htm>).

Des Forges, Alison (1999), *'Leave None to Tell the Story': Genocide in Rwanda*, New York: Human Rights Watch, and Paris: International Federation of Human Rights.

Galtung, Johan (1996), *Peace by Peaceful Means: Peace and Conflict, Development and Civilization*, Oslo: International Peace Research Institute and Thousand Oaks, CA: Sage Publications.

Gourevitch, Philip (1998), *We Wish to Inform You That Tomorrow We Will Be Killed with Our Families*, New York: Farrar, Straus and Giroux.

Granovetter, Mark S. (1973), 'The strength of weak ties', *American Journal of Sociology*, **78**, 1360–80.

Grootaert, Christiaan (1998), 'Social capital: the missing link?', Social Capital Initiative Working Paper 3, Environmentally and Socially Sustainable Development Network, World Bank, Washington, DC.

Lemarchand, René (1970), *Burundi and Rwanda*, New York: Praeger.

Narayan, Deepa with Raj Patel *et al.* (1999), 'Bonds and bridges: social capital and poverty', Policy Research Working Paper 2167, Poverty Division, Poverty Reduction and Economic Management Network, World Bank, Washington, DC.

Narayan, Deepa (2000), *Voices of the Poor: Can Anyone Hear Us?*, Oxford and New York: Oxford University Press for the World Bank.

Nathan, Laurie (1998), 'Crisis resolution and conflict management in Africa', paper commissioned for a conference on 'The Nexus between Economic Management and Civil Society in Countries Emerging from War in the SADC Region', sponsored by the Centre for Conflict Resolution and the World Bank Post-Conflict Unit, Cape Town, South Africa, 11–13 October.

Newbury, Catharine (1988), *The Cohesion of Oppression: Clientship and Ethnicity in Rwanda 1860–1960*, New York: Columbia University Press.

Prunier, Gérard (1997), *The Rwanda Crisis: History of a Genocide*, New York: Columbia University Press.

Reno, William (1998), *Warlord Politics and African States*, Boulder, CO: Lynne Rienner.

Uvin, Peter (1998), *Aiding Violence: The Development Enterprise in Rwanda*, West Hartford, CT: Kumarian Press.

Woolcock, Michael (1998), 'Social capital and economic development: towards a theoretical synthesis and policy framework', *Theory and Society*, **27** (2), 151–208.

Index